Magento 1 DIY

Viktor Khliupko

Apress®

Magento 1 DIY

Viktor Khliupko
Duesseldorf, Germany

ISBN-13 (pbk): 978-1-4842-2456-4   ISBN-13 (electronic): 978-1-4842-2457-1
DOI 10.1007/978-1-4842-2457-1

Library of Congress Control Number: 2016961761

Managing Director: Welmoed Spahr
Acquisitions Editor: Louise Corrigan
Development Editor: James Markham
Technical Reviewer: Richard Carter
Editorial Board: Steve Anglin, Pramila Balan, Laura Berendson, Aaron Black, Louise Corrigan, Jonathan Gennick, Todd Green, Celestin Suresh John, Nikhil Karkal, Robert Hutchinson, James Markham, Matthew Moodie, Natalie Pao, Gwenan Spearing
Coordinating Editor: Nancy Chen
Copy Editor: Kim Burton-Weisman
Compositor: SPi Global
Indexer: SPi Global

Distributed to the book trade worldwide by Springer Science+Business Media New York, 233 Spring Street, 6th Floor, New York, NY 10013. Phone 1-800-SPRINGER, fax (201) 348-4505, e-mail orders-ny@springer-sbm.com, or visit www.springer.com. Apress Media, LLC is a California LLC and the sole member (owner) is Springer Science + Business Media Finance Inc (SSBM Finance Inc). SSBM Finance Inc is a **Delaware** corporation.

For information on translations, please e-mail rights@apress.com, or visit www.apress.com.

Apress and friends of ED books may be purchased in bulk for academic, corporate, or promotional use. eBook versions and licenses are also available for most titles. For more information, reference our Special Bulk Sales–eBook Licensing web page at www.apress.com/bulk-sales.

Any source code or other supplementary materials referenced by the author in this text is available to readers at www.apress.com. For detailed information about how to locate your book's source code, go to www.apress.com/source-code/.

Printed on acid-free paper

Contents at a Glance

Contents

About the Author

Viktor Khliupko is an ecommerce expert, consultant, and developer. He is also a traveler and metal music fan. He has built successful Magento-based ecommerce businesses and startups worldwide. He is the founder of the Firebear Studio.

About the Technical Reviewer

Richard Carter is a seasoned web designer and front-end developer based in the North of England. His interest in SEO comes from a desire to help clients fully understand the implications of the ways websites are built and how they perform in search engines.

Richard lives in Newcastle upon Tyne. He is the founder of established UK web design agency Peacock Carter. He has worked with clients that include the University of Edinburgh, NHS, City & Guilds, University College Dublin, and the Scottish government.

CHAPTER 1

Setup

The book was written by Viktor Khliupko[1] in a collaboration with the Firebear team. Andrii Pechatkin, Demyd Maiornykov, Rita Aloshkina, Konstantin Sokolov, Oleg Pomjanski, and Andrey Nikolaev contributed much to make this happen. They shared their ideas and edited my thoughts. The following are the members of our team:

- Andrii Pechatkin[2] - lead editor, co-author

- Rita Aloshkina[3] - editor

- Demyd Maiornykov[4] - editor

- Oleg Pomjanski[5] - art direction, design

- Konstantin Sokolov[6] - consulting, editor

- Andrey Nikolaev[7] - Magento consulting

- Jewgeni Faktorov[8] - business support

- Ewgenij Sokolov - legal advisor

---

[1]https://www.linkedin.com/in/bi0tech.
[2]https://ua.linkedin.com/pub/andrii-pechatkin/103/bb/50a.
[3]https://ua.linkedin.com/pub/rita-aloshkina/a3/1a7/a6.
[4]https://ua.linkedin.com/pub/demyd-maiornykov/b5/1a4/952.
[5]http://op-original.de/.
[6]https://www.linkedin.com/pub/konstantin-sokolov/106/8a3/89/.
[7]https://www.linkedin.com/in/andreynikolaev.
[8]https://www.linkedin.com/pub/jewgeni-faktorov/105/454/55a.

The Magento platform is constantly changing, so it is impossible to create a book that will cover all of its aspects. Therefore, go to the Firebear blog[9] and sign up for updates. All the latest news, reviews, and advice on Magento 1 and Magento 2 are available there.

The next thing I'd like to mention is the release of Magento 2. Although the new version of the ecommerce platform offers a plethora of improvements, it won't outperform 1.x within the next few years. This time is required for the creation of an ecosystem with all the necessary extensions, themes, third-party software solutions, and developers. Thus, I recommend that you start your ecommerce business with the latest available version of Magento 1.x, as it is the most robust tool for online retail. When Magento 2 is mature, you will be able to migrate from your current version without any headaches.

As for Magento setup, it is a very complex procedure that starts with downloading and installation. Then you should set up the server and hosting. The next two big stages are related to the proper use of templates and extensions. Once you have completed these steps, you can start importing product and other data into your new website.

At this point, you have a complete ecommerce store, but it is still far from launch. The next essential stages include performance improvements, security implementation, and SEO optimization. If you think that it is the end of the setup procedure, however, you are mistaken. The last important step is a pre-launch.

In this chapter, I show you how to pass all the aforementioned stages with maximum efficiency, and at the same time, with minimal headaches. Let's start with downloading and installation.

Downloading and Installation

When it comes to the Magento download, you should first check the official source at `https://goo.gl/IdSktD`.

On this page, you will find the latest version of Magento Community Edition, the open source ecommerce platform. It also has the latest patches, which you should download and install separately. That's why I also recommend checking FireGento's GitHub mirrors with the latest patched version of the platform at `https://goo.gl/fssCe6`. It already includes all the patches and improvements. The benefit is obvious: you have a single installation and download procedure combined instead of two separate processes.

When you know where Magento Community Edition is situated, I can tell you a few useful things about the installation. You can utilize local hosting during development (it is described next). It helps you to reduce costs and get the necessary experience. According to the official guide (you can find it here: `http://goo.gl/wwVZZm`), you need to create the prerequisites found here: `http://goo.gl/4bls9m`.

You should also set up your server. I appeal to the official guide once more: `http://goo.gl/EJvYwA`.

Now you can run the installation procedure; see `http://goo.gl/PpOZzq`.

---

[9]`https://firebearstudio.com/blog/`.

Be proud of yourself. You've just installed Magento! Your ecommerce website is still far from being finished, but one of the most responsible and complicated stages is already behind you. If you have any questions, I recommend checking the following resources:

- Official wiki (http://goo.gl/PSveyi)

- Official forums (http://goo.gl/jn27KR)

- Magento Stack Exchange (http://goo.gl/u87Uer)

- The official resource list (http://goo.gl/A5KL1Y)

You can also read more about the Magento community on Firebear Studio[10], "The power of Real Magento Community," at http://goo.gl/sznMw1.

And of course, I'd like to mention the official Magento user guide. The *Magento Community Edition User Guide* should be your number-one handbook. You can find information on it at http://goo.gl/VpV5dm.

Server/Hosting

In this part of the chapter, I tell you about the crucial aspects of the Magento setup, such as the server and hosting. Here, you will find the best solutions optimized for Magento.

Good Magento optimized hosting guarantees a fast and stable store. In the article at http://goo.gl/hNXFn0 you can find the best 16 solutions optimized for Magento, but I recommend that you pay attention to Nexcess.

Nexcess (https://goo.gl/8NeYTe) offers secure, stable, and scalable built-in hosting solutions for Magento. The company provides several solutions called the Secure Isolated Platform (SIP). Each SIP is a fine-tuned, self-contained ecommerce hosting environment. Each platform includes a ready-to-launch optimized Magento website. Nexcess provides complete Magento hosting options only in the United States, the United Kingdom, and Australia. But it is still a reliable solution for other regions.

The cheapest solution is SIP 100. Its price starts at $19.95 per month if you pay for the whole year, but if you pay monthly, an additional $5 per month are charged. SIP 100 offers 2x Quad Core E5620, 7.5GB of free space, 16GB RAM, 75GB of data per month, one IP, nine additional stores, and 30 accounts per server.

I recommend that you not waste time and use SIP 200 instead, as it is the most powerful and reliable Magento-optimized server solution, at $75 per month. It provides enough resources for running a robust mid-sized ecommerce store. You can launch demos of all the proposed platforms to compare with other Nexcess solutions, but SIP 200 is the optimum solution.

CloudWays[11] offers reliable cloud hosting that is optimized for Magento. Being both fast and secure, it offers the following features:

- Installation focused on performance

- The ability to install unlimited number of websites

---

[10]https://firebearstudio.com/blog/.
[11]http://www.cloudways.com/en/magento-managed-cloud-hosting.php.

- Daily managed backups

- Dedicated servers

- Firewall

- Reliable support and monitoring 24/7

- Git and SSL

The cheapest plan starts at $5 per month.

EboundHost[12] offers managed Magento-dedicated servers. The cheapest CE server costs $99 per month and offers Intel Xeon E5-2630; 50GB SSD (RAID) 4 CPU Cores, 4GB of RAM, and JetRails™ Lite. EboundHost provides 24/7 support, lightning-fast SSD storage, and various optimizations specific to Magento.

Local Hosting

Local Magento web development is another important step in your ecommerce setup. With local hosting, you can install Apache, PHP, MySQL, and other useful tools right on your computer and use it like a web server. Thus, you will be able to install a Magento store right on your PC. You just need one of the following tools.

These are the benefits of local hosting:

- First, you can get enough practical skills before releasing your store on hosting.

- Second, an essential aspect is the ability to reduce costs required during development, as you don't need hosting during this stage.

MAMP (https://goo.gl/k5HAxM) provides a bunch of technologies composed of free, open source, and proprietary commercial solutions. MAMP is the acronym for Mac OS X (but it also works on Windows), Apache, MySQL, and PHP, Python, and Perl. The solution is based on a similar software set for Linux, called LAMP. There are also various AMP packages for different operating systems. MAMP is designed for all CMS platforms, so you can set up a local development environment with ease. You can get MAMP for free; the Pro version costs EUR 39.00.

XAMPP (https://goo.gl/qRNcm3) is a free and open source cross-platform web server solution that consists of Apache HTTP Server, MySQL database, and scripts interpreters written in PHP and Perl. The X means *cross-platform*. The development tool allows programmers to test their projects on computers without any Internet access by creating a corresponding development environment. In addition, XAMPP provides support for creating databases in SQLite and MySQL. You can download XAMPP for Windows, OS X, and Linux.

---

[12]http://eboundhost.com/magento/.

Magento Templates

Magento themes and templates offer a huge boon to your online business. By installing the correct product, you will provide your customers with a rich shopping experience. Created by professional and experienced web designers and developers, Magento themes and templates can bring your online store to an absolutely new level.

A good design increases the conversion rate, turns visitors into buyers, and buyers into regular customers. That's why it is important to understand the latest design trends: this knowledge will help you choose the right template. Note that template developers often provide support. It can be both free or paid, so you should check the information on every template.

I wouldn't recommend that you create your own template, because it is unreasonably expensive. You can utilize the existing templates instead, since it is possible to enhance them with corporate identity features related to your business. So what are the best sources of Magento themes and templates?

There are numerous theme marketplaces all over the Internet. You can spend days searching for the right source of content. Therefore it is necessary to know the major websites with themes and templates. They are all listed next.

Marketplaces

ThemeForest is the number-one marketplace for themes and templates. It offers premium content for Magento and other platforms. You can easily build your ecommerce store after having visited this marketplace, as ThemeForest offers more than 500 different Magento templates and themes.

Magento Themes on ThemeForest

ThemeForest Themes reviewed in our Blog[13]

Another reliable source of Magento templates is TemplateMonster. There are dozens of different ecommerce themes and templates within this marketplace. TemplateMonster provides its customers the ability to choose between different categories. Of course, this feature is also available at ThemeForest, but TemplateMonster provides more precise search options.

Buy Magento Templates at TemplateMonster

TemplateMonster Themes reviewed in our Blog[14]

Magento Connect is the official Magento marketplace. In addition to Magento extensions, you can also purchase themes and templates here. To find the best free options, sort them by price from lowest to highest (Price: Lowest - Highest), or choose Free among All, Free, and Paid themes.

---

[13]https://firebearstudio.com/blog/tag/ThemeForest.
[14]https://firebearstudio.com/blog/tag/TemplateMonster.

Magento˙cɔnnect

Figure 1-1. *Magento Connect*

Install Magento Themes from Magento Connect

RocketTheme offers an extensive collection of modern Magento themes. Take into account that the right one will help you engage your customers and showcase products in an attractive way. All the Magento themes available at RocketTheme were crafted with elegance and efficiency in mind. At the same time, they are powerful and easy to use. RocketTheme's library of Magento templates is constantly growing. Currently, there is only one free solution.

Download Magento Themes from RocketTheme

Unlike previous marketplaces, Ubertheme offers a developer package, all Magento themes, for $350. As a developer, you will get one-year access to the package. Moreover, the solution includes free complimentary extensions and the unlimited domain installation. There are more than 70 themes at Ubertheme, including two free solutions.

Get Magento themes and templates at Ubertheme

EMThemes is another source of premium themes for Magento. If you are looking for free solutions, EMThemes has four absolutely free themes in its library. Moreover, the company organizes giveaways, so you have chances to get a premium template for free.

Download Magento Templates from EMThemes

You can also check the selection of the best Magento templates on the Firebear blog here: http://goo.gl/Bc5BJG.

Top eCommerce Website Design Trends

Every successful ecommerce web developer or ecommerce website designer tries to follow the top web design trends. As an ecommerce store owner, you should do this because understanding the latest innovations is also crucial for your business growth. Everyone benefits from following the new standards: developers and designers provide competitive services and produce high-quality websites; ecommerce website owners get a better understanding of how to catch new customers and make the existing audience more loyal. Next, I tell you about the top ecommerce website design trends of 2015, so get ready for a long journey into the world of innovation. After reading this part of the chapter, you will be able to select a Magento template that will become the best solution for your ecommerce needs.

New Requirements for the Responsive Design

Responsive design is among the most essential elements of web design. Thousands of different smartphones, tablets, and phablets require a unique approach to provide customers with maximum accessibility on whatever devices they use. The difference between 2015 and previous years is in the appearance of new devices and platforms. Smart watches and home appliances, smart TVs, and smart glasses make the definition of responsive design much broader than before.

Scrolling over Clicking

With the popularization of smartphones and tablets, scrolling became more popular than clicking. Compared to clicking, it is more convenient and takes less time for a page to load because you get everything within one page and don't need to open additional elements on new pages. Thus, scrolling also provides users with the ability to get all the information they need without any unnecessary actions on additional screens and windows.

The Importance of Typography

Content was always extremely important, but every year customers, search engines, and competition provide stricter requirements and new trends. It is obvious that in 2015, typography will play a more essential role in ecommerce website design. Simplicity, bold elements, and large images are going to be among dominating design trends this year. We can even speak of *responsive typography,"* a new approach to typography with strong emphasis on a responsive design. Typographic flexibility and webkits are other key features of typography as an ecommerce website design trend.

Ghost Buttons

Ghost buttons have a chance to become a new favorite web element. They are nice, minimal, and useful. Ghost buttons look good and attract shopper's attention in a subtle way. They are not really a call to action but a useful addition to every ecommerce website. You can see the example of ghost buttons in the image (Mission, Play, Touch).

Material Design by Google

Mobile commerce also has its own trends. Material design is a design direction that Google implemented. It relies on *skeuomorphism* and entirely flat design. Material design covers different platforms and has its influence on ecommerce website design.

Microinteractions

"Microinteractions are contained product moments that revolve around a single use case—they have one main task. Every time you change a setting, sync your devices, set an alarm, log in, or "like" something, you are engaging with a microinteraction." They revolve around a single use case, when a customer interacts with a website. Microinteractions are incorporated in the improvement of customer engagement. During 2015, we will see more useful and sophisticated microinteractions.

Card Design

Card design is an integral part of responsive websites. The card approach to ecommerce website design provides the ability to organize and arrange things more effectively. In addition, cards allow visitors to get more information easier than any other solutions. Card design is simple, clear, and informative.

Background Images and Videos

The background is always among the most attractive parts of every website. Keep in mind that great content looks better over a stunning background image. That's why background images and videos are always important. They have become a trend with ecommerce website design.

Hidden Menus

The popularization of mobile devices has a great influence on the design of websites. Because of small screens, smartphones require some site elements to be hidden, but a user can always reach them. That's why global or product navigation is absent in its full size until you hit a special button. Thus, hidden menus are becoming more popular. These elements are widely used, even on relatively larger screens. Still, many people don't understand the meaning of hamburger menu icon, so there is a possibility that ecommerce website designers will use it in a tandem with the word *menu*.

Large Photography

Large images always had a negative impact on the site speed, so website designers tried to avoid using them in recent years. But everything has changed with an improved responsive design. New techniques and adaptive images make it possible to serve fast-loading even with large images. Of course, better content can help ecommerce websites sell more; therefore, the community expects larger images on home and product detail pages.

Nearly Flat Design

Thanks to Google, Apple, and Microsoft flat design occupied major mobile platforms. Of course, this idea isn't new, but it is fresh for ecommerce websites. The trend continues to expand its influence, because flat design is more pleasing to the customers and easier to understand, develop, and make it responsive. Another advantage of the flat design is the focus towards the content. The core principles of skeuomorphism make such elements as call-to-action buttons unobtrusive. The same holds for the use of shadows. With the flat design, ecommerce web developers can bring an element to the front of the screen and make it an integral part of the site. The "less is more" principle continues to enhance its influence, becoming one of the leading ecommerce website design trends.

Device Agnostic

Modern ecommerce website should be device agnostic. It's unacceptable to design web pages for particular devices. They must function properly on all screen sizes. Today, ecommerce web developers must take into account the amount of screen resolution variations, all the possible input methods, connection speeds, and browser requirements to create a universal experience for every visitor. With device-agnostic design visitors will leave the ecommerce website wanting to return. Users will be able to navigate through the site and complete the checkout without any need to pinch the screen or aim at buttons.

Tile Navigation

Images always were more time-saving and captivating than text boxes. The "less is more" principle lies at the heart of modern navigation. Instead of the standard bar, ecommerce websites are implementing tile navigation. By using image tiles instead of lists, web designers provide users with a preview of what they're going to see. Keep in mind that tile navigation is more user-friendly than any ordinary solution. It has a huge potential to grab the attention of visitors after the first few seconds of interaction with an ecommerce website. Tailed navigation recreates the feel of walking into a brick and mortar store, so visitors stay entertained as long as possible.

Parallax Scrolling

You have probably already seen websites with tantalizing background animation or parallax effect. It can be very impressive, but there is a problem when parallax turns into distraction. The ecommerce website loses its main goal, and instead of presenting products it demonstrates impressive design effects. Keep in mind that design should be beautiful and at the same time useful. Animations, images, and effects should support sales, not overshadow products.

The following websites provide examples of the most inspiring ecommerce web designs. They illustrate the most modern, beautiful, and practical solutions.

- Webdesign Inspiration

- Awwwards

- Inspirational shops

Now, when you are familiar with ecommerce design trends and know major marketplaces, you can look for the Magento template, but don't spend too much time on choosing the right solution, next I will tell you about the must-have extensions and how to install them.

Magento Extensions

Developing Magento extensions is not for everyone, but regardless of coding experience everyone can utilize the end product of this complicated process. It's just important to know which Magento extensions to choose and how to install them correctly. Next, I cover the best Magento modules and teach how to install them. The modules are divided into six groups: performance, SEO, front end, UI, usability, loyalty and referral campaigns, system back end, and marketing and sales. The installation procedure is described in three different ways: via Magento Connect, FTP, and SSH.

You can get a free support with paid extensions. Such services often have time limits, but you can always get a consultation from specialists. Don't be afraid to ask them!

But why do we use extensions?

Extensions

Magento extensions or modules offer tons of extra features and opportunities. Magento provides a lot (out of the box), but the default functionality is not enough for running a successful ecommerce business. That's why there are tons of both paid and free modules on Magento Connect, GitHub, and other websites. The following extensions introduce the basic level of improvements. They are just an example of what to use. Of course, you can choose your own modules.

The Magento extensions described next are not enough for receiving the maximum return from your ecommerce website. Check the other sections of this chapter to find out how more reliable improvements look like. For instance, there are sections dedicated to SEO and performance.

Performance

Being a part of customer relationships, good performance is the key to a growing revenue and profit. This significant aspect positively affects customer loyalty and search engines ranking, and as a result your cash flows. You can improve your Magento store performance by using proper settings and extensions.

If Magento store is not set up correctly, it becomes slow and alienates customers. Sometimes even experienced web developers could miss some settings, so it is necessary to monitor if everything is set up correctly. The probability for correct settings can be increased with the help of extensions. Several correct extensions can dramatically change the speed of your Magento store. The most reliable solutions will be discussed next.

Fooman Speedster is your performance tool number one. It combines multiple JavaScript files into a single one. The same holds also CSS files. As a result, you get shorter page load time. The other feature of the Fooman Speedster extension is the ability to reduce the total size of all the files required for loading empty and primed caches. In addition, Fooman Speedster reduces the number of HTTP requests. The extension doesn't require any gzip support on the server; therefore, all files are compressed without any additional tunings. Fooman Speedster is fully automated, supports multistore capabilities, and uses the Minify library. You can install Fooman Speedster here for free.

Merged with Fooman Speedster

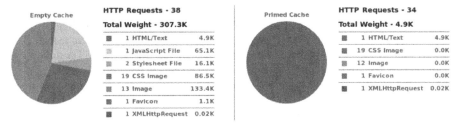

Empty Cache	HTTP Requests - 38	
	Total Weight - 307.3K	
	1 HTML/Text	4.9K
	1 JavaScript File	65.1K
	2 Stylesheet File	16.1K
	19 CSS Image	86.5K
	13 Image	133.4K
	1 Favicon	1.1K
	1 XMLHttpRequest	0.02K

Primed Cache	HTTP Requests - 34	
	Total Weight - 4.9K	
	1 HTML/Text	4.9K
	19 CSS Image	0.0K
	12 Image	0.0K
	1 Favicon	0.0K
	1 XMLHttpRequest	0.02K

Figure 1-2. Fooman Speedster

Lesti::Fpc is another useful module designed for performance improvements. It is an internal full page cache for Magento, which works with events. One of the most important features of Lesti::Fpc is its simplicity: the extension doesn't need any external software. Being an internal cache, Lesti::Fpc replaces dynamic blocks before sending a response to a customer. You can find more information on the extension and install Lesti::Fpc here.

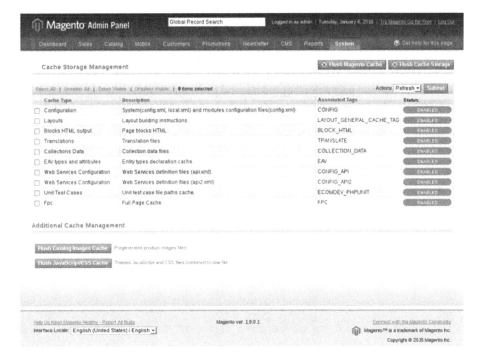

Figure 1-3. Lesti_Fpc

More Performance Extensions[15]

CloudFlare is a world-leading content delivery network that is optimized for Magento. With the Control for CloudFlare Magento extension, you are able to integrate your store with this service. As a result, dozens of JavaScript, CSS, and image files loaded from your server during every page view (even if you use Full Page Cache and minification) are loaded from distributed servers around the world. This will dramatically reduce server load and provide your customers with an amazing page load speed. The additional features of this extension include resource caching, DDoS protection, additional forms and files security, and async JS load. You can download the Magento extension here: Control for CloudFlare. And don't forget to check CloudFlare's plans. There is a free one.

SEO

According to Wikipedia, SEO is the process of affecting the visibility of a website in a search engine's organic search results. The earlier and the more frequently your Magento store appears in the list of search results, the more visitors come to your website. That is why SEO optimization is crucial for your ecommerce business. There is a SEO guide discussed in this chapter, but nevertheless, at this point I will explicitly discuss the key SEO extensions. Magento is SEO-friendly right out of the box, but you can always enhance the default capabilities with the help of proper modules.

Creare SEO for Magento adds a lot of new features to your ecommerce Magento store. By installing this extension, you will enhance your website with the following features: HTML sitemap; Noindex on category filters; unique category headings; default metadescriptions and page titles for products and categories; config-editable .htaccess and robots.txt; 301 redirects for discontinued products; Twitter cards for product pages; the ability to disable keywords and metadescription tags; an SEO checking page in the admin; a performance cleanup script; a breadcrumbs schema; XML sitemap fix; canonical product redirect; a product attribute validator; and duplicate product button removal. You can install Creare SEO for free here.

---

[15]https://firebearstudio.com/blog/the-best-must-have-magento-extensions-2014-performance-seo-frontendui-loyaltyreferral-campaigns-systembackend-marketingsales.html#performance.

Figure 1-4. CreareSEO

Schema.org is another must-have tool for SEO optimization. The extension adds metadata to the product pages of your ecommerce store. The product name, its description, price, stock status, ratings, and a non-cached image path are used in addition to the default information about every product page of your website. The extension is compatible with such search engines as Google, Bing, and Yahoo!. Check this page for additional information.

With SEO Pagination extension, you can provide search engines the ability to properly understand the structure of your Magento store. This leads to a higher keyword ranking in search results. The extension allows you to implement Google recommendations to target pagination issues in SEO with rel="prev" and rel="next" markup tags. It means that the category pages of your Magento store will be optimized for most search engines robots. Having installed the extension, search engines will receive a strong hint to treat pagination within the category pages as a logical sequence. By providing search engines with the information on how to work with the pages of your webstore, SEO Pagination helps to avoid duplicate content issues. You can download SEO Pagination here.

More SEO Extensions[16]

---

[16]https://firebearstudio.com/blog/the-best-must-have-magento-extensions-2014-performance-seo-frontendui-loyaltyreferral-campaigns-systembackend-marketingsales.html#seo.

Front End, UI, Usability

The front end, user interface, and overall usability are closely related. Since the front end is responsible for collecting data from the visitors, think of it as of an interface between your customers and the back end. The user interface is the place where interaction between customers and the store occurs. As you can see, front end and UI are closely connected and have significant influence on overall usability. By using the following extensions, you can improve the front end, the UI, and the usability of your Magento store. The following modules are designed to improve the usability of your ecommerce store. They add lots of new features, making the user experience better.

One Page Checkout Magento module significantly reduces the steps required during the checkout. In ecommerce, fewer steps mean that your customers are more likely to complete the full checkout process. Thus, One Page Checkout extension allows users to checkout without any hesitation. Moreover, the extension provides numerous configurations, so the new checkout process can be modified to fit your webstore needs. Learn more about One Page Checkout.

Social Connect is another important Magento extension. It adds Google, Facebook, and Twitter buttons to your login page. As a result, customers experience a much faster login and registration options. They just have to hit one button to complete login or registration. Information from their Google, Facebook, or Twitter accounts is used. Thus, the overall process becomes easier and dramatically faster. You can find more information about Social Connect Magento extension here.

Figure 1-5. Social Connect

14

Toogas Featured Popup extension provides you with fully customizable options for pop-ups. All of these options appear in Magento's admin. With this module, you make the pop-up windows within your ecommerce store nice and friendly. The corresponding image and its dimensions, the associated store views, and several other settings, such as opacity and priority, are offered by this extension. Toogas Featured Popup is absolutely free and you can download it here.

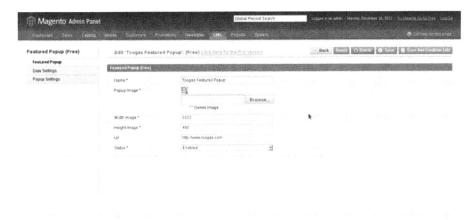

Figure 1-6. *Toogas Featured Popup*

Improved Navigation: the name of this extension speaks for itself. The default navigation within Magento store is far from being top-notch, but with Improved Navigation by Amasty you will make your store much more user-friendly. Your customers will easily find the way from the main page of your Magento store to the products they are looking for. Thus, you will be able to increase revenue and customers loyalty. Improved Navigation offers such features as SEO-layered and Ajax-layered navigation, navigation filters, advanced menu categories, price slider, and so forth. For additional information, look here.

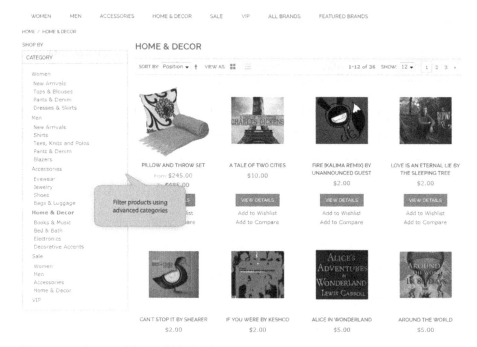

Figure 1-7. Improved Layered Navigation

By installing the AddThis extension, you enhance the usability of your Magento store with the help of a sharing tool. Thus, your customers are able to share content from your ecommerce website to more than 350 social media services. You can even see some sharing stats with an AddThis account. The tool provides information on the number of shares among your visitors, services used for sharing, shared content, and even copied text. You can install AddThis extension from here.

Figure 1-8. AddThis

The Easy Lightbox extension is a special tool designed for installing a Lightbox widget for your Magento website. It replaces the default product image zoomer with an attractive lightbox window. With the extension you can install and configure Lightbox within five minutes. The process is free and extremely easy, since no coding experience is required. Moreover, you don't even have to replace the existing files. Hit this link for additional information.

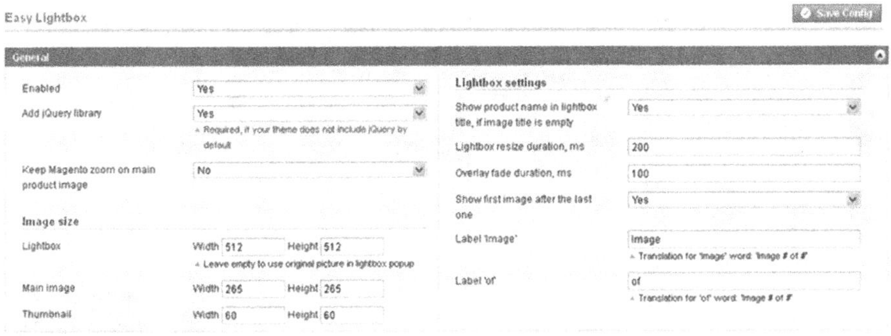

Figure 1-9. *Easy Lightbox*

Quick Contact extension provides your customers with the ability to leave feedbacks about your ecommerce website. Using this module, you will be closer to your customers. Furthermore, you will always know why your visitors are dissatisfied. The tool is absolutely free, upgradable, customizable, and easy to install. You can download Quick Contact extension here.

Figure 1-10. *Quick Contact - Free Extension*

Banner Slider extension is the most powerful banner management tool among all similar Magento modules, since it offers 36 available positions for displaying banners and slideshows. The extension supports ten banner rotator effects and a customizable slider. Banner Slider provides an easy banner management due to the following parameters: URL, showing time, image, appearing order, and so forth. You can download Banner Slider here.

Figure 1-11. *Banner Slider*

Applying the Advanced Product Options module, you can specify the available number of every standard custom option offered on Magento. The extension also provides the ability to upload images for all these options, so you can represent your goods in a more convenient and affordable way. The Advanced Product Options Magento module is used by thousands of ecommerce merchants all over the world. It is a time-tested reliable solution designed to make your store more user-friendly. Visit this page to purchase the extension.

More Frontend Improvements[17]

---

[17]https://firebearstudio.com/blog/the-best-must-have-magento-extensions-2014-performance-seo-frontendui-loyaltyreferral-campaigns-systembackend-marketingsales.html#frontend.

Loyalty and Referral Campaigns

It is extremely important to increase visitor loyalty to turn buyers into returning customers and create buzz within social networks. When different stores sell similar products, loyalty means almost everything, since the growing loyalty paves the way to an increase in sales. Posts from random users on Facebook or Twitter have become one of the most trusted forms of advertising. Thus, there is no question of whether to start a referral campaign. The question is how to do it with maximum output. I recommend that you begin with the following extensions.

Sweet Tooth Loyalty and Reward Points Magento extension provides you with the ability to create reward points programs developed to increase loyalty, and as a result, sales. Sweet Tooth offers tons of customizations and unique features. You will be able to turn your visitors into buyers, buyers into returning customers, and returning customers into brand advocates that bring friends to your ecommerce store. Note that Sweet Tooth is available on a monthly subscription basis. For additional information, go here.

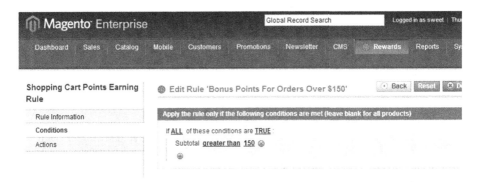

Figure 1-12. Sweet Tooth

Refer a Friend by aheadWorks is another reliable tool when it comes to loyalty and referral campaigns. As you might have guessed by its name, it is established to stimulate customers to invite other people to your ecommerce website. A buyer gets a reward for every new invited customer. It can be a percentage or flat discount on a purchase. While you are getting new customers, your revenue is growing. You can get more information about Refer a Friend by aheadWorks here.

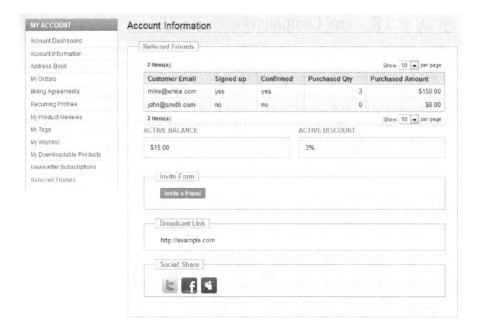

Figure 1-13. *Refer a Friend*

By using the Unirgy_Giftcert Magento extension, you provide your customers with the ability to use gift certificates within your store. Moreover, these gift certificates support custom gift messages. There are no transactional fees or other hidden payments. For more information, visit this page.

Figure 1-14. *Unirgy_Giftcert*

By installing the Gift Registry module, you can help your customers get the gifts they want. The extension allows them to create and manage gift registries with the information about their wishes for special occasions. Of course, these gift registries are often posted on social networks in order to inform friends about the desired gifts. As a result, you get lots of new visitors and additional buyers. You can purchase the Gift Registry extension here.

Figure 1-15. *Gift Registry*

More Loyalty Tools[18]

---

[18]https://firebearstudio.com/blog/the-best-must-have-magento-extensions-2014-performance-seo-frontendui-loyaltyreferral-campaigns-systembackend-marketingsales.html#loyality.

System and Back End

There are also some extensions developed for system and back-end enhancements. Usually, they simplify the work of administrators, providing some new features and extra customizations. As a result, you spend less time on different routine processes. Thus, you can concentrate on other vital aspects of your ecommerce business. Next, I show you the most reliable solutions, which can make the back end of your store better.

By installing the Enhanced Admin Grids Magento extension, you obtain extra customization options for most admin grids. As a result, administrators receive many new useful features, new columns, and a powerful editor. The module provides the ability to edit values directly in grids, shows hidden columns, and offers several rendering options. With the Enhanced Admin Grids Magento extension, you are able to customize such column base values as header, width, and alignment. Moreover, the module's drag-n-drop feature simplifies the columns order modifications. You can find more information about the Enhanced Admin Grids (+ Editor) module here.

Figure 1-16. *Enhanced Admin Grids*

The Pulse Storm Launcher is a Magento analog of the Spotlight app. This extension is designed to save countless hours previously spent on traveling through the Admin menus. It is a free, fast, and highly productive tool for the Magento admin console. Get one-click access to the system with the Pulse Storm Launcher. You will be able to save your time and money. For more information, look here.

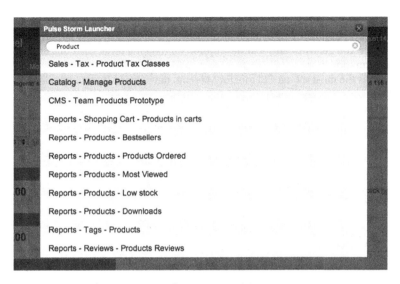

Figure 1-17. Pulse Storm Launcher

The Improved Import extension enhances the ability of the default Magento import procedure. By installing this module, you will add the most requested import features to your ecommerce store. The extension works with the out-of-the-box Magento Dataflow import/export from CSV files. It allows you to import multiple product images from external URLs along with product custom options and tier prices. Check this page for the full list of features.

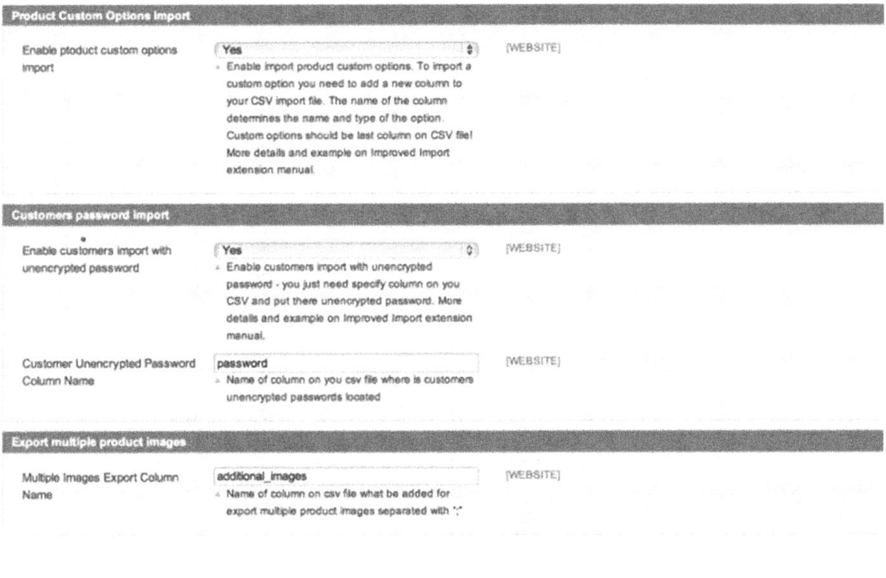

Figure 1-18. Improved Import

The Seamless Delete Order module features the easiest way to delete orders on the back end. It adds a new option into the Action drop-down box from the native Order Manager. As a result, you get a fast and seamless option for deleting orders. Hit this link for additional information.

n98-magerun is the most robust CLI tool for Magento developers. It provides a large set of tested commands that save hours simplifying common processes. All commands are extendable via a module API.

- Description[19]
- Official Website[20]
- GitHub[21]

More Backend Modules[22]

Marketing and Sales

There are also Magento extensions that can be used in various marketing campaigns. They have different purposes, but the same final goal. Such extensions are aimed at the implementation of a successful marketing campaign and a sales increase.

For instance, Ebizmarts provides many opportunities for the email marketing, since it is an official extension for Mandrill and MailChimp integration. With the aid of this Magento module, you will be able to utilize Mandrill to send transactional emails—up to 12,000 per month for free. Additionally, you will obtain such features as an email Autoresponder and Abandoned Carts Recovery. The extension is absolutely free and you can download it here.

---

[19]https://magently.com/what-is-n98-magerun-and-why-you-should-use-it/.
[20]http://magerun.net/.
[21]https://github.com/netz98/n98-magerun.
[22]https://firebearstudio.com/blog/the-best-must-have-magento-extensions-2014-performance-seo-frontendui-loyaltyreferral-campaigns-systembackend-marketingsales.html#loyality.

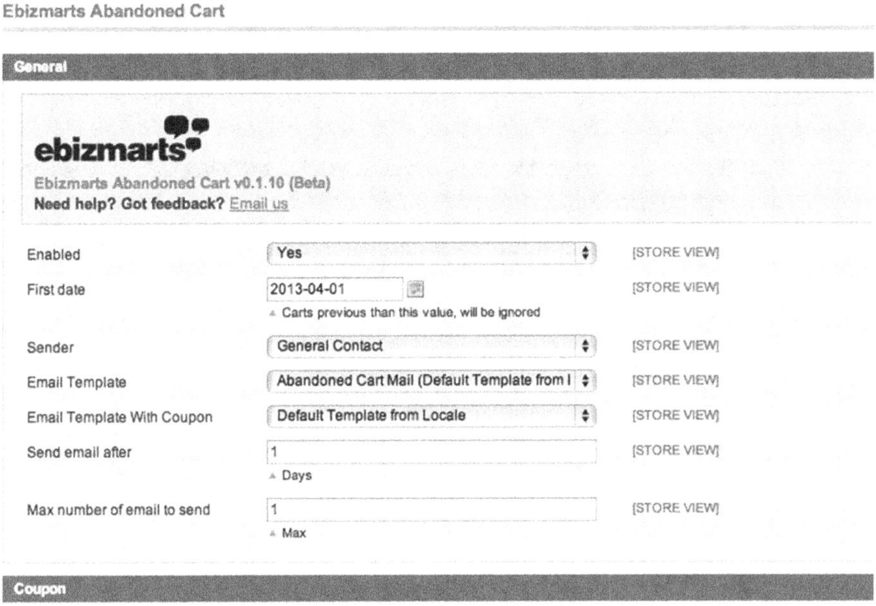

Ebizmarts Abandoned Cart

General

ebizmarts

Ebizmarts Abandoned Cart v0.1.10 (Beta)
Need help? Got feedback? Email us

Enabled	Yes	[STORE VIEW]
First date	2013-04-01	[STORE VIEW]
	▵ Carts previous than this value, will be ignored	
Sender	General Contact	[STORE VIEW]
Email Template	Abandoned Cart Mail (Default Template from	[STORE VIEW]
Email Template With Coupon	Default Template from Locale	[STORE VIEW]
Send email after	1	[STORE VIEW]
	▵ Days	
Max number of email to send	1	[STORE VIEW]
	▵ Max	

Coupon

Figure 1-19. *Mandrill and MailChimp integration*

Improved Newsletter is another reliable marketing tool. It is designed for collecting customer emails. With the aid of this module, you can easily create a large database required for a successful email marketing strategy, as well as autosubscribe customers to your newsletter with their registration. In addition, the tool can detect unsubscribed customers and subscribe them while they are placing orders. The module is really powerful. You can purchase it here.

Figure 1-20. *Improved Newsletter*

Another important group of marketing extensions is represented by Advanced Reports. This module creates a complete picture of your ecommerce business. It provides reports related to sales, customers, and other marketing data. The default Magento solution is limited, so I strongly recommend that you use this third-party solution. You can find more information on Advanced Reports here.

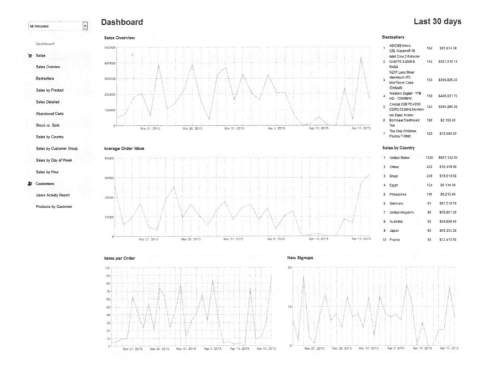

Figure 1-21. Advanced Reports

LUKA Google AdWords Conversion Tracking is developed for seamless integration with Google AdWords. By installing this module, you will be able to add Google conversion tracking codes to every page of your store. The extension is absolutely free. Take a look at this page for additional information.

Blog is another core tool for your ecommerce business. You can post recent news, promotions, and information about upcoming products. The Blog extension by aheadWorks not only provides your customers with this data, but it also brings new visitors to your Magento website and helps with search engine optimizations by building relevant SEO-friendly text links. The Blog module provides wide opportunities for building successful sales strategies. In addition, it can be used for gathering feedbacks from your customers. You can find more information here.

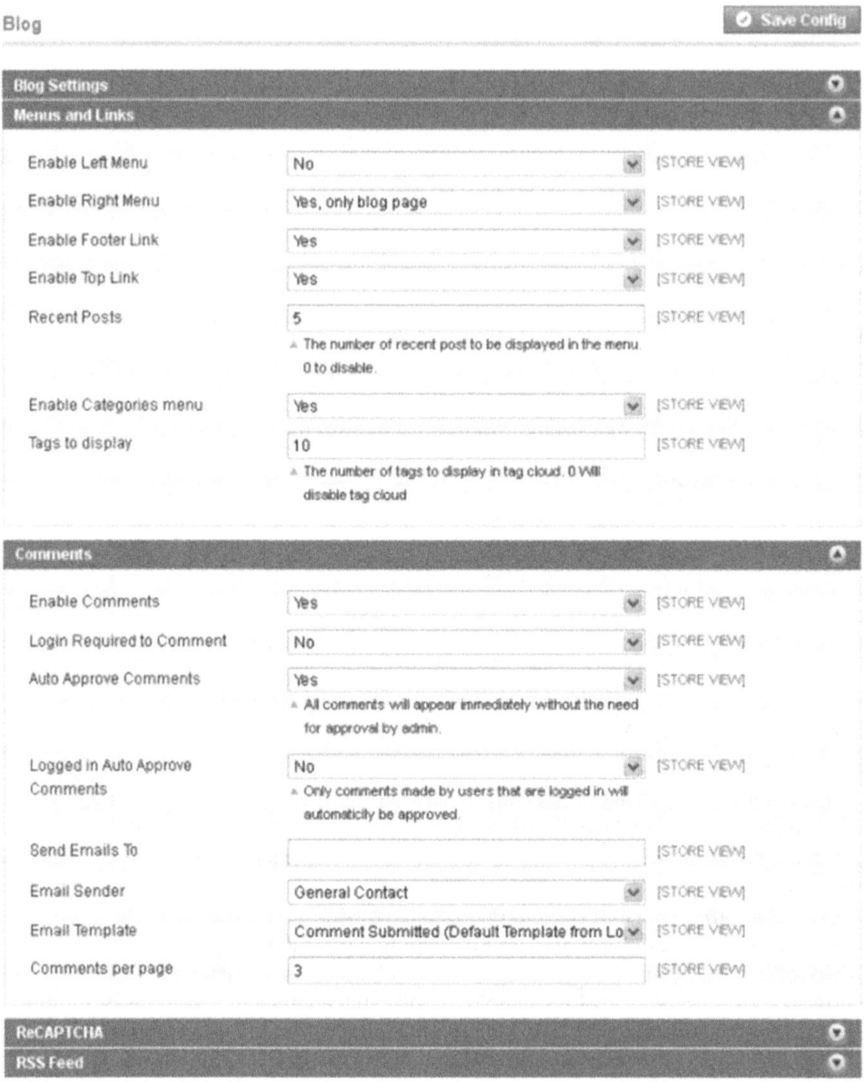

Blog   ⊘ Save Config

Blog Settings   ⊙

Menus and Links   ⊙

Enable Left Menu   No   ⌄   [STORE VIEW]

Enable Right Menu   Yes, only blog page   ⌄   [STORE VIEW]

Enable Footer Link   Yes   ⌄   [STORE VIEW]

Enable Top Link   Yes   ⌄   [STORE VIEW]

Recent Posts   5   [STORE VIEW]
                            ▲ The number of recent post to be displayed in the menu.
                              0 to disable.

Enable Categories menu   Yes   ⌄   [STORE VIEW]

Tags to display   10   [STORE VIEW]
                            ▲ The number of tags to display in tag cloud. 0 Will
                              disable tag cloud

Comments   ⊙

Enable Comments   Yes   ⌄   [STORE VIEW]

Login Required to Comment   No   ⌄   [STORE VIEW]

Auto Approve Comments   Yes   ⌄   [STORE VIEW]
                            ▲ All comments will appear immediately without the need
                              for approval by admin.

Logged in Auto Approve   No   ⌄   [STORE VIEW]
Comments
                            ▲ Only comments made by users that are logged in will
                              automaticlly be approved.

Send Emails To   [STORE VIEW]

Email Sender   General Contact   ⌄   [STORE VIEW]

Email Template   Comment Submitted (Default Template from Lo ⌄ [STORE VIEW]

Comments per page   3   [STORE VIEW]

ReCAPTCHA   ⊙

RSS Feed   ⊙

Figure 1-22. *Blog*

Related Products Manager is a special Magento extension that uses existing shopper data to generate related items, cross-sells, and up-sells for your ecommerce store. This is another must-have module for your ecommerce store. It not only gains sales, but also helps with growing a customer loyalty. The tool is free, but for shops with more advanced needs, there is a paid version. You can get the Related Products Manager extension here.

More Marketing Extensions[23]

Magento Hackathon Extensions

And don't forget about Magento Hackathon extensions. Magento Hackathon is a series of community-driven events where Magento community enthusiasts create amazing open source Magento extensions and tools within just a couple of days. The core aspect of all Magento Hackathon events is intensive team collaboration: the best specialists develop top-notch solutions during short periods of time. The most prominent results of such cooperation are listed next. Please note that all Hackathon extensions have been tested by a broad Magento community, so you can easily use them not only during development, but also in production (if a project is stable, of course).

Magento Hackathon Extensions[24]

Installation

Congratulations! Now you know which extensions to install, so it's time to show you how to do it. Next, I have described three different types of installation. The second one is the easiest, but it can only be used with free extensions. The other installations are more complex, but that shouldn't frighten you. Let's start with a manual installation via FTP.

How to Install Magento Extensions Manually via FTP (Six Universal Steps and Troubleshooting)

The following FTP (File Transfer Protocol) guide is designed for basic webserver setup: MySQL, Apache, and PHP. For a server with a more advanced setup, you have to adjust these steps. Ask your system admin about the details. You can also automate the installation process with the help of a command-line equivalent.

I strongly recommend that you use a test site to install modules. You might get into trouble even with the best Magento extensions, so you should check how they work without doing any harm to your live store. Therefore, install your modules in a test environment first. If everything is OK, repeat the installation on a live site.

Now I'll explain how to install Magento extensions while avoiding Magento Connect. I have described the most common problems with a manual installation and show how to fix them. The following are the six universal FTP steps:

1. Turn off compilation.

2. Turn on cache.

3. Perform installation.

---

[23]https://firebearstudio.com/blog/the-best-must-have-magento-extensions-2014-performance-seo-frontendui-loyaltyreferral-campaigns-systembackend-marketingsales.html#marketing.
[24]https://firebearstudio.com/blog/the-best-magento-hackathon-extensions-free-open-source.html.

4. Refresh cache.

5. Re-enter back end.

6. Turn on compilation.

Turn off Compilation

If your Magento compilation mode is enabled, you have to turn it off; otherwise, your ecommerce store and its admin could be inaccessible after you install an extension. To disable the Magento compilation procedure, go to System ➤ Tools ➤ Compilation.

If you prefer working with the command line, you should use this equivalent:

```
1   php -f shell/compiler.php -- clear
```

In addition, I recommend that you create a backup of all Magento files. Thus when something goes wrong, you will be able to fix all problems with ease. You can also refresh the cache and check if your website works well. Don't start the installation if there are issues with your ecommerce website.

An optional step is a database backup. You should create it for additional safety purposes. You can take your website offline or keep it live. In the second case, you will have to re-add orders manually after you create the backup.

Turn on Cache

Now, you have to turn on the configuration cache to prevent an early installation, as it could be the reason of errors. Go to System ➤ Cache Management.

Perform Installation

When you've found an extension that is necessary for your ecommerce website, you have to read its installation instructions first. That way, you get all the essential information for a successful installation. Don't ignore this advice.

When you know all the nuances, you can download a Magento extension and unzip it into a separate folder.

You have to upload the unzipped content to a server via SFTP or FTP. Connect to your Magento server. Go to the root directory. Upload the appropriate files to the root folder. The root folder includes such subfolders as app, downloader, errors, and so forth.

One of the best free FTP tools is Filezilla. You can freely use it to simplify the installation.

Note that the uploaded files have to be readable by a web server. This means that they must have the same permissions as the existing ones.

Refresh Cache

Now you should go to System ➤ Cache Management once again and refresh Magento's cache. This step is necessary for providing Magento with the ability to register a new extension.

Re-enter the Back End

To prevent the Access Denied error, you have to re-enter the back end. Log in with a full administrator account to get new permissions.

Check whether your ecommerce website works as always. If you've turned off the store, you should bring it online.

Turn on Compilation

If you are using the compilation mode, which was previously disabled, you have to turn it on. Go to System ➤ Tools ➤ Compilation and hit the Run Compilation Process button.

You could also use the command line instead:

```
1   php -f shell/compiler.php -- compile
```

▪ **Warning!**   In order to prevent potential conflicts, you have to install only one extension at a time.

Troubleshooting

Next, I explain how to fix the most common errors related to the Magento extension installation.

I have done everything as described but I can't find my extension.

There is a possibility that Magento will not be able to read the Name.xml file, which has to be associated with the module's name or developer.

1. First, check System ➤ Configuration ➤ Advanced ➤ Disable Modules Output. If the extension is not there, you have two more ways to fix the problem.

2. Check the permissions of the uploaded files one more time. They must be readable by Magento.

3. Flush the cache and delete the contents of var/cache (in rare cases, this content can be cached in the tmp/ folder).

An error page with a reference number at the bottom occurs.

This number corresponds to a file from a server. The file is situated in <MAGENTO_-ROOT_FOLDER>/var/report/.

To get more information about the error, you have to open this file. If files from the includes/src folder are mentioned in the report, it's likely that you've failed in the first step of the guide. Now you do not have an access to your admin.

Luckily, you can fix the problem by editing the includes/config.php file. Change the following:

```
1    define('COMPILER_INCLUDE_PATH', dirname(      FILE    ).DIRECTORY_
     SEPARATOR.'src');
```

to this:

```
1    #define('COMPILER_INCLUDE_PATH', dirname(__FILE__).DIRECTORY_
     SEPARATOR.'src');
```

The Magento back end should be functional again, so you can rerun the compilation process, as described in the sixth step.

If this doesn't help, contact the extension developer.

I've refreshed the cache but there are still no new configuration options

Once again, check whether Magento can read the permissions of the uploaded files. Flush the cache and delete the contents of var/cache.

I see a white page after the installation

This is a fatal error that occurred while the page was loading. You have to check the details of this problem in the server's error log. It is often necessary to contact the extension developers and show them this log in order to fix the issue.

How to Disable a New Extension

The following explains how to disable a new extension.

1. Go to the app/etc/modules folder.

2. Change the file name ending .xml in
   <companyname>_<extensionname>.xml to .off,
   for instance. You should get the following result:
   <companyname>_<extensionname>.off.

3. Refresh the Magento cache. Go to the var/cache folder and
   delete its content.

You can always re-enable an extension by renaming the file name to end with .xml. Take into account that the Disable Modules Output option disables a block output only, so uninstall extensions in a proper way.

Now you know how to install extensions via FTP. As you can see, this process is not difficult, but it requires some attention. Next, I discuss an even simpler procedure—installation via Magento Connect.

How to Install Free Extensions via Magento Connect

Please note that you must use the previous guide for commercial extensions.

Some specialists don't recommend using Magento Connect. Although it is the easiest way to install an extension, there are several drawbacks:

- By using the same key at different installations, you can install the wrong version of a module.

- It is unsafe to use Magento Connect Downloader with the 777 permission.

- You don't have any ability to inspect code.

- By using Magento Connect Manager, you can accidentally trigger the upgrade of the Magento core.

If these aspects don't deter you, then you should perform the following steps:

1. Go to the profile of a preferred extension.

2. Check supported versions of the platform.

3. Select your platform (e.g., Community).

4. Hit the **Install Now** button.

5. Choose the Magento Connect channel: 1.0 for Magento CE 1.4.x and below; 2.0 for Magento CE 1.4.2.0 beta; CE 1.5+; EE 1.9.0.0-RC2+.

6. Don't forget to check the license agreement box.

7. Get an extension key.

8. Copy the key by clicking **Select Key**.

9. Log in to the admin of your Magento store.

10. Go to **System ➤ Magento Connect ➤ Magento Connect Manager**.

11. Paste the key into the appropriate field.

12. Click the **Install** button.

13. Now you can cancel or proceed to the installation. Click **Proceed**.

14. A console box will appear. It shows the installation process and displays issues (if there are any).

15. Hit the **Refresh** button to finish the installation.

Troubleshooting

If there is any trouble with the Magento Connect Manager installation, you should make sure that the correct extension key was used. Stability is another discrepancy factor. It is impossible to install beta extensions if your system is set to Stable. The following explains how you should change your stability settings in Manager:

1. Go to your admin panel and choose **System ➤ Configuration**.

2. Enter your Magento Connect account.

3. Hit **Settings**.

4. Choose the necessary option from the pull-down menu.

5. You can select among stable, alpha, or beta.

6. Click **Save**.

Read the Magento Connect FAQ for help with other issues and troubleshooting. That was easy. Follow these steps for uninstallation:

1. Open the Magento Connect Manager.

2. Go to the Manage Existing Connections section.

3. Choose an extension.

4. Choose **Uninstall** from the drop-down menu under the Actions column.

5. Hit the **Commit Changes** button.

6. End the process with the help of **Refresh**.

Next, I shed light on more complicated methods. The previous two are enough for running an ecommerce store successfully, so you can skip the following guides. If you want to get more advanced knowledge, see the following tutorials.

How to Install Magento Extensions via SSH

Another installation method is based on using SSH (Secure Shell). It is a little complicated, but you can still utilize it.

1. Go to the directory with your installed Magento.

2. Run these commands:

```
1   chmod +x mage
2   ./mage mage-setup .
3   ./mage config-set preferred_state stable
4   ./mage install http://connect20.magentocommerce.com/REPO PACKAGE_NAME
```

Note that you must replace REPO and PACKAGE_NAME with values related to your extension.

For Magento 1.4.x or earlier use the following commands:

```
1   chmod +x pear
2   ./pear mage-setup .
3   ./pear config-set preferred_state stable
4   ./pear install EXTENSION_KEY
```

You have to change EXTENSION_KEY with a new value related to your extension.

■ **Warning!**   It is required to install core Magento extensions for Magento 1.4.x or earlier versions of the platform; otherwise, Magento will upgrade your ecommerce website to the latest version.

You can use Magento Connect to check if core Magento extensions are installed. Just log in to get this information.

How to Install Magento Extensions with Composer

I also recommend that you check these tools because they significantly simplify the installation: Magento Composer Installer and Composer Installers.

The purpose of Magento Composer Installer is to enable Composer to install modules and integrate them into a Magento installation automatically. It adds Composer's vendor autoloader ability; as a result, Composer-compatible third-party tools can be used. Read about the project here: Magento Composer Installer[25].

Another useful tool is Composer Installers. You can examine it here: Composer Installers[26]. Composer Installers also simplifies your daily routine by installing extensions or modules on Magento.

If the aforementioned information is not enough, check these manuals on module installation:

- How to install Magento extensions[27]

- How to install a Magento module[28]

Congratulations! Now you can install Magento modules. Now it's time to choose a payment gateway for your ecommerce website

---

[25]https://github.com/Cotya/magento-composer-installer.

[26]https://github.com/AOEpeople/composer-installers.

[27]https://firebearstudio.com/blog/how-to-install-magento-extensions-magento-connect-ftp-ssh-modman-composer.html.

[28]http://fbrnc.net/blog/2014/11/how-to-install-a-magento-module.

Payment Gateways

It's obvious that an ecommerce website should support online payments, but what payment gateways suite best for the needs of your business? There are hundreds of online payment services on the Internet, so it is difficult to choose a right one. Therefore, I will teach you how to select a payment gateway for your business.

It's critical to understand all nuances related to online payment processing so that you get a solution that is the most suitable for your ecommerce business.

- **Payment gateways and merchant accounts**. A *payment gateway* approves or declines payments. A *merchant account* is a place where your money is held before being transferred into a bank account. There are services that provide both tools within one platform, and there are companies that offer only one solution.

- **Different types of checkout**. There are several types of payment gateways. *Hosted* solutions are gateways that take your customer out of your website during the checkout. *Non-hosted* solutions let your buyers stay in your store while entering credit card information. In order to cover the needs of all of your customers, you should offer both solutions.

- **Fees and payments**. Every credit card payment gateway charges a different amount of money for its implementation. There are three major types of fees: setup fees, monthly fees, and transactional fees. Some payment services charge only transaction fees, whereas others try to gather as much money as possible. Thus, it is important to know all the fees in the payment gateway of your choice.

- **Anti-fraud protection**. Unfortunately, there are gateways without strong antifraud protection. Take into consideration that these payment solutions are not secure. You should choose gateways that provide data encryption and allow CVV2 verification.

- **Payment methods**. Some gateways are limited to certain payment methods. You should always check if they provide payment methods that are common within your target market.

- **Prohibited items**. Please note that there can be a prohibited items list in every payment gateway. If you sell products from this list, the gateway will not work on your ecommerce website.

- **High-risk businesses**. Features such as high-risk credit card processing or high-risk merchant account maintenance are not provided by all gateways. If you operate in gambling, ebooks, electronic cigarettes, adult content, or other risky sectors, you should check if the chosen payment service will work on your website.

- **Payment turnarounds**. You don't want to spend several days waiting for your money, right? That's why you should check payment turnaround. Ideal gateways provide a rapid payment turnaround time, but be prepared for more realistic solutions.

- **Chargebacks**. Chances are that your customers will request chargebacks from time to time. Thus, you should be able to provide them with this opportunity. Keep in mind that this feature must be supported by your payment gateway; otherwise, you will experience a lot of unnecessary issues.

- **Customer support**. Imagine a situation where you have a problem that should be solved immediately, but appropriate customer support doesn't work. This situation could lead to money loss or even a spoiled reputation, so 24/7 customer service is a must.

- **Localization**. Localization is also vital. Some gateways support multiple languages and currencies, whereas others provide limited opportunities. If your business provides localization, you should offer the same conditions during the checkout. That's why you need a payment solution that supports localization.

- **Scalability**. Please note that some ecommerce payment gateways have limited transactions and other restrictions. Thus, they can be used with small businesses only. Check whether your chosen gateway is scalable to avoid future problems.

- **Contract**. Beware of a contract! Some companies want you to sign a two-year contract, so you would not be able to change your gateway during this period. Pay close attention to a contract offered by the payment solution that you choose.

- **Reputation**. Don't forget to first check the reputation of the payment gateway providers that you are considering. Try researching social networks or forums.

You know how to choose a payment gateway, so you can also check our list of the best payment solutions for your website: Best Payment Gateways for Modern eCommerce[29].

The leading payment gateways are PayPal, Stripe, and Authorize.net. PayPal is the most popular and reliable solution. It is widely used among ecommerce merchants in all platforms, including Magento. PayPal supports almost all types of payments, as well as related operations: web payments, mobile payments, eBay integration, online invoicing, and so forth.

---

[29]https://firebearstudio.com/blog/best-payment-gateways-for-modern-ecommerce.html.

Stripe is the most prominent gateway among recent market players. Since Stripe is designed for ecommerce websites, online marketplaces, mobile apps, and subscription services, it is a perfect solution for multichannel enterprises. This gateway offers all the features that you will ever need.

Authorize.net is another giant in the payment gateway market. It is the most powerful and well-known payment solution. It offers custom payment forms and extra security.

This section covered market leaders, but you can easily choose another payment solution. Otherwise, let's go the next stage of the chapter, which covers the core topic of shipping.

Magento Shipping

Shipping is a constant part of every ecommerce business. In order to make this process flawless, you can utilize Magento extensions. Custom Shipping Methods And Rules[30] discusses a set of tools that can help you avoid headaches with delivery, rates, and other aspects of custom shipping methods and rules.

Considering the following questions can help you determine the best shipping provider for your specific needs.

- Where are you shipping to? Does your provider support these countries?

- What types of products are you shipping? What is the average size of your orders?

- What is the shipment processing speed offered by your shipping provider?

- Does it support tracking?

- Are there insurance options?

- Does it feature live rates integration?

You should understand your shipping options and needs. For instance, multiple shipping options let your customers choose a provider from among a list of the providers that you work with. There is also free shipping. Customers like this option, so you should think about its implementation. Another key option is flat rate shipping. You can offer it instead of free shipping by charging a flat rate for deliveries for every package. This option can also ranges for various order totals or weights.

Real-time carrier rates are much more complex than other shipping solutions. They depend on various factors, such as package weight and shipping location, but at the same time charges the exact amount of money that your provider will charge you. The customer needs to add a product to his cart to see the most accurate price.

---

[30] https://firebearstudio.com/blog/top-magento-extensions-for-custom-shipping-methods-and-rules.html.

I should mention the click-and-collect option. The concept of click-and-collect or the instore pickup business model is very simple and at the same time counter-intuitive. A customer buys goods on a company's website and rather than wait for the postman several days later, picks up these goods at a local brick-and-mortar store. More about this option can be found here: Click & Collect (In-store pickup) Magento extensions[31].

Note that all the leading market players, such as UPS, DHL, and FedEx, offer all of these options. Moreover, they provide integration with Magento.

With installed extensions, a reliable payment gateway, and convenient shipping options, your store is ready for the data import procedure, which is required if you are not new to ecommerce and already have an ecommerce website on another platform. To get all of your products within the Magento website, read the next part of this chapter.

Data/Product Import

Figure 1-23. Product import

In this section, I explain one of the most advanced tasks of the Magento store management: product import. The following guide includes a description of the CSV file structure and all of its columns, as well as detailed information about product attributes related to the import procedure.

The Magento import is necessary if you are going to migrate from another ecommerce platform. The procedure described next helps transfer products, clients, and orders from an existing online store to a new Magento website. Even if you are not familiar with ecommerce, the following part of the chapter will be useful to you, since it describes core aspects of Magento, but you can easily skip it and return later.

---

[31]https://firebearstudio.com/blog/click-collect-in-store-pickup-magento-extensions.html.

CSV File Structure for the Magento Products Import

For working with CSV (comma-separated values) files, I strongly recommend that you use OpenOffice.

Minimum Required Columns for a Simple Product Import

The easiest way to understand what data is required in a CSV file is to export some products from your Magento store. If you don't have any ecommerce stores based on this platform, you can always use several products for a test. Fill in all product information, add images, and then try to export them. Just go to Magento admin ➤ System ➤ Dataflow profiles ➤ Export all products. As a result, you will get a CSV file with dozens of columns. Let's take a closer look at them. Next, I provide a brief description of a CSV file's parts.

- **websites**. A website entity is associated with a product. In default Magento and in most other cases, it is "base."

- **store**. A store entity is associated with a product. In default Magento and other cases, it is "admin."

▪ **Warning!**   websites and store can be the reason behind a problem when products are not displayed on the front end or the Magento admin panel after your import. So you should check if the values used there are correct. If you are not sure what values to use, you can try the default ones: base and admin (Magento admin ➤ System ➤ Manage stores).

- **type**. The types of a product: simple product, grouped product, configurable product, virtual product, bundle product, downloadable product.

- **attribute_set**. The "default" or another attribute set used for a product. See it in Magento Admin ➤ Catalog ➤ Attributes ➤ Manage Attributes sets.

- **tax_class_id**. Product tax classes: None, Taxable goods, Shipping. You can manage them in Magento Admin ➤ Sales ➤ Tax.

- **status**. The status of a product can be enabled or disabled. If a product is disabled, it will not be displayed on the front end.

- **weight**. The weight of a product; just use 1 if you don't need it.

- **sku**. A unique product identification.

- **name**. The name of a product.

- **price**. The price of a product.

- **description**. A full description of a product that is displayed on a product page.

- **short_description**. A short description is displayed on a product page and on other pages, depending on template settings.

- **visibility**. The visibility of a product on the front end: Not Visible Individually / Catalog, Search / Catalog / Search.

- **category_ids**. Magento category ids are associated with different products. They are created in Magento admin ➤ Catalog ➤ Categories. To get a category id, check it in Magento admin.

- **qty**. The available quantity of a product. It is used to control the in-stock/out-of-stock status of a product.

- **is_in_stock**. Sets up a default status of a product (boolean value 1 or 0): in stock (1) or out of stock (0). Out-of-stock products are not displayed on the front end and can't be sold.

- **image, small_image, thumbnail**. First, you have to upload images into the media/import folder in your Magento installation folder, and then enter an image file name prepended with a slash. You can use the same large image for all three types of product images; Magento will scale it to other required sizes.

■ **Tip**   Images are required for successful product import in Magento, but if you want to import products without images you can use a trick with the default Magento product image placeholders located at skin/frontend/default/default/images/catalog/product/placeholder. You can find three images there: image.jpg, small_image.jpg, and thumbnail.jpg . Copy and paste them to the media/import folder and use them for your products. Product images can be updated during the next import procedure.

To import multiple product images and galleries, you have to use the Improved Import[32] extension, since Magento does not provide this feature out of the box (more extensions follow).

CSV File sample consists only of the columns described. If you've decided to give it a try, you need a category with id=3 and placeholder images copied from skin/fron-tend/default/default/images/catalog/product/placeholder to the media/import folder.

---

[32]https://firebearstudio.com/blog/improved-import-extension-manual.html#multiple_images.

Extended Import with Additional Features

To get the full list of columns, you can just export existing products, as well as imported earlier (as in CSV sample). Appropriate export options are situated in Magento admin ➤ System ➤ Import/Export ➤ Dataflow ➤ Profiles ➤ Export all products.

Now you can get a complete list of default columns used in Magento product import. You can use them for the import procedure which includes column names and example data. In most cases, it is not difficult to understand what data can be placed there.

store, websites, attribute_set, type, category_ids, sku, has_options, name, meta_title, meta_description, image, small_image, thumbnail, url_key, url_path, custom_design, page_layout, options_container, image_label, small_image_label, thumbnail_label, country_of_manufacture, msrp_enabled, msrp_display_actual_price_type, gift_message_available, price, special_price, weight, msrp, status, is_recurring, visibility, enable_googlecheckout, tax_class_id, description, short_description, meta_keyword, custom_layout_update, special_from_date, special_to_date, news_from_date, news_to_date, custom_design_from, custom_design_to, qty, min_qty, use_config_min_qty, is_qty_decimal, backorders, use_config_backorders, min_sale_qty, use_config_min_sale_qty, max_sale_qty, use_config_max_sale_qty, is_in_stock, low_stock_date, notify_-stock_qty, use_config_notify_stock_qty, manage_stock, use_config_manage_stock, stock_status_changed_auto, use_config_qty_increments, qty_increments, use_config_enable_qty_inc, enable_qty_increments, is_decimal_divided, stock_status_changed_automatically, use_config_enable_qty_increments, product_name, store_id, product_type_id, product_status_changed, product_changed_websites, additional_images

Full CSV File sample

Magento Product Import Tips and Tricks
Product Import Custom Options

Unfortunately, default Magento lacks custom options for product import. But you can solve this problem by using the Improved Import[33] extension. With the help of this module, you can get new options and a new column in a CSV file. This column includes the following specific options: name, type, and price.

Product Attributes

Magento doesn't provide you the ability to import product attributes and values out of the box. But you can use this solution: Import Product Attributes into Magento[34].

---

[33]https://firebearstudio.com/blog/improved-import-extension-manual. html#custom_options.

[34]http://insidethe.agency/blog/import-product-attributes-into-magento#.VZ6ftPmqqko.

Products with Multiple Attribute Values

You can import products with multiple attribute values if you have attributes with values in the Magento admin and you want to associate them with existing imported products.

Import Multiple Product Images and Images from External URLs

By default, you are not able to import multiple product images and images from external URLs, but it's possible with the Improved Import extension. With this Magento module, you can add as many images as you need in an additional CSV column and upload them to the media/import folder. The same process is suitable for images from external URLs.

Product Tier Prices Import

You can easily import product tier prices from different customer groups with the Improved Import extension.

Product Import Errors and Solutions

The following describes some potential product import errors and their solutions.

Image Does Not Exist

If you've got an "Image does not exist" error in any product images required for import, you didn't properly set that image in the CSV image column in your media/import folder. To solve this problem, you can use the trick described earlier (import everything without images) or use the Improved Import extension to find out which product images are missing.

Products Are Not Displayed on the Front End After Import

If products are not displayed in your front end after import, you must check "columns = values" in your CSV file. Check the following column descriptions:

- websites = base
- store = admin
- status = Enabled
- visibility = Catalog, Search
- category_ids = NUMBER (must be valid enabled category id in you store)
- qty > 1
- is_in_stock = 1

Products Are Not Displayed on the Back End (Magento Admin) After Import

Primarily, you have to check "websites = base" and "store = admin" in your CSV file. If everything is alright there, you should go to the next step of this guide and perform some cleanup in Magento.

Strange Stacks and Other Errors

If nothing else helps, use the Magento cleanup tools. Read this article: `http://goo.gl/izm1Zo.` It shows how to clean up Magento after a failed import process. Before using this method, make sure that you've double-checked your CSV files according to the requirements described.

Magmi

Another complex Magento import solution is Magmi, an open source tool with dozens of features and settings that makes Magento import flawless. It is extremely powerful, but not easy to use. You can download Magmi here: `http://goo.gl/aF7nd.`

Excel Import to Magento with Cobby

Cobby[35] is another useful tool designed with productivity and usability in mind. It connects your Magento website with Excel in real time, so you can edit all of your attributes and add new products without any headaches. Thus, Cobby is one of the most reliable and user-friendly ways of importing data to Magento on a daily basis.

The following are some other import extensions:

- Improved Import

- Import + Export Bulk Product Attributes / Attribute Sets / Attribute Options / Multiple Attributes

- Stock / Inventory Import Module

- Custom Bulk Product Import + Export with Tier Pricing / Product Custom Options / Configurable Products / Bundle Products / Grouped Products / Downloadable

- Extended Grid / Export - Orders, Invoices, Shipments, Products

- Import Products categories, multiple images, and custom options

- Fast Products Import

---

[35]`https://www.cobby.io/.`

- AvS_FastSimpleImport

- Bulk Category Import / Export

- Import Export Categories Extension

You can find their detailed descriptions here: `http://goo.gl/ZFNPB9`.

You are now familiar with Magento downloading and installation, what to do with a server and hosting, which templates and extensions to choose and how to install them, and how to import product data into your Magento store. So, it's time to talk about a key topic of this chapter: performance.

Performance

Performance is extremely important for every website—and ecommerce web stores are not an exception. Statistics differ from market to market, but the negative impact of slow speed is obvious. According to Summit.co.uk, in 2013, slow websites cost UK online retailers more than £8 billion. At the same time, there is information about the US market's $3 billion ecommerce sales loss.

Website performance tests by Summit.co.uk showed that over 90% of the 230 leading online retailers were failing to meet the industry's benchmark of a three-second page load. Furthermore, it took some about eight seconds to display a page. But how does this affect a visitor's behavior?

Forty-four percent of online customers think that a transaction has failed if the checkout is slow. As a result, many of them (33%) abandon their carts to look for ecommerce stores with better performance. A transaction with a two-second delay results in a high shopping cart abandonment rate, which is more than 80%.

The Metrics

There are new and existing consumers on every ecommerce web store. Thus, we can speak about two types of interaction: first view and repeat views. Both have three specific metrics: time to first byte, render start, and load time.

With *time to first byte,* you measure the amount of time required for servers to react to a request of a browser to send data. With *render start*, you measure the amount of time necessary for the first page element to be displayed in a browser. *Load time* means the total amount of time required to load all elements of a page.

The metrics should be measured under normal and peak loads conditions. You can use Webpagetest.org to do this. A report indicates what is slowing down your ecommerce website. The most common reasons are heavy images and interactive page features, site build shortcuts, a poor hosting environment, and so forth. These are Amazon's results for the first view:

- First byte: 0.285 sec

- Render start: 0.944 sec

- Load time: 2.071 sec

These are the results for the second view:

- First byte: 0.285 sec

- Render start: 0.833 sec

- Load time: 1.346 sec

Such results are an example of top-page load speed metrics to some extent. Next, I talk about all the solutions designed to optimize Magento ecommerce site performance and to achieve the aforementioned results.

This Magento Performance Ultimate Guide[36] is written for all versions of Magento (including Magento 2). It is suitable for the both Community and Enterprise editions. Additionally, it is useful for PHP and MySQL applications.

Magento Server-side Performance

You will find information about Magento server optimization in this section of the chapter. I show all the core aspects of this process.

Magento Optimized Hosting Services

You need to choose a hosting service for your Magento store. With a web hosting service, you make your ecommerce Magento store accessible via the World Wide Web. Th hosting service greatly influences performance. For example, a poor hosting solution can noticeably slow down your website. You can check our "Best Magento optimized hosting" blog post to find out the best solution for you. I would now like to draw your attention to Nexcess and Rackspace.

With Nexcess, you get full hosting options for your Magento website. The basic plan is $19.95 per month, but you have to pay annually if you want this exact price. If you choose a monthly payment, Nexcess costs $24.95 per month. For both solutions, you get one IP, 7.5GB of free space, 16GB RAM, 2x Quad Core E5620, 75GB of data per month, 9 additional stores, and 30 accounts per server. You can launch a demo for all proposed Nexcess plans.

This hosting service is the cheapest and the most stable and reliable among all Magento-optimized hosting services. I highly recommend that you try Nexcess SIP 200 as the perfect Magento hosting solution for both small and middle-sized Magento stores.

Rackspace is another top-notch hosting provider. The company has been on the market since 2008. Today, it includes more than 1,000 Magento clients worldwide. The cheapest Rackspace solution costs $499 per month. It best suits stores with 100 concurrent visitors and 150,000 products. For this money, you will get one quad core processor, 1 x 146GB 10K SAS, 4GB of RAM, Cisco ASA 5505 firewall, and 2TB Bandwidth every month.

---

[36]https://firebearstudio.com/blog/magento-performance-ultimate-guide-mysql-opcache-cache-cdn-nginx.html.

Nginx as a Magento Web Server

Magento Nginx configuration

Official manual on Magento wiki

You can always use LAMP as a simple hosting solution for your Magento store, but there are cases when the usage of Apache with mod_php is not the best idea. For instance, when your ecommerce Magento store has dynamic content generated by PHP scripts in addition to static files. For such situations, Nginx with PHP-FPM can be a better idea.

For simultaneous HTTP/HTTPS connections, Apache uses a large quantity of RAM and CPU cycles. The problem is particularly acute for the standard Apache configuration and the mod_php prefork. Since each Apache child process generally requires around 100MB RAM for every request, a dedicated 16GB RAM web server is limited to just 150 concurrent requests.

One of the major advantages of Nginx is its event-based structure (Apache is process based). Thus, Nginx doesn't require any new process to increase the level of concurrency. As a result, the memory footprint of Nginx is very low. In addition, Nginx exploits asynchronous and nonblocking I/O.

Nginx is operated by a pre-set number of worker processes, and each of them exists in the form of a single isolated process. Due to the event-driven and non-blocking architecture, Nginx allows every single worker process to handle requests from multiple clients.

You can benefit from Nginx even if you aren't going to handle thousands of requests at the same time. This server solution scales in all directions: from the smallest VPS to servers' clusters.

Nginx handles about 10,000 HTTP/HTTPS requests per second. It uses just 10MB to 20MB of RAM and averages 10% to 15% of CPU. Notice that in HTTPS, the usage of CPU is higher because of decryption/encryption routines.

The biggest drawback of Nginx is the absence of mod_php or its analogs designed for the direct execution of PHP apps. Being a static content web server and a reverse HTTP/FastCGI proxy, Nginx can't run Magento directly. In order to do so, it must utilize other means. The most reliable solution of this problem is PHP-FPM established for running high-load websites with PHP web apps. PHP-FPM consumes a small amount of resident memory and offers some unique features, such as adaptive process spawning, advanced logging with a slow log for slowly executing PHP scripts, the ability to start workers with different php.ini and "uid/gid/chroot/environment", an emergency restart for an accidental opcode cache destruction, real-time data on performance, and server activity.

To use Nginx with your Magento store, you need the front end enhanced with the following:

- Caching

- Reverse FastCGI proxy, which handles all HTTP/HTTP connections

- All static file delivery

- PHP-FPM

In this case, Nginx performs as a reverse FastCGI proxy for all dynamic content requests. All of them are proxied to a back-end PHP-FPM app and delivered back to a visitor after a response.

The usage of Nginx as a load balancer (one Nginx front end plus several PHP-FPM back ends) leads to a back-end failover and both high scalability and availability for the Magento installation. And you eliminate the need to utilize a hardware load balancer or any other associated expenses.

Monitoring Tools and Analyzers

A slow page or other negative user experiences could be the reason for leaving a webstore long before getting to checkout. Luckily, there are a lot of different monitoring tools and analyzers designed to identify a problem in time.

New Relic can be used to mark various operations, such as key transactions, for example triggers for custom alerting. Another function of this tool helps observe the slowest queries. Thanks to the "app map" feature, New Relic provides a clear view of the application dependencies that occur on your Magento ecommerce site. This feature also works along with third-party extensions and external services. With the app map feature, you can easily find the "weakest link" in your application chain. However, there are two other features that should be mentioned: Apdex scoring and alerting. With the aid of Apdex scoring, New Relic evaluates how well the Magento app is performing according to industry standards. Since the feature is combined with alerting, you will be always notified when the performance of your Magento store is challenged, due any variety of reasons.

Debugging Magento Performance with New Relic

Magento New Relic Integration on GitHub

Yireo New Relic Magento Extension

With the AppDynamics platform, you get full visibility of Magento-based PHP app performance. The solution provides rapid installation and high scalability. AppDynamics automatically discovers the Magento application topology. The tool provides the ability to customize a monitoring process by choosing which transactions to include or exclude from a real-time view. It also distinguishes web and mobile experiences, and expands visibility from the user to a database by correlating the performance of the database to originating transaction performance metrics. In addition, you are able to monitor root-cause errors and exceptions in real time.

Magento MySQL-Optimized Configuration

Proper MySQL configuration is among the most robust enhancements made to ensure the supreme performance of a Magento store. It requires an understanding of your hardware–primarily the available RAM. Next, I discuss the most reliable solutions elaborated to optimize Magento and that enhance a website's performance with the help of proper MySQL configurations.

This is an example of proper MySQL configurations:

```
1    ######################################################################
     ###################\
2    ####
3
4    ##  http://dev.mysql.com/doc/refman/5.6/en/innodb-parameters.html  ##
5
6    ##  https://raw.githubusercontent.com/rackerhacker/MySQLTuner-perl/
     master/mysqltuner.pl  ##
7
8    ## https://launchpadlibrarian.net/78745738/tuning-primer.sh ##
9
10   ## yum install mytop / apt-get install mytop ##
11
12   ######################################################################
     ###################\
13   ####
14
15   [mysqld]
16
17   ### MyISAM #
18
19   key_buffer_size = 16M # keep it low if no myisam data
20
21   myisam-recover-options = FORCE,BACKUP
22
23   ### SAFETY #
24
25   innodb = force
26
27   max_allowed_packet = 150M
28
29   max_connect_errors = 100000
30
31   bind-address = 127.0.0.1
32
33   skip-name-resolve
34
35   ### CACHES AND LIMITS #
36
37   back_log = 200
38
39   interactive_timeout = 7200
40
41   wait_timeout = 7200
42
43   net_read_timeout = 120
```

```
44
45   net_write_timeout = 300
46
47   sort_buffer_size = 2M
48
49   read_buffer_size = 2M
50
51   read_rnd_buffer_size = 16M
52
53   join_buffer_size = 4M
54
55   tmp_table_size = 128M
56
57   max_heap_table_size = 128M
58
59   query_cache_type = 1
60
61   query_cache_size = 128M
62
63   query_cache_limit = 4M
64
65   max_connections = 150
66
67   thread_cache_size= 32
68
69   open_files_limit = 65535
70
71   table_definition_cache = 4000
72
73   table_open_cache = 4000
74
75   ### INNODB_ #
76
77   innodb_thread_concurrency = 0
78
79   innodb_lock_wait_timeout = 7200
80
81   innodb_flush_method = O_DIRECT
82
83   innodb_log_files_in_group = 2
84
85   innodb_log_file_size = 256M
```

```
86
87    innodb_log_buffer_size = 16M
88
89    innodb_flush_log_at_trx_commit = 2
90
91    innodb_file_per_table = 1
92
93    innodb_io_capacity = 400
94
95    innodb_read_io_threads = 8
96
97    innodb_write_io_threads = 8
98
99    innodb_buffer_pool_instances = 8
100
101   innodb_buffer_pool_size = 4G
102
103   ### LOGGING #
104
105   #log_error = /var/log/mysql/mysql-error.log
106
107   #log_queries_not_using_indexes = 1
108
109   #slow_query_log_file = /var/lib/mysql/mysql-slow.log
110
111   ### BINARY LOGGING #
112
113   #log_bin = /var/lib/mysql/mysql-bin
114
115   #expire_logs_days = 14
116
117   #sync_binlog = 1
```

MariaDB Instead of Default MySQL

MySQL is not a necessity, so you can always move out of it. There are two popular alternative solutions: MariaDB and Percona. The first one is a fork of MySQL developed by the Magento community. MariaDB was created under GNU GPL. Its goals are as follows:

- Maintain high MySQL compatibility

- Ensure a drop-in replacement capability with a binary equivalency

- Match with MySQL commands and APIs

MongoGento by Smile Open Source Solutions

There is also an opportunity to use the NoSQL database instead of MySQL. Therefore, all you need is MongoGento by Smile Open Source Solutions. Since this module provides your Magento store with the ability to use MongoDB, you will reduce the size of your database and the Magento EAV model impact. The second reason of these two improvements is heterogeneous catalogues, designed for millions of products. At the same time, you retain the flexibility of a document model.

Another strong point of MongoGento is its performance. The combination of SolR, MageCache, and MongoDB makes both the front end and the back end extremely fast. I need to mention that MongoGento is an open source, scalable, and secure alternative to MySQL that has a quick installation.

The only drawback is a conflict among MongoGento and some other modules. For example, product catalog rules are not able to handle some attributes if you use MongoGento. For more information, go to MongoGento's GitHub or official web page:

MongoGento on Ecommerce-Performances

MongoGento on GitHub

MySQL and InnoDB Optimized Configuration

The following are the general options in a MySQL and InnoDB optimized configuration:

- **max_connections**: The maximum number of connections to allow. Watch this value: max_used_connections.

- **thread_cache**: Cache to prevent the creation of excessive thread. The good value is 50–100. Watch threads_created.

- **table_cache/table_open_cache**: Opens table instances cache. Multiple entries for single table are possible. Watch this status value: opened_tables and start with 4096.

- **open_files_limit**: Up to two file handlers are required for MyISAM tables. Each connection is file handler. It is safe to set to 65535 for the most systems.

- **table_definition_cache**: Cache table definitions and use only one entry per table. Opened_table_definitions to watch. Set + 10% to the number of tables unless there are 50K+ tables.

- **back_log**: Adjustment for many connections/sec is required. The reasonable value is 2048.

- **max_allowed_packet**: Sets a limit for the maximum query size and internal string variable size. The good value is 16MB.

- **max_connect_errors**: Prevents password brute force attack. Can be a cause of a Host Blocked error message. The good value is about 1000000.

- **skip_name_resolve**: Helps avoid DNS lookup on connection. Don't use host names for GRANTs.

- **old_passwords**: This shouldn't be enabled. It causes the use of insecure password hash.

- **log_bin**: Enable this parameter for replication and point in time recovery. To avoid default naming, you should set it to mysql-bin.

- **sync_binlog**: Make Binlog durable. Set to 1 for RAID with BBU or Flash. It turns slow drives into a performance killer.

- **expire_log_days**: Purges old binary logs after the set number of days. A good value is 14. Don't forget about weekly backups.

- **tmp_table_size**

- **max_heap_table_size**: Typically set to same value. Created_tmp_disk_tables status variable. BLOB/TEXT fields cause on disk table of any size.

- **query_cache_size**: Enable this parameter only if it is tested to provide considerable gains. It often causes stalls and contention. Remember, you should not set it over 512MB.

- **sort_buffer_size**: Used for sorting in memory buffer. Watch sort_merge_passes. Set within sessions for large queries. Good value is up to 1MB. Larger values hurt small queries performance.

- **join_buffer_size**: Use for better performance of joins with no indexes. But it is better to get rid of such joins. The reasonable value is 8MB.

- **default_storage_engine**: It uses the InnoDB engine for tables if nothing else is specified.

- **read_rnd_buffer_size**: A buffer for reading rows in sorted offer. It specifies the maximum value. Use values around 16MB, because they often make sense. Do not mix with read_buffer_size.

- **tmpdir**: Specifies location of temporary directory. It is often a good choice unless a very large temporary space is needed. tmpdir=/dev/shm.

The following are MyISAM options:

- **key_buffer_size**: Caches MyISAM indexes, but doesn't cache data. Requires up to 30% of memory if using MyISAM only.

- **myisam_recover**: Automatically repairs corrupted MyISAM tables after crash. The good value is BACKUP,FORCE.

- **myisam_sort_buffer_size**: Buffer used for building MyISAM indexes by Sort. Good values are between 8MB and 256MB

- **low_priority_updates**: This parameter allows higher concurrency for SELECTs. It may starve update queries.

- **bulk_insert_buffer_size**: A buffer for bulk inserts optimization. Values of 1/4 of key_buffer_size make sense. The value is per connection.

The following are the InnoDB memory settings:

- **innodb_buffer_pool_size**: This is the most important setting. About 80% of memory is allocated here.

- **innodb_buffer_pool_instances**: Reduces contention. Set it to 4+ in MySQL 5.5+.

- **innodb_log_buffer_size**: A buffer for log files. Good values are between 4MB and 128MB.

- **innodb_ibuf_max_size**: Controls the size of the insert buffer. 1/2 of buffer pool by default. Smaller values are good for SSD.

The following are the InnoDB IO options:

- **innodb_flush_log_at_trx_commit**: Controls durability. Use 1: flush and sync; 2: flush; 0: neither.

- **innodb_flush_method**: this parameter controls how InnoDB performs IO. O_DIRECT is a good value for most servers.

- **innodb_auto_lru_dump**: Percona Server feature designed for quick warm up. The good value is 300 (seconds).

- **innodb_io_capacity**: Controls InnoDB assumption about disk performance. Increase it for faster drives,

- **innodb_read_io_threads**:

- **innodb_write_io_threads**: Controls the number of threads by doing reads and writes. Since MySQL 5.5 has async IO, very high values might not be needed; 4 is a good default value.

- **innodb_flush_neighbor_pages**: Percona Server feature designed to control how flushing work. Disable it for SSD by setting to 0.

The following are other InnoDB options:

- **innodb_log_file_size**: sizes of redoes log file. Larger logs provide better performance, but with longer recovery.

- **innodb_log_files_in_group**: Leave it at 2.

- **innodb_file_per_table**: Store each InnoDB table in a separate file.

- **innodb=force**: Enable so MySQL is disabled to start if InnoDB could not initialize. Otherwise it might start but with the error on access to all InnoDB tables.

- **innodb_lock_wait_timeout**: Waiting time for row-level locks before bailing out.

- **innodb_old_blocks_time**: Use to make buffer pool scan resistant. Good values are around 1000.

- **innodb_file_format**: Sets the file format that InnoDB will use. The default legacy format is Antelope. Barracuda allows you to use new features.

- **innodb_stats_on_metadata**: Update statistics on metadata access (Information_schema queries). To disable it for more workloads, set to 0. InnoDB will refresh stats when the table changes significantly.

- **performance_schema**: Enables Performance Schema in MySQL 5.5+ and watches potential overhead.

- **log_slow_queries**: Enables Slow Query Log.

- **long_query_time**: With this parameter set to 0 periodically, you can get sample of the load.

- **log_slow_verbosity=full**: more data about queries in Percona Server.

- **low_warnings=2**: Warnings about disconnects in an error log.

- **userstat_running=1**: Advanced Table and Index usage statistics for both Percona Server and MariaDB.

MySQL Settings Optimization with Tuning Primer

The Tuning Primer shell script allows developers to review the MySQL settings of a Magento store and make adjustments to them for database stability and performance increase. The script analyzes MySQL stats and provides recommendations on tuning a MySQL server. The uptime required to correctly work the script is more than 48 hours. The Tuning Primer script is developed for all MySQL versions, starting with version 3.23.

Although there are a lot of articles about Magento performance, I advise you to pay attention to Magento on Steroids. Its author shares his best practices related to his daily work with Magento performance issues; he makes a strong emphasis on Magento server optimization.

Zend PHP Accelerator Configurations (Performance Improvements with OPcache)

As a code caching module, OPcache can significantly improve PHP performance and the performance of an entire store. OPcache uses shared memory to store a precompiled script bytecode, eliminating the need to load and parse scripts on every request, which is common for PHP. Thus by optimizing OPcache settings, you improve the performance of your Magento website. Check the article Enhanced Magento Performance with Optimized OPcache Settings to find out more about the optimization of OPcache settings.

Note that there are several other PHP accelerators developed to improve webstore performance. You can find the most useful and reliable solutions in our blog post The Best PHP Accelerators.

How to Use Redis with Magento

Redis (**Re**mote **di**ctionary **s**erver) is an open source, networked, in-memory data structure server that stores keys with optional durability. Being one of the most popular key-value stores, Redis is suitable for Magento. The ecommerce platform currently provides support for various cache back ends with file systems; but most of them cannot cope with a growing number of requests, thus they provide terrible scaling.

Moreover, some of them suffer from other limitations. A good example of such restrictions is the lack of support to group cache entries. To solve this problem, you can tune your Magento to a Redis store.

The current Memcached has no significant advantages over Redis. Both solutions are extremely fast, and all major features of Memcached are now offered by Redis. However, Redis surpasses Memcached. The latest version of Redis offers out-of-the-box clustering. The other useful tools are replication and Sentinel. With this combination, Redis offers a bunch of advantages over Memcached. The following features turn Redis into a real data store (Memcached is just a cache):

- Data types with powerful commands: sorted sets, hashes, lists, and so forth

- Default persistence to disk

- Optimistic locking transactions (WATCH/MULTI/EXEC)

- Extremely fast pub/sub

- Values are limited to 512MB (1MB per key in Memcached)

- Built-in clustering (as of 3.0)

- Lua scripting (as of 2.6)

Furthermore, Redis is more flexible than Memcached. It provides higher scalability, availability, and administration. Redis is not only a better solution for use cases associated with Memcached, but it is also suitable for new occasions.

The process of the Redis implementation as a cache and session back end is fully described on Inchoo: Redis cache backend and session storage in Magento.

There is another useful article related to this topic: How to Use Redis with Magento. Don't miss this PDF tutorial: Redis as a Cache Backend in Magento.

There are two useful projects on GitHub as well. The first one is Cm_RedisSession. It is a Redis-based session handler designed for Magento. Cm_RedisSession has a lot of useful features.

Go to Cm_RedisSession for a detailed description of this tool. There, you will also find an installation tutorial and an example of configurations.

With Cm_Cache_Backend_Redis, you get a Zend_Cache back end with Redis and tags support. The back end makes it possible to turn every Redis server into a central cache storage. Keep in mind that with Cm_Cache_Backend_Redis, full tags support doesn't require the use of TwoLevels cache. Thus, this back end is best suited for use in a cluster or on a single machine. Cm_Cache_Backend_Redis works with any Zend Framework project, all versions of Magento are supported as well.

How to Use CDN with Magento

A *content delivery network* (CDN) is a complex of servers with multiple data centers around the world and across the Internet. The main goal of every content delivery network is to provide content to end users with the highest possible performance and availability. CDNs work with different web objects and store downloadable content. They also provide faster access to apps, streaming media, and social networks. Thus, CDNs play an important role in modern online content delivery. There are dozens of possible solutions, but I would like to draw your attention to CloudFlare.

CloudFlare relies on recent hardware innovations, advanced network routing, and modern web server technology improvements. As a next-gen CDN, CloudFlare works better than its competitors. It is also more affordable and easier to set up. This CDN solution provides your website with a load speed that is twice as fast (regardless of the location of your visitors). I should also mention that CloudFlare works well with both static and dynamic content. Furthermore, the company guarantees that your Magento store will always be online. Last but not least, there is support for IPv6 networks and other CDNs. To set up your web store to use this CDN, you can utilize our CloudFlare control extension.

Get access to CloudFlare CDN[37]
Control for CloudFlare® Magento extension[38]
The Best CDN Services[39]

Magento Application-side Performance

The speed of your Magento website is among the key aspects of your success in online business. Since speed is taken into account by every search engine, it influences rankings. Thus, sites with better performance have advantages over the slower ones. That's why Magento's application-side performance also plays a crucial role.

Full Page Cache Magento Extensions

There are a lot of full page cache Magento extensions designed to improve website speed and reduce page load time. All modules from this group are based on the same principle explained next. Magento automatically generates and delivers pages to first-time visitors. These pages are copied and saved to cache. At some point, all the pages of your Magento store get cached copies, and the necessity to generate new pages from scratch is eliminated. Therefore, the full page cache extension reduces the load from the database and the server, and decreases page load time.

---

[37]https://www.cloudflare.com/.
[38]https://firebearstudio.com/cloudflare-control.html.
[39]https://firebearstudio.com/blog/the-best-cdn-services-and-extensions-for-magento.html.

You can find a complete list of the Full Page Cache extensions here: The Best Magento Full Page Cache Extensions[40].

The best free solutions among these is Lesti; whereas the most robust paid FPC Magento module is Extendware.

The Lesti::Fpc Magento extension (https://goo.gl/NHxxDs) doesn't require varnish or any other external tools and solutions. It works with events, replaces dynamic blocks before sending a response to the visitor, and caches cms_page_index, cms_index_index, catalog_product_view, and catalog_category_view pages by default. The module supports multiple stores and currencies. Additionally, Lesti::Fpc provides mobile themes and custom price groups. Hit this link for further information. Please note that the extension is good for small projects, but if you have a growing store, I definitely recommend that you use Extendware Full Page Cache.

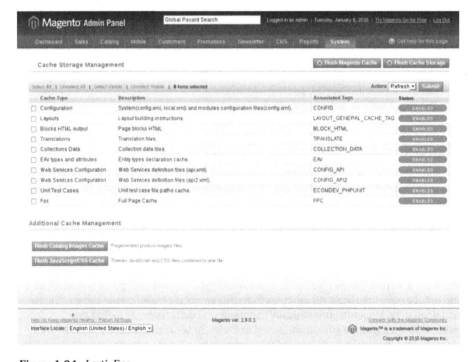

Figure 1-24. *Lesti_Fpc*

---

[40]https://firebearstudio.com/blog/the-best-magento-full-page-cache-extensions.html.

This solution possesses a positive reputation and tons of reviews from professionals. It features several add-ons that make it even faster, offers support for Redis, and provides reliable customer service. By using this full page cache, you will be able to receive help from Extendware specialists. Here are the core features of the module:

- Extendware Full Page Cache does not use the database, handling 90% of all requests. Thus, you can see the same speed as in Varnish, but with a better cache hit rate and easier configurations.

- The module enables entire page cache, groups of pages, or just specific pages related to an affected product. Thus, you don't flush what you don't really need to.

- Moreover, Extendware Full Page Cache fully supports catalog sorting. Please note that other similar extensions do not support the default Magento sort order changing in the catalog, which is the reason for incorrect caching in the default category sort order.

- There is multi-level cache support. The Full Page Cache extension offers three cache systems combined in one. Primary Page Cache increases server throughput by more than 100+ times. Secondary Page Cache offers hole punch support for logged users or visitors with products in a cart. Lightening Page Cache is 2–200 times faster than the primary cache level.

Don't forget to check other features in our Extendware Full Page Cache review: Extendware Full Page Cache Magento Extension Review[41]. You can also purchase the extension there.

Magento Cache Crawler/Warmer Extensions

It's extremely necessary to enhance your Full Page Cache Extension with a warmer/crawler module. This module crawls your ecommerce store to ensure that all pages load as fast as possible. In addition, a warmer/crawler extension refreshes old cached pages. Thus, all of your customers get the newest content at the fastest speed.

Moreover, cache warmer/crawler extensions help improve a website's cache hit rate by pre-caching uncached pages. As a result, you get more cached and less uncached requests. A list of warmers is here: The Best Full Page Cache Warmers/Crawlers For Magento[42]. I recommend that you use a solution offered by maverick193. You can get it for free. The best paid module is Extendware, which provides more robust features.

---

[41]https://firebearstudio.com/blog/extendware-full-page-cache-magento-extension-review.html.
[42]https://firebearstudio.com/blog/the-best-full-page-cache-warmerscrawlers-for-magento.html.

CSS and JS Minification

Another method of the Magento speed optimization concerns JavaScript and CSS files. It is possible to combine, compress, and cache them to enhance Magento's performance. I recommend that you use the Fooman Speedster Advanced Magento extension for the aforementioned operations. The module combines multiple JavaScript files or CSS files into a single file. It reduces the total size of loadable files and the number of HTTP requests, so you get a shorter page load time. You can download the Speedster Magento extension for free.

Merged with Fooman Speedster

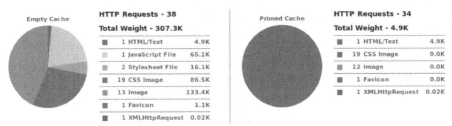

Figure 1-25. *Fooman Speedster*

Download Speedster Advanced Magento extension
Speedster Magento extension on GitHub
Extendware Minify JS / CSS / HTML Magento Extension[43]

Magento Cleaning

Due to an excellent logging system, the details of every request in Magento are logged. This leads to an oversized database, however, which slows down the website. Fortunately, there are many Magento cleaning solutions. Maintaining a database through log cleaning leads to a dramatic improvement in latency and performance. Nexcess explains how to optimize a large Magento database and increase the performance of an ecommerce store. You can take a look at a useful guide on Magikcommerce and these tips from different specialists. And don't forget to protect yourself from future headaches with the Yireo_DisableLog Magento module. Since this tool stops Magento from logging things, you get a neater database that will never decrease the performance of your website.

---

[43]https://firebearstudio.com/blog/extendware-minify-js-css-html-magento.html.

Faster Re-index

Fast re-indexing is another aspect of the Magento server optimization. It reduces server loads by speeding up saving products in a catalog. As a result, you increase the performance of your online store.

By installing the Improved Indexing Magento module, you will significantly improve the speed of the back end. Thus, saving products and categories will be much faster with this extension, and your administrators will be able to perform more tasks in a minimal amount of time.

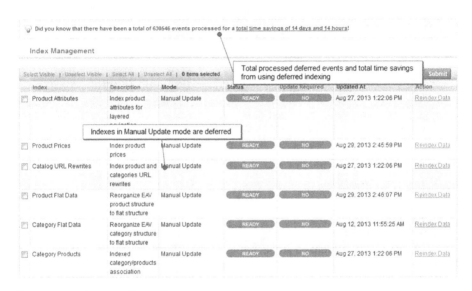

Figure 1-26. *Improved Indexing*

With the Fast Asynchronous Re-indexing extension, you will also boost the performance of your Magento website. This module reduces peak loads on a server by speeding up admin-related processes. When someone adds a new product or changes an existing one, a query to re-index goods occurs. With the Fast Asynchronous Re-indexing extension, a cron process performs data re-indexing in the background. Thus, admins can work continuously without any need to wait until re-indexing is finished.

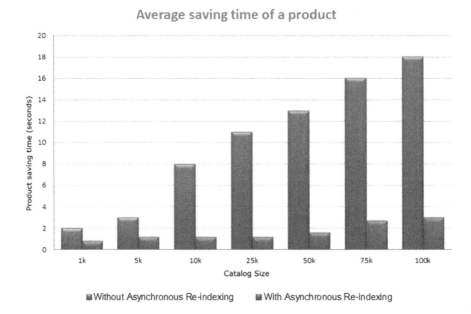

Figure 1-27. *Fast Asynchronous Re-indexing*

Varnish Cache

Varnish is designed to minimize a number of contentions between threads. It stores data in virtual memory. The selection of what data goes to disk and what is stored in the OS cache occurs. As a result, you can avoid a situation where the data is cached by the operating system and at the same time moved to a disk.

The Turpentine Magento Extension is developed to improve Magento's compatibility with Varnish. With the aid of Turpentine, you can improve your website's performance by adding a fast-caching reverse proxy to its system. Unfortunately, the default solution doesn't cache requests with cookies, so Magento's front-end cookies cause a near zero hit-rate with Varnish. By installing the Turpentine Magento extension, you provide the system with Varnish configuration files (VCLs) and improve Magento's behavior. Thus, Varnish works with Magento.

Turpentine on GitHub

You can use the official manual to learn how to use Magento + Varnish Cache. And don't forget to check a comparison of Full Page Cache vs. Varnish Cache on Amasty.

Improved Magento Catalog Search

A reliable searching tool is useful for every ecommerce store. Luckily, there are a lot of extensions designed for providing visitors with the ability to find the desired content. I recommend that you pay attention to the Sphinx Search Ultimate and Managed Elasticsearch Magento extensions.

The Sphinx Search Ultimate extension helps you improve the quality of a search. The module supports more than 660 stop words and understands more than 60,000 synonyms. It provides your customers with the ability to perform a searching query by category names, tags, and product SKUs. The extension costs $149.

Mirasvit Sphinx Search Ultimate Review[44]

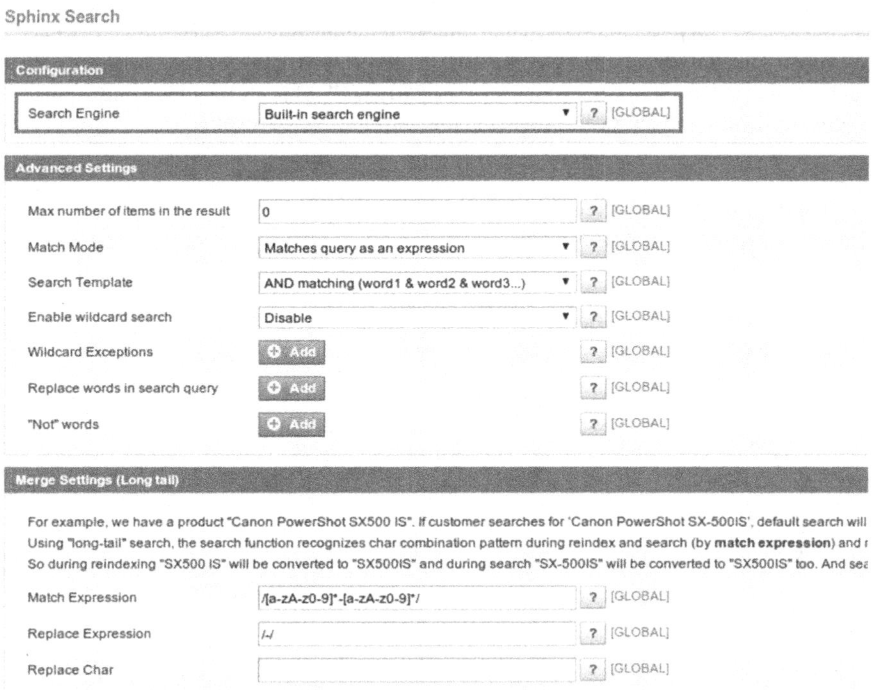

Figure 1-28. *Sphinx Search Ultimate*

The Managed Elasticsearch Magento extension provides one of the most powerful full-text search options available as an open source product. With this Magento module, you provide your customers with precise and reliable search results. Additionally, there is the opportunity to configure attribute names, descriptions, and SKUs as searchable attributes with this extension.

Download Managed Elasticsearch

---

[44]https://firebearstudio.com/blog/mirasvit-sphinx-search-ultimate-for-magento-1-and-2.html.

How to Improve Checkout and Add to Cart Speed in Magento

Although you can cache static CMS pages, like products and categories, with Full Page Cache, along with a fast back-end cache storage, such as Redis or Memcached, you will still have slow dynamic pages. Thus, it is vital to increase checkout and add-to-cart speed in your Magento setup. There are also problems related to PHP/web server, which slow down your store. Next, I'll teach you how to improve default performance, making your customers loyal to your brand.

One Step Checkout

First, I'd like to draw your attention to One Step Checkout extensions, since they are more user-friendly than a default solution. There is an appropriate list of such modules on the Firebear blog (The Best One Step / Page Checkout Extensions For Magento[45]). The best free tool is One Step/Page Checkout by IWD (`https://goo.gl/72qrA8`). The most reliable paid solution is One Step Checkout (`http://goo.gl/2MjSf`). By installing one of these extensions, you significantly improve the time required for checkout.

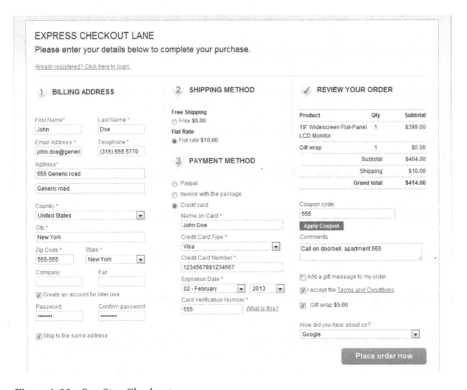

Figure 1-29. *One Step Checkout*

---

[45]`https://firebearstudio.com/blog/the-best-one-step-page-checkout-extensions-for-magento.html`.

PHP Accelerators

Another crucial aspect that helps to increase site speed is the usage of PHP accelerators designed to improve the performance of PHP apps. Most of them cache compiled opcode/bytecode to avoid overhead caused by compiling source code during each request. The cached code is stored in a shared memory and executed from there. As a result, PHP accelerators minimize the amount of slow disk reads and decrease memory copying at a runtime. The best PHP accelerators are described here: The Best PHP Accelerators[46].

Cache Back End

You can easily improve your cache back end with the help of the Performance Cache Backends extension by Extendware. The module provides improved file-based and Redis-based caches optimized for tag flushing. As a result, you get a faster add-to-cart process, checkout, and product savings. The extension costs $149 and you can check its review here: Extendware Cache Backends / Faster Checkout Magento Extension[47].

Indexing

Improved Indexing is another extension by Extendware aimed at improving the performance of your Magento store. The module increases the speed of the administrative back end. It reduces all slowdowns that occur when saving products or categories. As a result, you can perform the same amount of work faster. The price of Improved Indexing is $139. You can check the extension here: Extendware Improved Indexing Magento Extension Review[48].

The Most Reliable Community Advice

By monitoring different forums, I've highlighted the following important steps:

1. To increase the speed of Magento checkout, disable the Mage_Rss module, since it forces a "cache clean" four times during a checkout process slowing down your website.

2. If you aren't using downloadable products, turn off Mage_Downloadable. This will help to increase the checkout speed, as well as reduce the time necessary for cart actions when there are multiple items in a cart.

---

[46]https://firebearstudio.com/blog/the-best-php-accelerators.html.
[47]https://firebearstudio.com/blog/extendware-cache-backends-faster-checkout-magento-extension.html.
[48]https://firebearstudio.com/blog/extendware-improved-indexing-magento-extension-review.html.

3. Set your indexes to **manual** and disable cache tag storage. Both changes provide a huge impact on performance as they prevent Magento from flushing out caches and re-indexing for each order. Unfortunately, these actions can make your content stale.

4. Perform some profiling and wire up xhprof/xhgui.

Disable Some Core Extensions

The following are some of the core extensions that need to be disabled.

- Mage_Adminnotification
- Mage_Authorizenet
- Mage_Bundle (if it is not used on your website)
- Mage_Downloadable
- Mage_GiftMessage
- Phoenix_Moneybookers
- Mage_Paygate (along with disabled Mage_Paypal, Mage_PaypalUk, and Mage_Authorizenet)
- Mage_Poll
- Mage_Rating (if it is not used on your website)
- Mage_Rss
- Mage_Sendfriend
- Mage_Tag (if it is not used on your website)
- Mage_Weee (along with disabled Mage_XmlConnect)

You can turn off more core extensions, depending on your project, but these are the ones that should be disabled most often. Just make sure that you don't break the stability of your Magento.

Always clean the cache and do full end-to-end store testing after disabling to make sure that everything works well and there are no errors.

Enterprise-Class Magento Performance Solutions

This section discusses Enterprise-class Magento performance solutions.

Dedicated Magento Multi-Servers/Clusters

Magento Enterprise Clusters by Nexcess offers the highest possible performance. All solutions utilize the latest security and performance enhancements. Each cluster is individually built, optimized, and customized for Magento, and all of them include access to Nexcess' CDN. A basic solution is Two-Node Cluster, both a web application server and a database server. With this solution, you can split your Magento store load into two independent servers. In addition, you will get such features as extra firewalling and staging environments. Two-Node Cluster starts from $1,499 per month.

Similar to Nexcess is Rackspace. It hosts more Magento sites than any other competitor. The company provides simple and powerful templates for self-service management. Other advantages of Rackspace include flexible architecture options, end-to-end support, and exceptional customer experience.

Mgt-commerce also offers Enterprise-class performance solutions for Magento and provides first-rate hosting services. By choosing this option, you get additional time for managing your business, since Mgt-commerce offers four types of multi-server environments optimized for blazing speed. The basic solution starts at $249.

And don't forget to look at Dedicated Magento Cluster by Byte. It also aims at enhancing the performance of your website. The basic solution costs $1,800 per month.

How to Scale Magento in a Multi-Hosting Environment

In this tutorial on severalnines, the author shows how to cluster Magento, Nginx, and MySQL on multiple servers. The article is full of useful tips, demonstrative visual materials, and examples. There are also articles on Stack Exchange that show how to scale Magento in a multi-hosting environment. I recommend that you pay attention to a post by Valentine Okafor. It describes the process of moving a Magento database to a different server.

Now your Magento store has an incredible performance range but it is still insecure. Hackers can steal vital data from your website, turn off the ecommerce store, and even digitally rob your customers. Next, I explain how to avoid these problems by turning your Magento store into a fortress.

Security Guide

Thousands of Magento websites were infected with the Guruincsite malware, so it is extremely important to find out if your store is infected and to prevent it from the virus. For further information, check this article: Guruincsite Magento Disaster[49].

---

[49]https://firebearstudio.com/blog/guruincsite-magento-disaster.html.

SUPEE-6788 was released to help solve the Guruincsite problem. For further information about how to download and install the patch to remove the problem, visit our Magento security patches[50] post.

Eighty percent of Magento shops worldwide are still vulnerable. Check the following infographic by Byte for further information. Alternatively, you can read the entire article related to the problem (the infographic is the illustration of the article). It describes the reason why people do not patch their Magento websites, so it might change your opinion about the security problems. 80% of Magento shops worldwide still vulnerable[51].

Fortunately, you can easily scan your Magento shop for known security vulnerabilities on MageReport[52].

Although Magento is the safest ecommerce platform, there are still additional security tricks that make it even safer. Thousands of Magento websites have been hacked during the past few years. Luckily, there are several useful methods developed to fix all the major problems. Next, the most important security tips and reliable security extensions are described. You can also check this guide: Magento Security Ultimate Guide[53].

Name and Password

You should make all of your Magento passwords unique and strong. The same goes for your admin name. This simple step can help you improve the security of your website. Just create a password that is longer than eight characters and to some extent, you will prevent your store from being hacked. Note that passwords should combine numbers, letters, and special characters. Indeed, do not use weak usernames such as "admin" or "administrator". If you are using an insecure name and password, you can always change them in System ➤ My Account.

Custom Path for Admin Panel

A default path to an admin panel has the following construction: http://storename.com/admin. Everyone knows it—consequently, it is among Magento security vulnerabilities. By changing it to more complex path—for example, http://storename.com/superadmin, you push the security of your ecommerce website to a new level. This small step is the best defense against broken authentication and session management attacks.

You can always change the Magento admin path in the app/etc/local.xml file. Find the line which contains <![CDATA[admin]]> and create a new string instead of admin, for instance, superadmin. The new code should look as follows: <![CDATA[superadmin]]>.

---

[50]https://firebearstudio.com/blog/magento-critical-security-patches-supee-5344-and-supee-1533-shoplift.html.

[51]https://www.byte.nl/blog/80-of-magento-shops-worldwide-still-vulnerable.

[52]https://www.magereport.com/.

[53]https://firebearstudio.com/blog/magento-security-ultimate-guide.html.

Two-Factor Authentication

Another reliable security technique is two-factor authentication. It adds an additional security layer to an existing one. The system requires two separate authentications to provide users with access. Thus, your Magento website becomes two times more secure. You can provide your admins with the two-factor authentication solution using one of these Magento modules: Xtento Two-Factor Authentication[54] or Extendware Two-Factor Authentication[55]. More Admin Login Security Tools[56].

Encrypted (HTTPS/SSL) Connection

Another essential security improvement is the usage of the HTTPS/SSL–secure URLs. By being HTTPS/SSL–encrypted, your ecommerce website is PCI-compliant as well. This means that you will get a secure data transfer between your site and server. Otherwise, there is a risk that data (database information and login details) will be intercepted by hackers.

To enable the HTTPS/SSL secure URLs, you should go to System ➤ Configuration ➤ General ➤ Web. Then, it is necessary to change "http" to "https" in the base URL, and enable the "Use secure URLs for both Frontend and Admin" feature.

File Upload with Secure FTP

In addition to HTTPS/SSL–secure URLs, you can also take care of the FTP connection with your server. Use SFTP because it provides an additional encryption of user credentials. This protocol uses a private key file for authentication. Make sure that file permissions are not set to 777; otherwise, anyone will be able to rewrite them.

Pre-Defined IP Addresses for Administrators

Magento provides the opportunity to set predefined IP addresses for accessing the admin panel, which is a robust security enhancement. You just have to create a list of IPs. This way, users with other addresses won't be able to access the admin panel of your website.

To implement this security feature, find your .htaccess file and enter the following code:

```
1    AuthName "Protected Area"
2    AuthType Basic
3    <Limit GET POST>
4    order deny,allow
5    deny from all
6    allow from 172.161.132.13
7    allow from 153.119
8    </Limit>
```

---

[54]https://firebearstudio.com/blog/xtento-two-factor-authentication-for-magento-2-and-1.html.
[55]https://firebearstudio.com/blog/extendware-two-factor-authentication-magento-extension-review.html.
[56]https://firebearstudio.com/blog/admin-login-security-extensions-for-magento.html

Hence, you implement the user permission to access your admin panel with the 172.161.132.13 IP address, and for everyone whose IP address starts with 153.119. This technique supports an unlimited number of IP addresses.

Then, you should go to the Magento root directory and create a new folder called admin. Copy the index.php file of your Magento and paste it there. Now, you have to change relative paths to the config.php and Mage.php files. Change the following lines:

```
1   $compilerConfig = '../includes/config.php';
2   $mageFilename = '../app/Mage.php';
```

You should only add '../'.
Now go to the. htaccess file and enter the following lines:

```
1   Redirect permanent /index.php/{admin_path} /admin/index.php/{admin_path}
2   Redirect 301 /index.php/{admin_path} /admin/index.php/{admin_path}
```

Therefore, you will direct users coming to our admin to a new directory. {admin_path} indicates the new admin path that was manually changed.

This security step works only with static IP addresses. If your ISP assigns dynamic IP addresses, you shouldn't implement this technique.

Malicious PHP Functions

There are malicious PHP functions that should be disabled. You can use more secure alternatives instead. To disable these functions, find your php.ini file, open it, and add the following code:

```
1   disable_functions = "apache_child_terminate, apache_setenv,
    define_syslog_variables, escap\
2   eshellarg, escapeshellcmd, eval, exec, fp, fput, ftp_connect, ftp_exec,
    ftp_get, ftp_login\
3   , ftp_nb_fput, ftp_put, ftp_raw, ftp_rawlist, highlight_file, ini_alter,
    ini_get_all, ini_\
4   restore, inject_code, mysql_pconnect, openlog, passthru, php_uname,
    phpAds_remoteInfo, php\
5   Ads_XmlRpc, phpAds_xmlrpcDecode, phpAds_xmlrpcEncode, popen,
    posix_getpwuid, posix_kill, p\
6   osix_mkfifo, posix_setpgid, posix_setsid, posix_setuid, posix_setuid,
    posix_uname, proc_cl\
7   ose, proc_get_status, proc_nice, proc_open, proc_terminate, shell_exec,
    syslog, system, xm\
8   lrpc_entity_decode"
```

Take into account that you can disable other functions in your php.ini file, as well as omit important functions from the code.

Directory Listing

Directory listing is among common server loopholes. It provides everyone with the ability to see the directory structure and location of all of its files by simply entering a website's URL. Therefore, you should disable directory indexing by adding the following code in your .htaccess file:

```
1   Options -Indexes
```

MySQL Injections

Since every Magento website has many form fields for user data input, hackers can easily steal this data by injecting MySQL statements. To protect your store from such a threat, you should use web firewalls (several apps are described next).

To solve this problem, update your Magento to the latest version because it always provides a lot of improvements, bug fixes, new features, and security enhancements. At the same time, there is the possibility of new, undiscovered problems related to the latest update.

- **Create backups of your Magento store regularly**. This helps you decrease every hack damage level and you will be able to restore your Magento website faster.

- **Fix all email loopholes**. Keep in mind that your email should not be widely known. It should be protected by a unique and secure password as well.

- **Check the security of your Magento website regularly**. This will help you find all issues at early stages.

- **Always update your antivirus software**. Older versions are not able to protect your store from the latest threats.

- **Find out where your browser comes from**. The browser stores a lot of necessary information about your Magento website. Try not to save passwords in it because any access to your computer allows hackers to easily get your credentials.

- **Hide the local.xml file from public access**. It contains sensitive data, such as database information and the encryption key. Hide it. You can do it by changing file permissions for local.xml to 600(-rw) or blocking a web access to the entire app directory.

- **Upgrade your OS to the most recent version**. It should provide new security improvements.

- **Install Magento security patches**. They are developed to fix all current security problems on your store. When writing this guide, SUPEE-6285 was the latest.

- **Make sure that your hosting provider is reliable and secure**. Note that some hosting providers are not prepared for hacker attacks.

- **Provide limited permissions for files and documents**. For downloadable documents, set only read permissions, so that no program will be able to modify them.

- **Disable Magento Connect Manager** after installing extensions. This prevents any random changes.

- **Use only trusted Magento extensions** from reliable sources, such as Magento Connect.

- **Change passwords for outside developers**. You can reset your original passwords after work is done.

- **Check web server logs for errors or suspicious activities**. This way, you will be able to detect threats at early stages.

- **Block unwanted countries if you are not shipping worldwide**. You can utilize the GeoIP Legacy Apache module.

See the PDF for more tips.

Magento Security Extensions

First, check Amasty Security Suite for Magento[57], since it is an all-in-one solution. Next, examine the following list.

- The ET IP Security extension restricts access to your Magento website by IP addresses or IP masks, so you don't have to implement this security technique manually. The module redirects customers without access to a page specified in settings (it can be just a blank page). The extension is free. Download ET IP Security Magento Extension.

---

[57]https://firebearstudio.com/blog/amasty-security-suite-for-magento.html.

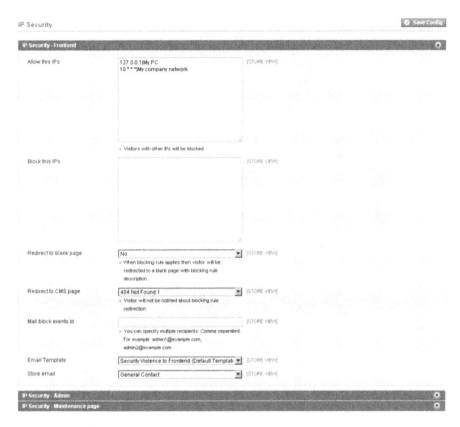

Figure 1-30. ET IP Security

- With the SecureTrading Magento module, you will be able
  to integrate your ecommerce website with STPP - The
  SecureTrading Payment Pages. This gateway provides a secure
  acceptance of online payments. Your store doesn't even have to
  be PCI-compliant (but it should) with this module, since all of
  your customers will be redirected to the servers of SecureTrading
  to enter card information. This solution relies on iframes and
  custom CSS/JavaScript. It provides two payment methods:
  Payment Pages, which is based on redirection to Secure Trading,
  where credit card information is captured, and API, where all
  information is captured on your server (less secure). The module
  is also free. Download SecureTrading Magento Extensions.

- With the help of Trusted Shops with Trustbadge, you provide your customers with insight into the reliability of your store. The extension shows a trust badge, which displays such information as reviews, trustmarks, and money-back guarantees. Although the module doesn't provide any security fixes, it shows that your Magento store is a secure place. And you can download it for free. Download Trusted Shops with Trustbadge Magento Extension.

- Authorize.Net CIM is designed for the improved payment security of your ecommerce website. It supports all Magento payment actions and allows customers to save payment information for future usage. As a result, they can enjoy a rapid checkout without disregarding PCI compliance. I should also mention that Authorize.Net CIM supports ACH and recurring profiles. The extension costs $599. Download Authorize.Net CIM with Recurring Profiles.

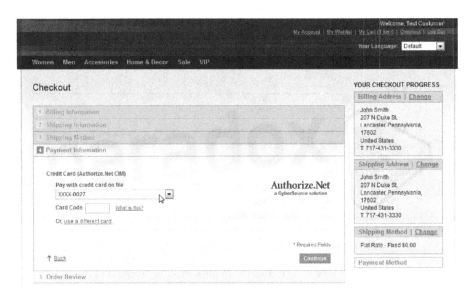

Figure 1-31. Authorize.Net CIM

- With the Enhanced Admin Security: Two-Factor Authentication Magento module, you are able to enhance the security of your store by utilizing two-factor authentication. Thus, your admins will have to enter a username, password, and security code to log in to the system. The code, which is generated by an application on a smartphone, can be used only once within 30 seconds. You can download the Enhanced Admin Security Magento extension for $69. Download Enhanced Admin Security Magento Module.

Magento
Log in to Admin Panel
User Name:
Password:
Security Code:
Forgot your password?
Login
Magento is a trademark of Magento Inc. Copyright © 2012 Magento Inc.

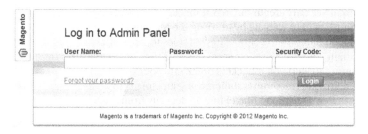

Figure 1-32. *Two-Factor Authentication*

- Magento: Two-Factor-Authentication is a free alternative to the previous solution. With this module, back-end users with access to Magento's protected resources are asked to enter a one-time security code after standard authentication. The code is generated by the Google Authenticator application. Download Magento: Two-Factor-Authentication from GitHub.

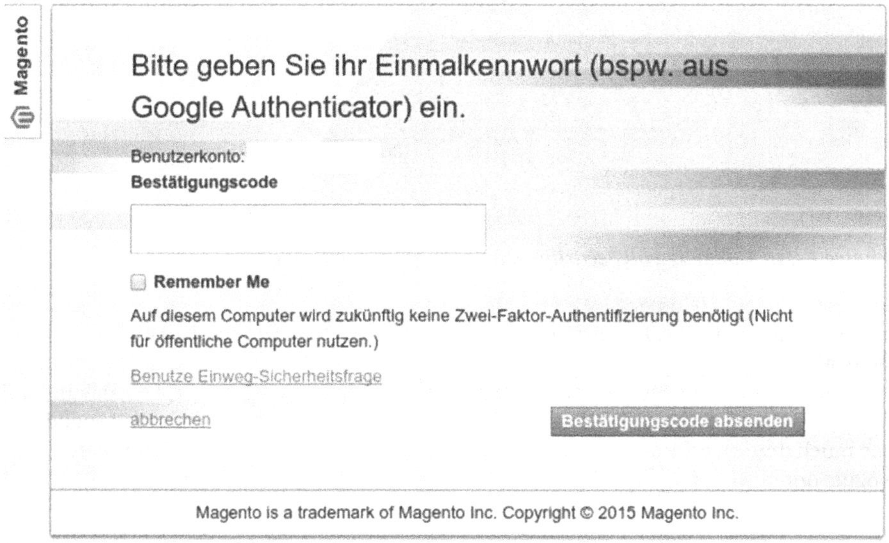

Magento
Bitte geben Sie ihr Einmalkennwort (bspw. aus Google Authenticator) ein.
Benutzerkonto:
Bestätigungscode
Remember Me
Auf diesem Computer wird zukünftig keine Zwei-Faktor-Authentifizierung benötigt (Nicht für öffentliche Computer nutzen.)
Benutze Einweg-Sicherheitsfrage
abbrechen
Bestätigungscode absenden
Magento is a trademark of Magento Inc. Copyright © 2015 Magento Inc.

Figure 1-33. *Magento Two-Factor-Authentication*

- • MageFirewall Security creates an additional layer of security around your Magento website by utilizing the Magento firewall. This extension relies on the Ninja Firewall rules to block attackers, blacklist them, and prevent their access to your site. MageFirewall uses a scanner to alert you if hackers break into your website. In addition, it provides recommendations on your store setup. The extension is free. Download MageFirewall Security from Magento Connect.

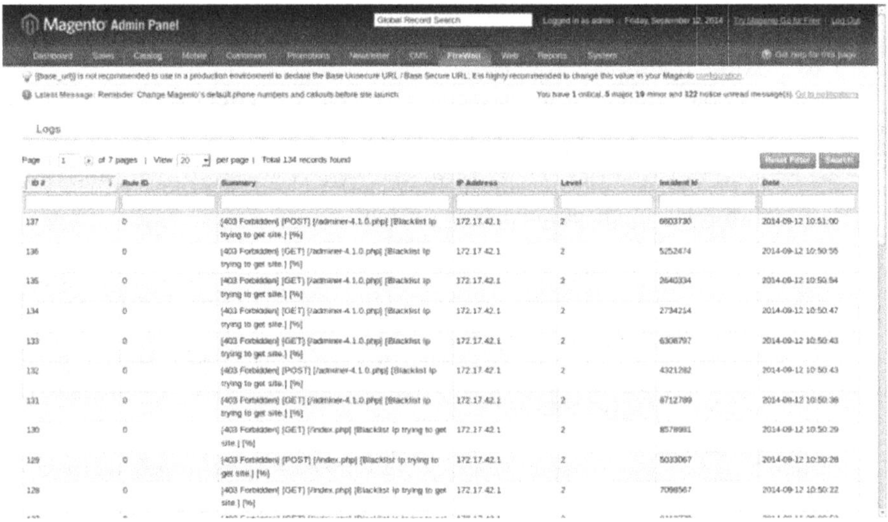

Figure 1-34. *MageFirewall Security*

Don't forget to check an important article regarding Critical Security Patches, located here: http://goo.gl/JTXc83. Security problems described in this article can be solved by installing the latest versions of the platform or manually. In this article, I shed light on all the solutions and provide relevant information about the problem. But don't spend too much time on critical security patches; there is still a lot of work to do with search engine optimization (SEO).

SEO

Search engines provide your potential customers with a list of search results, where your ecommerce website is shown. This list often consists of hundreds of pages. You want to see your Magento store at the top; otherwise, it will be lost among the others, and your potential customers will never visit it. The only helpful solution to this problem is *search engine optimization*. I have gathered everything that you need to know about this process.

You can start your search engine optimization with the Magento extensions described earlier. You can also find the best solutions in this post: Best Magento SEO Extensions[58]. Additionally, you can check Magento Connect for more modules—just hit this link. If you need a single reliable solution, pay attention to the Creare SEO Magento extension. The module is free, but at the same time it is one of the most robust SEO solutions. It enhances your store with several new features, such as an HTML sitemap; unique category headings; Noindex on category filters; config editable .htaccess and robots.txt files; default page titles and metadescriptions for categories and products; discontinued products and 301 redirects; the ability to disable keywords and meta description tags; Twitter cards for product pages; a script for performance cleanup; the Breadcrumbs schema; a SEO checking page in admin; an XML sitemap fix; a product attribute validator; the canonical product redirect, and so forth. You can download Creare SEO from Magento Connect here. Hit this link for additional information about the extension.

Take into consideration that search engines love fast websites, and ecommerce stores are not an exception. So you can improve your rankings by making your store faster.

Just enhance the performance of your Magento website and you will get better SEO results. Moreover, you will make your customers more loyal, because they, as well as search engines, have a better opinion of faster websites.

In addition to extensions and performance, there are plenty of tips and tricks for guaranteed search engine optimization on every website. Next, you will find the most popular SEO solutions taken from this post: Ultimate Guide to Magento SEO[59]. Also check our DIY SEO articles[60].

Stay Away from Manufacturer's Descriptions

Many ecommerce merchants use manufacturer's descriptions in their initial state. As a result, hundreds of web stores post the same content. Of course, this provides a negative impact on SEO, since search engines want to index only unique content. Add something new to the description of your goods, and you will get better rankings. I strongly recommend that you avoid copying content from other websites. Spend additional time (or money) on rewriting product descriptions.

---

[58]https://firebearstudio.com/blog/best-magento-seo-extensions-2014.html.
[59]https://firebearstudio.com/blog/ultimate-guide-to-magento-seo.html.
[60]https://firebearstudio.com/blog/diy-seo-on-firebear.html.

Extract Benefits from Your Image Alt Tags

There is an "alt" property in the image HTML tag that was originally designed for slow Internet connections. But now it has a new purpose. The image alt tag can be used for the search engine optimization of your Magento store. Google relies on the content of alt tags to define what is on the page (mostly images). That's why you should create small descriptions in the alt property in order to improve SEO.

Tool up with Link Building

A proper link-building strategy will significantly improve the SEO optimization of your Magento store. Also don't forget about cross linking within your website. Check our blog post on Link Building Strategies to find out the core SEO improvements that you can perform with the help of this set of tactics.

Get More Profit from Similar Products

Let's imagine that a visitor has landed on the web page of a product that he doesn't want. You can still save the day by proposing similar products on the same page. Thus, the customer does not leave your site immediately and won't provide a negative impact on your rankings. Moreover, you will be able to upsell by offering similar goods. Check this list of the Best Related Products Magento Extensions for additional information.

Utilize Popular Products Properly

Use your homepage to display products that are popular on the market or within your store. This will help engage your returning visitors immediately.

Make Discontinued Products Work for You

Some products from your ecommerce store probably no longer exist. But don't be in haste deleting their pages. Instead, redirect your visitors from old pages to new ones by using the server 301 redirect code. You will preserve all of your page rankings this way, so don't make obvious mistakes by deleting useful content.

What Should I Do with the 302 Redirects

Whereas the 301 redirect is a real SEO savior, the 302 redirect is a harmful one because it doesn't pass any link juice to a new page (301 does). Thus, you lose traffic and rankings if you use the 302 redirect. However, it's good to apply it with compare links, wish list links, geolocations, and currency switch links. Visit this page to find out more about the 302 redirect.

Create a Perfect 404 Page

Deleted page links stay in search engines for a certain amount of time. When a customer clicks such a link, the 404 error page is displayed. I recommend that you customize your 404 page to help visitors find the products that they are looking for. That's why a custom 404 page can save you from losing traffic.

Better SEO Results with Good Navigation

When a random user visits your Magento store from a search engine page, but leaves it to perform another query, he provides a negative impact on your rankings. The core reason for such behavior is navigation. Provide your visitors with a proper user experience and you will prevent your Magento SEO from this negative impact. Therefore, make it easy for users to find the desired products within your store.

Clean up Your URLs from Store Codes

With default configurations, Magento adds store codes to URLs. These unique identifiers are good for locating products within your database, but they are inappropriate in URLs. Disable store codes by setting "Add Store Codes to URLs" to No. Go to the Configuration menu, select Web, and then Search Engine Optimization. You will see an appropriate option there.

Optimize your Magento Store Wisely with Google Analytics

With Google Analytics, you can get all the information that is essential for SEO optimization. Luckily, there is an opportunity to connect this service to your ecommerce store without any headaches, since Magento supports GA integration. Be wise and get more from available resources.

Turn Your Visitors into Buyers with the Aid of the Right Keywords

Keywords influence the effectiveness of optimization. Some keywords are more for "buying" than others. Pay attention to this nuance, and you will be able to gain more from your Magento website.

Unleash the Power of Blogging

By adding a blog to your digital store, you are able to improve its SEO. Post unique and relevant content, communicate with your visitors, provide them with useful information, and you will engage more customers.

Get More from Rich Snippets

Due to rich snippets, you can integrate different HTML5 components into your products, improving their SEO. For example, ratings and reviews integrated into products appear in search engine results and provide you with competitive advantages over other ecommerce websites (if they are a five-star ratings).

Enhance SEO with the Help of Security

Use SSL certificates to provide both customers and search engines with a sense of security. You will learn how to use SSL later in this chapter.

Never Forget About Your Robots.txt File

It is extremely important to make a custom robots.txt file. All ecommerce stores are different, so a generic robots.txt file is unacceptable. I strongly recommend that you consider applying the Google Webmaster Tool before using it on a web store.

Stay Mobile-Friendly

If you have an audience of mobile users, then you should provide them with a mobile-friendly version of your Magento store. According to Google's policy, websites with a responsive design (or with a mobile version) get better rankings in a mobile search. Check our posts about Mobilegeddon and Responsive Design for a better understanding of the problem.

Be the King of Social Media

Utilize the power of social networks. You will not only improve your SEO, but you will get many more new buyers. Pay attention to the fact that Facebook and Twitter can become the driving forces of your sales. You just have to use them properly.

That's all in regards to small SEO tips. More robust optimization is waiting for you next!

More Complex Search Engine Optimizations

If the preceding information is not enough for your ecommerce store, and you plan to implement more robust changes to improve SEO, then this section of the chapter is for you.

1. Start with the Basics

1.1. General Configurations

Magento is not only one of the safest ecommerce platforms, but it is one of the most SEO-friendly solutions and you can always make it even more SEO optimized.

I recommend that you update your store to the latest version of the platform and enable Server URL rewrites. Just go to System, open Configuration, click the Web options, and make an improvement in the Search Engines Optimization section. On the same screen, set Add Store Code to URLs (under URL Options) to No.

You can choose between a www and a non-www version of your website URL. But which version is more SEO-friendly?

There is no definite answer to this question, so you should decide which one is better for you. I only recommend that you create a 301 redirect if you change this setting. Use .htaccess with mod_rewrite, because it prevents Magento from adding SID queries to URLs.

1.2. Header

"Magento Commerce" is the default title of your Magento store. To improve your SEO, you should change this. You can do it in Configuration ➤ Design ➤ HTML Head. Change the default title to a new one that describes your store.

You can also add a store name to all of your website's page titles in the Title Suffix field. Keep Prefix, Default Description, and Default Keywords fields empty.

There are production and non-production environments on your Magento store. Both have default robots. For non-production applications, you should set NOINDEX, NOFOLLOW; for all others, set INDEX, FOLLOW.

Don't forget about canonical URLs. You can set them using one of these modules.

1.3. CMS Pages

To get better rankings, you can optimize your Magento store's CMS pages. When they are filled with decent content, take both a page title and a SEF URL identifier, go to the Metadata tab, and create descriptions for the CMS pages that you are going to work with.

Keep the Keywords field empty. Please note that you should create descriptions with your customers in mind, because the descriptions are displayed on search results pages. Use only informative descriptions that you've written. Avoid using autogenerated descriptions.

1.4. Category

To prevent duplicate content issues associated with categories, you should disable the "Use categories path for product URLs" option. Go to System, open Configuration, find the Catalog options, and click Search Engine Optimization. Set the parameter to No.

To set category information, go to Catalog ➤ Manage Categories and Descriptions in Meta Description fields and create a short description. At the same time, use keyword-rich URLs in URL Key field. Keep the Page Title empty.

1.5. Product Pages

The optimization of product pages is almost the same as with categories. Keep in mind that Meta Title overwrites the title of a page.

Additional search engine optimization includes work with images. You should use the alt tag to make your Magento website more SEO-friendly.

2. Make the Most out of the Magento Template

2.1. Headings

Let's start with the logo. In a default template, it is the <h1> tag, which should be used on the front page only! For other pages, use the <h3> tag or lower. Keep in mind that it is extremely important to use an <h1> tag for the title of content.

Don't use headers in side columns and make all text relevant to your shop. Replace all <h4> tags for keywordless titles in <div> with <strong> tags.

Use an <h3> tag for product names and <h1> for a category name on category pages. In every product page, put the name of a product in an <h1> tag.

2.2 Clean up Code

Optimize your template file by moving JavaScript and CSS to external files. Keep your templates clean to get better SEO.

2.3. Speed up Your Store

If you don't want to deal with a complicated tutorial, you can implement the following Magento SEO tips:

1. Enable caching features in System ➤ Cache Management.

2. Optimize host and server configurations.

Also, decrease the number of external files! This will help you improve Magento performance. You can even merge several external files into one.

3. The Curse of Duplicate Content

Your Magento store has a lot of duplicate content. Due to layered navigation and sorting options, every product can be available on up to four pages. You should get rid of copied content; search engines must spider it without indexing.

3.1. Noindex

Install this extension[61] (or you can use an alternative solution) for the implementation of Noindex.

Go to Settings to check if the indexing of all non-content pages is prevented.

Set all options to Yes. Now, search engines can follow all the links from a set of pages but don't show them while indexing.

3.2 Nofollow

Now it's time to optimize your non-content pages (it can be painful). To prevent a negative impact from login and checkout pages, wish lists, RSS feeds, layered navigation, and other similar pages, go to your template files and manually add Nofollow to the appropriate links.

3.3 XML Sitemap

Use XML sitemap to provide search engines with information about your content. Furthermore, your store will be indexed faster. Go to Catalog ➤ Google Sitemap ➤ Add Sitemap to create a sitemap manually. Don't forget to create a new XML sitemap every time you change your inventory.

4. Dealing with Layered Navigation

Layered navigation is one of the biggest optimization nightmares because it is the core reason for duplicate content. Therefore, I've decided to make a separate section related to this problem.

4.1. Canonical Tag

A canonical tag is the number-one remedy for layered navigation. It shows the URLs that are available for indexing purposes, so search engines index only appropriate content from your website. It is also necessary to mention the simplicity of the canonical tag implementation, so don't be afraid to utilize this technique.

4.2. Parameter Handling

There is a Parameter Handling resource in the Google Webmaster Tool. You can utilize it to make your store even more SEO-friendly. The Parameter Handling resource tells Google how to interact with your Magento website pages. It's a very powerful tool and you should combine it with the following technique.

---

[61]https://www.creare.co.uk/blog/news/creare-seo-magento-extension.

4.3. Meta Rules

Use Meta Rules to curb layered navigation. They were partly described along with Noindex and Nofollow.

4.4. Ajax Navigation

Ajax navigation is the most complex and effective solution. It relies on filters to avoid the duplicate content issue. Thus, you don't have to optimize Ajax navigation for better SEO results.

Integration with Google Services

Magento Integration with Google Services is another key part of search engine optimization. Next, I explain how to connect your store with Analytics, WebMaster, and AdWords.

Google Analytics Magento Integration

Google Analytics is one of your major analytics tools. This freemium service provides the ability to track big data related to the traffic of your ecommerce website. You can easily review online campaigns and see what happens on your online store in real time. With the help of the following Magento extensions, you will be able to integrate Google Analytics with your ecommerce website and enhance default abilities of the platform. See our blog post Magento Integration with Google Analytics and other Services[62].

Google Analytics+ adds new features and advanced capabilities to the default module. The extension supports Universal Analytics and dynamic remarketing tags; helps improve conversions; tracks checkout process and AdWords conversions; and filters reports by different customers. Furthermore, you will be able to track data in a secondary profile and combine several sites in one account with this extension. The module is free.

Download the Google Analytics+ Magento Extension.

With the Google Universal Analytics by Aromicon module, you can also enhance your ecommerce store with Google Universal Analytics. The extension offers ecommerce tracking as well, so you don't have to spend time on its manual implementation. In addition, you will get funnel tracking for checkout. Google Universal Analytics by Aromicon is compatible with Magento CE 1.4+ and Magento EE 1.10+. The module adds an appropriate script to the head or before the body end. You can download it free of charge.

Download Google Universal Analytics Magento Extension

Also see the Extendware Google Analytics Dashboard[63]. It helps you integrate the Google Analytics dashboard into the Magento back end.

---

[62]https://firebearstudio.com/blog/magento-integration-with-google-services-merchant-center-analytics-webmaster-adwords-trusted-shops.html.
[63]https://firebearstudio.com/blog/extendware-google-analytics-dashboard-magento-extension-review.html.

If the methods described are not enough for you, read the following guidelines. The following five steps show how to implement all the ecommerce capabilities built into Google AdWords.

Magic with a new Universal Google Analytics Tracking Code

Get a new Universal Google Analytics tracking code and place it on your Magento store. Here are the steps to do so:

1. In the Google Analytics admin, find the **Property** column.

2. Choose the property that you're going to work with.

3. Go to **Tracking Info** and select **Tracking Code**.

4. Copy and paste a new Universal GA tracking code into the source code of your website.

Every page of your Magento website has the html/head.phtml file with a child theme in it. You should paste the new code there before the closing tag. Don't forget to place it on all the pages in your website; otherwise, data will be tracked imprecisely.

Use developer tools in a browser to check if the code was added in a proper way.

Preparation in Magento Admin

Now you should enable the Google API in your Magento store. In admin, navigate to Configure, find Sales, and go to Google API. You can enable Google Analytics API there.

Adding Google Analytics Demographics to the Game

Congratulations! You have implemented the standard Universal Google Analytics tracking code, but this is just the beginning. Unfortunately, you still don't have the ability to see demographics data. Additional coding work is waiting for you next. Note that you will have to verify it under Audience-Demographics-Overview tab. I recommend that you check the following Google articles; each offers a detailed description of this process:

- Enable Remarketing and Advertising Reporting Features in Google Analytics

- About Advertising Features

Enabling eCommerce Tracking

The following information will help you set up ecommerce tracking based on Google Analytics. First, you need to enable a reporting view with ecommerce data:

1. Sign in to Google Analytics.

2. Use the **Account ➤ Property ➤ View** drop-down menu to navigate to the desired view.

3. Find the **View** column and select **Ecommerce Settings** there.

4. Enable an appropriate option by setting a toggle to **ON**.

5. You can also turn on **Enhanced Ecommerce**.

6. Submit all the aforementioned actions.

7. Go to **Property Settings** under **Property column** to find out your tracking id.

8. Now it's time to work in Magento Admin. Navigate to **System** ➤ **Configuration** ➤ **Google API** ➤ **Google Analytics**. Paste your tracking id into the **Account Number** field.

9. Set **Enable** to Yes.

10. Save new configurations by clicking **Save Config**.

To properly use Google Tag Manager, check this setup guide. Note that you have to add basic page tracking. For third-party shopping carts and transaction tracking across separate domains, check this guide. Take into consideration that the feature is unnecessary if your ecommerce website and shopping cart software are on the same domain.

Keep in mind that you will have to work with JavaScript in order to collect ecommerce data from your website. Therefore, check this Google Analytics documentation on Ecommerce Tracking and this one on Enhanced Ecommerce Tracking.

To gather ecommerce data from Android and iOS apps, read this official documentation. I recommend that you check this post on an Internet-connected device, such as POS.

Setting up Conversion Tracking

In order to set up conversion tracking, take the following steps:

1. Go to the **Account** and **Property** columns in the Analytics admin.

2. Select your property.

3. Navigate to **Tracking Info-Tracking Code**.

4. Get a code.

5. Add it to the Magento HTML head in **Configuration-Web-HTML Head**.

However, you can also add the code manually, as follows:

1. With the aid of an FTP client, go to the /checkout/success. phtml file.

2. Use an editor to open the file.

3. Place the GA tracking code in the bottom of this file.

4. Save and upload the file.

Test that everything is OK with the URLs. You can do it under Real Time-Conversions. If a particular goal is not working, you should navigate to Admin-Goals and check that the URLs are correct. Take into account that destination should be set to the final success page.

Google Webmasters Magento Integration

With Google_Webmasters, you will get all the necessary data and a set of tools for making your Magento store Google-friendly. If you rely on traffic from this search engine (and I know that you do), the Google Webmasters integration is inevitable. Next, I will show you two ways of Google Sitemap Magento Implementation.

How to Manually Create Google Sitemap in Magento

The following explains How to Manually Create Google Sitemap in Magento

1. Log in to the Magento admin.

2. Navigate to Catalog-Google Sitemap.

3. Create a sitemap with the following URL: `http://www. example.com/sitemap/sitemap.xml`.

4. Required conditions: Set FTP to your server and sitemap folders chmoded to 777.

5. Navigate to the Magento admin and hit the Add Sitemap button.

6. Set up the default values.

7. Go to System ➤ Configuration ➤ Catalog ➤ Google Sitemap and configure the sitemap.

8. Check XML Tag definitions here.

9. Enter the following URL manually to begin the creation of the sitemap: `http://www.example.co id/actualSitemapID`.

I also suggest that you check this How to Set Up a Cron Job article.

Creare HTML Sitemap for SEO

With the help of this extension, you will be able to replace a default Magento paginated sitemap with an SEO-friendly one that lists all the categories of your ecommerce website in a cascading style. The Creare HTML Sitemap for SEO Magento module lists all CMS pages, as well as a few static pages. Thus, the categories in your online store are indexed correctly. In addition, you get an XML checker. To check the new sitemap, go to the following URL: yoursite.com/sitemap.

Download Creare HTML Sitemap for SEO

Also, take a look at the MageWorx Sitemap Suite[64] and the Amasty SEO Toolkit[65].

Google AdWords Magento Integration

Next, I explain the benefits of Magento integration with AdWords and show how to connect both systems together.

Google AdWords management and conversion tracking shows the effectiveness of ad clicks. If your Magento website is connected to AdWords, you can easily get data about website purchases, app downloads, phone calls, newsletter sign-up, and other conversions. Invest in your ecommerce store wisely and optimize your campaigns according to business goals with the aid of AdWords. You can easily integrate your Magento store using the LUKA Google AdWords Conversion Tracking Magento extension.

The LUKA Google AdWords Conversion Tracking Magento extension simplifies integration with AdWords. You just have to install the module to enable Google AdWords Conversion Tracking on your Magento website. Check the source code of LUKA Google AdWords Conversion Tracking on GitHub here. Note that the module is absolutely free. Download LUKA Google AdWords Conversion Tracking Magento Extension.

How to Check a Conversion Tracking Tag

To verify if AdWords "sees" a conversion tracking tag, go to your AdWords account. Find the Tools option. From a drop-down menu, choose Conversions. The tracking status is specified in front of every conversion action in the "Tracking status" column. The tag can be one of the following:

- Unverified (Google hasn't verified the tag on your website).

- No recent conversions (during previous 7 days).

- Recording conversions (everything is OK).

- Tag inactive (Google doesn't see the tag).

- Removed (the name speaks for itself). Check this article for additional information.

---

[64]https://firebearstudio.com/blog/mageworx-sitemap-suite-magento-2-extension-review.html.

[65]https://firebearstudio.com/blog/amasty-seo-toolkit-for-magento-2-and-1.html.

Google Merchant Center Magento Integration

Google Merchant Center is a service, designed to help you with store and product information integration into Google Shopping. In order to work with the Google Merchant Center, you have to use your Google account or create a new one. Every Google account can be associated with only one Google Merchant Center account, but you can add extra users to your Google Base. At this stage, there are also two other conditions. Initially, you have to configure your account and choose your location and then agree to the Terms of Service.

Having set up your account and verified your website URL, you have to submit your product data. Before uploading any data files into Google Merchant Center, it is necessary to create and register your data feed—a file that includes attributes that define your products in a special way. The data feed is built like a classic RSS feed, but it also includes specific XML tags. Of course, you can perform all the actions manually, but there are numerous Magento extensions designed to simplify your interaction with Google Merchant Center; for example, Simple Google Shopping.

This module is established for exporting a well-structured and valid data feed from your Magento store to a Google Merchant account. Simple Google Shopping is highly configurable, easy to use, and provides support for several stores, VAT rates, and currencies. Get Simple Google Shopping Magento Extension.

The Google Shopping Feed extension is recommended by Google reps. Using this module you will be able to create a feed according to Google's full specification. The main goal of the extension is to get as close as possible to a perfect data feed without maintaining it after the module's installation. Download Google Shopping Feed Magento Extension.

By using the Magento Product Feed Generator, you have the ability to create product feeds for Google, eBay, and GetPrice. The extension supports CSV, XML, TXT, and other formats. With its aid, you can also get product details right from your admin. Get Magento Product Feed Generator Extension.

Using the Product Feed by Amasty Magento extension, you are able to generate a product feed in a short period of time (not more than few minutes). And it will take a day or two to put your products on high-traffic shopping platforms. Moreover, Product Feed by Amasty provides the opportunity to create an unlimited number of product feeds and separate them for all of your Magento store views. The extension works with Shopping. com, Google.com, Getprice.com, Myshopping.com, Shopmania.com, Nextag.com, and Amazon.com. Purchase Product Feed by Amasty.

The Product Feed Creator/Shopping Feeds module is a feed generator that allows you to create custom data feeds and then submit them to various product search engines. Product Feed Creator generates feeds for Google Product Search, Amazon, Shopping. com, Yahoo! Store, Channel Advisor, and dozens of other services. You can create feeds for your customers as well. This feature is useful for dropshipping and wholesale businesses. Get the extension.

Product Tags as a Powerful Cross Linking Tool

With the constant growth of information on the Internet, it's becoming harder to sort it out by the various features. So, for example, if you find a picture of a nice pair of shoes and you decide to look for more like it, it will take you a lot of time, because you have no specific attributes for a search except for the shoes' shape and color. Today, the problem seems to be solved thanks to a widespread use of so-called tags that play the role of peculiar labels that can be attributed to any online content. The main advantage of tags lies in their ability to specify the category of the content so that you can easily understand its origin, characteristics, and the reason for publishing.

Although tags are mostly used in social networks and bookmarking sites, they can be of particular interest to the ecommerce industry as well. For instance, if you use content tagging for your product marketing strategy, you can significantly increase your chances to attract a target audience to your website. There are a lot of possibilities with efficient product tagging that Magento retailers can adjust for their everyday needs, so I suggest getting acquainted with the main tagging principles and their application for every Magento store.

Public tagging allows users to apply various keywords to describe the content they see online. This type of tagging is widely used on bookmarking websites such as 9rules.com or Digg.com. For a website owner, having public tagging available means automatically getting your items indexed, which is important in terms of better search results rankings. Moreover, public tagging often suggests submitting links to particular content with a subsequent possibility of creating tags related to those links. After it's done, it becomes possible for other users to find this content through entering tags in a search field.

In ecommerce retail, keyword research should be made first. Basically, a retailer has to understand which keywords are popular among the audience by checking their relevance in Google search requests. Furthermore, tags can become especially handy when dealing with a wide range of products. Although you can make traditional product categorization with the ability to search items by certain keywords, tagging allows you to set two or three keywords for each item that you have, so that if users click one of the tags, they are able to see the list of other items associated with the same keyword at once.

To make publisher tagging even more effective, you can also engage with book-marking websites. For this you should only be able to offer something useful to your customers. This could be thematic articles or any other business-related content, including infographics, event announcements, and photographs. You should note, however, that submitting clearly commercial content to bookmarking websites won't be appreciated by their owners and audience.

Thus, public and publisher tagging can be equally useful for satisfying your SEO needs, although the former should require proper quality control, and the latter, more thorough preliminary analysis of the relevant keywords.

The process of submitting links to content and connecting them with related tags is actively used in public and publisher tagging and can be actualized in various forms. In general, it can be called *cross linking* or *internal link building*. One of the most often used types of cross linking is a tag cloud, which is visually represented by a cluster of tagged keywords placed in a specific area of a website. Each tag in a cloud is in fact a separate link that directs the user to an internal search results list containing all the posts or items of the website where a tagged word or phrase is mentioned. Not only does this simplify the users' site navigation process, but it also is a good SEO approach in general.

You can find a full article about tags here: http://goo.gl/yyLQ2o. To summarize the material, I'd like to show you two useful extensions associated with product tagging.

With the help of the SEO Product Tag URLs extension, you can make your product tag links more efficient for a search engine to interpret them. For instance, if your internal links lack any keywords and instead consists of strange sequences of letters and numbers, their search engine readability will be quite low. SEO Product Tag URLs solves this problem by converting all of your links into nicely tagged URLs that make it much easier for a searcher to get to your product pages. Download SEO Product Tag URLs.

Admin Product Tagging gives you the opportunity to add as many tags as you want to your product pages from the very beginning of creating those pages. Unlike default Magento managing tools, which only make it possible to add tags after a product page has been created, this extension allows you to add tags every time you decide to edit a page. The main advantage of the extension is that you don't have to approve each new tag from the Admin panel individually. Rather, every newly created tag is automatically saved as approved. This, however, does not extend to user tagging, which means that all the public tags still have to be approved separately. But if you get tired of doing it all the time, there is an additional function in Admin Product Tagging with which you can simply disable tagging product pages by customers. Download Admin Product Tagging.

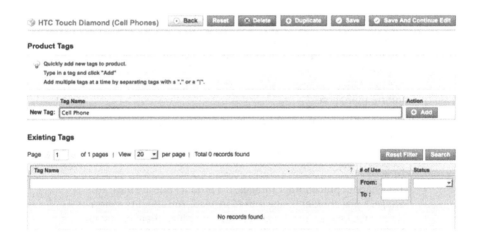

Figure 1-35. *Admin Product Tagging*

Now, your ecommerce store is almost ready for the first public launch, so it's time for final preparations. Since your Magento website is installed and optimized for work, has high performance, incredible security, and good SEO, it's time to learn more about the pre-launch checklist.

Pre-Launch Checklist

This is the final part of the chapter, which is based on the Complete Magento Pre-Launch Guide[66]. We all know that bringing any website live is a very stressful and responsible task, especially if it is a Magento ecommerce store. Your website should go live as soon as possible. At the same time, there are a lot of vital steps that you can easily forget about. If you don't want to miss anything, read over the following list of pre-launch actions.

- **Change the base URL**. The core_config_data database table stores URLs that should be updated when you move your Magento website live; otherwise, they refer back to a staging site. You can access these URLs through admin interface here: System ➤ Configuration ➤ Web. In this situation, it is essential not to miss a trailing forward slash.

- **Improve SEO with new HTML head settings**. The HTML head contains original settings. In order to improve your SEO, you should change them. Use your own title, set keywords, and metadescriptions. You can do this here: System ➤ Configuration ➤ General ➤ Design ➤ HTML Head.

- **Provide your visitors with relevant contact information**. An ecommerce website without email addresses and store information looks suspicious. By missing this little step, you can frighten your future customers, so don't make this mistake. Go to System ➤ Configuration ➤ General and System ➤ Configuration ➤ Store Email Addresses. You can add all the necessary information there.

- **Create a favicon**. Don't start your ecommerce store without having created a favicon. It will still work if you forget about this step, but that does not mean that you should overlook having a favicon.

- **Take care of placeholder images**. If a product doesn't have an image, a placeholder image is used instead. You should create a set of such images for your store. You can upload them in System ➤ Configuration ➤ Catalog ➤ Product Image Placeholders. Alternatively, you can place them in catalog/products/placeholder/image.jpg (small_image.jpg and thumbnail.jpg).

- **Improve your security with a custom admin URL**. The default Magento path to admin is insecure because everyone knows it. Luckily, you can always change it. Just go to the local.xml file and replace the admin frontname in the admin router with a custom one. Don't forget to delete cache before visiting a new URL.

---

[66]https://firebearstudio.com/blog/complete-magento-pre-launch-guide-go-live-check-list-items-qa-testing-overlooked-tips-and-tricks.html.

- **Provide your buyers with nice invoices**. All the information on your Magento website should look good. The invoices should also look good. Thus, take care of the logo. You should upload it to an appropriate folder.

- **Offer transactional emails with the correct logo**. It's not a surprise that transactional and default emails use different logos. Therefore, you should save the correct image (logo_email.gif) in the theme directory. Note that there are Magento themes that are based on hard-coded values and require manual changes.

- **Customize your 404 page**. What do you feel when you see a 404 page? You are a little bit disappointed, right? So are your customers. Don't make them more disappointed with the default Magento block—customize your 404 page. Go to CMS ➤ Pages and make it better.

- **Customize the error page**. Prevent your customers from seeing a default Magento error page. Adapt this page to the current Magento template by modifying files from the error directory. Additionally, you can disable stack trace printing. Open the errors/local.xml file and replace the print action with email. Set an email address.

- **Don't forget about test data**. You've probably created a lot of test data while testing your Magento store. Before going live, you should remove it. Products, orders, and customers created during development should be deleted.

- **Check tax settings**. Go to System ➤ Configuration ➤ Sales ➤ Tax to check your current tax settings. You can also use appropriate Magento extensions to optimize these settings for certain markets. Go to Magento Connect or check this blog post to find suitable tools.

- **Set the shipping origin**. Parallel to tax settings, you should set a shipping origin. Various countries require a different approach in providing the appropriate tax rates.

- **Import the right product inventory**. Make sure that the necessary configurations are set up. Note that you may have to perform an additional import of stock levels.

- **Check shipping methods**. Make sure that fixed products, cart fees, or other related features are configured. In a cart weight route, make sure that the weight is attached to all products.

- **Improve performance with this simple step**. Flush JavaScript to a single file in order to reduce load time. Go to System ➤ Configuration ➤ Developer ➤ JavaScript Settings and perform all the required actions there. Keep in mind that inline JavaScript requires its own file to avoid page load slowdown.

- **Don't ignore CSS minification**. You can always use a CSS compressor to minify CSS data. Create a minified version in addition to a readable one.

- **Consider this additional advice on CSS**. You can also combine your CSS files into a single one—just like in a JavaScript case. Take into consideration that this feature doesn't work well with all Magento websites. I recommend that you check it on a staging server before going live, since it can have some unwanted side effects. Go to System ➤ Configuration ➤ Developer ➤ CSS Settings to flush CSS into a single file. Or you can use the Fooman Speedster Magento extension. It functions with both CSS and JavaScript files.

- **Use the maintenance.flag**. Go to the root of your Magento installation and find the maintenance.flag file. It displays a holding page during your going online. Move the maintenance. flag file first, queueing the rest of Magento to transfer.

- **Inevitable index management**. Please note that after performing any catalog changes, you should also re-index.

- **Utilize the power of system compilation**. Reduce the load time of your ecommerce store by compiling the system. This will lead to a 50% performance increase in loading a page. You can find the necessary settings here at System ➤ Tools ➤ Compilation.

- **Enable caching**. Caching is usually disabled during the development stage. Thus, you should enable and refresh it before going live; otherwise, you will decrease the performance of your website.

- **Integrate your store with Google Analytics**. Magento supports integration with Google Analytics. You just have to set up your account and put its number in System ➤ Configuration ➤ Sales ➤ Google API ➤ Google Analytics.

... and with Google Base

Google Base integration is also supported by Magento. Check this article by Inchoo to find out more about this process.

- **Improve your SEO with Google Sitemap**. Go to "Catalog-Google Sitemap" and select "Create Sitemap." With the help of Webmaster Tools, point Google toward your sitemap.

- **Test how newsletter subscriptions work**. Do not test this feature on real customers. It's better to check how it works before going live. Test the opportunity to sign up and unsubscribe. Check whether newsletters can be sent out.

- **Make sure that your payment gateways work**. It is extremely important to check that a payment gateway is ready to go live with your store; otherwise, you can lose the first customers. Enable SSL Certificate because many payment gateways will not function without this security feature.

- **Go live with all Magento extensions**. Some modules from Magento Connect will not work without a license key. In order to go live with them, you should check if every key is still valid. Obtain new keys if necessary.

- **Take care of unnecessary modules**. Your ecommerce store probably doesn't need all default Magento features. Therefore, you can easily disable them. Go to System ➤ Configuration ➤ Advanced and turn off everything that you don't need.

- **Enable product import/export with right PHP configurations**. Keep in mind that the memory_limit and max_execution_time files should have only reasonable values. Restrictive values are often a reason of a product import/export fail.

- **Don't forget to turn on crons**. Some Magento components require regular updates, which run due to periodical scripts. You can find the needed configurations in System ➤ Configuration ➤ Advanced ➤ System. To modify the cron.php file, go to the root of your Magento installation. Check this page for a more detailed description of the process.

- **Clean logs**. A database that contains logs becomes bloated. Thus, you have to clean it from time to time. You can even set a daily cleaning. The appropriate option is situated in System ➤ Configuration ➤ Advanced ➤ System ➤ Log cleaning.

- **Regularly backup your store**. You can use the Automatic Database Backup Magento extension. This module will do everything for you. Just go to Magento Connect, install it, and get your backups.

Final Words About Performance

Before going live, test the performance of your site. As mentioned, a fast ecommerce store not only makes customers loyal, but also provides a positive impact on SEO. There are dozens of tools and extensions designed for checking the performance of your Magento website. You can use GTMetrix, YSlow, or any other convenient solution to find bottlenecks and fix them. Remember, your visitors always compare your store to other websites; that's why they will move to a competitor if you provide them with a low performance.

For the More Curious

If these checklists are not enough for you, see this blog post. That Magento Pre-Launch Checklist includes some additional advice.

Magento Store Audit

In brick-and-mortar retail, a store audit is an examination of information about the effectiveness of different parameters, such as price, sales, or advertising campaign compared to that of any competitors or common standards. As for ecommerce in general and Magento in particular, this process is more complicated, since it consists of a wider number of variables that require different approaches in calculation. Luckily, there are a lot of tools and materials that can help you with a Magento store audit. The following guide offers a store audit checklist, resources, and techniques necessary for running the procedure. Being useful for all kinds of Magento specialists and store owners, it teaches how to estimate efforts, collect information about your Magento website, and keep the installation clean and healthy.

When it comes to auditing a Magento website, the first difference from a brick-and-mortar store audit is the necessity to measure a site speed. That's where PageSpeed Insights[67], a product from the Google Developers kit, is helpful.

The next important difference is security. Although you can examine the safety of a brick-and-mortar store, this parameter is not as important as in ecommerce. In Magento, a store audit requires finding and fixing various security vulnerabilities. Chances are your website lacks some crucial patches or has other holes. You can find all of these security problems with the aid of MageReport, a free service that gives you a quick insight into the security status of your Magento store. Besides showing all current security problems, the service teaches you how to fix possible vulnerabilities.

Although the idea behind Mage Scan is to evaluate the security and quality of a Magento website, you don't have access to further work with a potential developer or a new client, you can easily utilize Mage Scan[68] in a Magento website audit.

Toolbox for Magento Shop Audit is another vital software solution. With the generate-reports.sh script, you can get various reports on a Magento installation. All of these reports are a vital foundation in a Magento website audit.

Toolbox for Magento Shop Audit requires copying files from its repository[69] right into your Magento installation. Then, you can easily run the script and get all the necessary data. The script downloads a clean Magento source from the Magento website to run the audit. The following are some useful articles related to the topic:

---

[67]https://developers.google.com/speed/pagespeed/insights/.
[68]http://magescan.steverobbins.com/.
[69]https://github.com/schmengler/magento-audit.

- Three-tier system for Magento quality analysis[70]

- Analyzing an existing Magento Shop[71]

- How do you give estimates for Magento upgrade?[72]

- Conducting Magento Store Audit[73]

Conclusion

Your Magento website is now live, but don't expect that this is the end of your development process. Chances are that your ecommerce store contains bugs, so you should be ready to discover and fix them as soon as possible. There are also a lot of SEO, performance, and security improvements to be implemented.

I strongly recommend that you create two separate versions of your Magento store. One should be directed at public, while the other one should become your laboratory. If experiments are successful and you are content with your results, push an improvement online. Thus, your customers won't see your fails, but your store will always get useful updates and fixes. What are these updates and fixes? I describe all of them in this book. Growth is the next step in your ecommerce development.

---

[70]http://magenticians.com/3-tier-magento-quality-analysis.
[71]https://www.integer-net.de/download/20130918_ShopAnalysis.pdf.
[72]http://magento.stackexchange.com/questions/99/how-do-you-give-estimates-for-magento-upgrade.
[73]https://firebearstudio.com/blog/magento-store-audit.html.

CHAPTER 2

Sales Generation

The newcomers on the field of ecommerce often tend to have problems with gaining enough traffic to their websites. It is quite difficult to attract customers if nobody even knows about your existence. Since making a profit online requires a lot of time, investments, planning, and management, you have to be patient and consistent to get your website out of the Google search abyss and increase your website traffic. In this chapter, I'll shed light on the most effective ways of sales generation in the context of a successful marketing campaign.

Evaluate Your Marketing Campaign

With the ecommerce industry exceeding $294 billion of profit in 2014, it is not surprising that digital commerce is worth being called a competitive market. This, however, must call for more actions, because retailers, who think that their marketing strategy can bring money steadily for years, are going to lose everything just within several months. Ecommerce marketing nowadays is a tough job requiring a lot of effort.

The most effective way of maintaining your business on the highest level is a constant control over the success of your current strategies, and if they fail in fulfilling a plan—the invention of better ones. Therefore, get ready for an intensive study of planning, implementing, and evaluating your marketing campaigns.

© Viktor Khliupko 2016
V. Khliupko, *Magento 1 DIY*, DOI 10.1007/978-1-4842-2457-1_2

Understand Your Goals

If you're not really sure what you want to reach with your marketing campaign, you will not succeed in it anyway. Even if you spend a great amount of money on numerous ads, believing that this is a successful campaign, you're wrong. Thus, it's important to make a clear plan of what you want to achieve by your strategy—for instance:

- Reach 1,000 orders per month

- Obtain 500 new customers

- Increase growth in revenues by 30%

Identify Metrics for Measuring Your Campaign

At the end of the first period, you can start measuring the results of a current strategy. For each aim established at the beginning, you will have to utilize appropriate metrics to calculate their value. For instance, if your aim was to gain more sales to your website, the following rates must be considered:

- Average number of product page views

- Percentage ratio of users that purchased your products to all users that viewed your website during a certain period

- Sum of total revenue

Implement Comfortable Metrics Tracking

Active ads allows you to easily monitor the number of visitors coming to your website and mostly all the activities performed by these visitors through the toolkit of your particular ad campaign. Thus, you're open to control all stages of a potential purchase from the very first view of a page to a complete product purchase. In fact, by using your ad stats, you will get the exact rates for performing final calculations. For example, to calculate an overall conversion rate of a particular product, you may simply divide the number of its purchases by the number of product page views for a given period.

Be Original with All Media Representation on Your Site

For each ad campaign, you should use different visual solutions to perfectly suit the social environment that you want to integrate your website with. For instance, if you create an ad on Facebook, make sure to use an unusual color scheme or imagery that is likely to attract the major audience of the network to your website. Sometimes you will even have to be minimalistic if you don't want to spoil your customers' impressions.

Use UTM Links to Direct Users to the Most Suitable Page

If you create ads on several websites or platforms, it would be nice if you could see which of them brings the greatest amount of customers. Thus, you can utilize *UTM links*, which are basically specific parameters assigned to the main link. They can help you with tracking the number of clicks performed on every ad, as well as analyzing their efficiency in your primary campaign.

There are numerous tools for creating UTM links, such as Google URL Builder and Terminus, but while the former is considered to be relatively easy to use, the latter contains a set of more advanced settings for experienced retailers.

The following are the main UTM parameters for adjusting to an ad link:

- Source (website at which your ad is located, e.g., Facebook)

- Medium (variation of your banner, e.g., banner variation 1)

- Campaign (name of your ad campaign, e.g., autumn collection)

The result should look like what's shown on the following web page:

```
http://yoursite.com/blog-post-fall-collection/?utm_source=facebook&utm_
medium=bannerverisio campaign=autumncollection
```

Add such link to all of your ads and publish it only if you're sure that it works properly.

Run Some Tests Before Publishing Your Ads

It is important to test how UTM links work and whether they direct users to the right place. Try to produce all the actions of a potential customer, starting with clicking ads, browsing various product pages, and ending with checkout. Then, go to your tracking page and see whether the metrics change their values. If everything is fine, proceed to the next step.

See the Results

In order to provide yourself with a convenient way of tracking your metrics, you can use several handy tools that will help you understand whether your goals are achievable. The following are the best solutions:

- **KISSmetrics**: A flexible medium for effective tracking of major campaign rates.

- **Google Analytics**: Good at dealing with UTM links.

- **Converto**: A more advanced tool that offers the ability to analyze the efficiency of all of your ads and redirect your resources to more profitable channels.

Keep in mind that even if your campaign fails, with these analytical add-ons at hand, you should identify which rates appear to be insufficient and calculate current losses. Using official ad tools on your advertising channels is also possible, but it often happens that rate values are different from what you might expect.

Make a Conclusion and Prepare for Further Campaigns

However, getting results is not your final destination. In addition to evaluating your campaign achievements, you should analyze each of your advertising channels to define which of them gained the biggest audience. For instance, you may discover that Facebook gave you 500 page views, among which 50 were purchases. Thus, I can suggest that Facebook is likely to be effective for attracting customers, but certain modifications to your ad campaign on this platform are required. If your Twitter ad campaign brought you just 200 page views, but 150 of those ones still ended up completing an order, this ad source is worth investing in. Those ad sources that brought you nothing but a few page views for the whole period should be discarded.

Finally, learn all of your achievements and failures from the current marketing strategy, so that the next time you can apply this knowledge to getting your business to the top positions in the ecommerce market.

The Main Traffic Sources

As a retailer, you might be curious about what traffic sources can bring you the desired number of customers. In fact, everything depends on the size of your business. For instance, it is not profitable for a small store to rely on direct traffic, so you have to look for other alternatives to achieve your marketing goals. Let's look at some traffic sources and define their pros and cons.

Direct Traffic

Direct traffic is a flow of users who come to your website by typing in the direct URL address in their browsers. To make this source valuable for you, it is important to become a popular brand offline and provide people with the ability to engage with you and your products by actually going to your brick-and-mortar stores. In this case, all the investments must be made for a high-quality PR scheme and the opening of an offline store chain. The principle disadvantage of this source is that it can only bring 10% to 15% of visitors. Besides, if you're generally doing well with your offline business, you can look for more advanced ways of driving extra traffic to your online store.

Email Marketing

This traffic source is considered to be one of the cheapest ones. Furthermore, it can be used for all possible kinds of business. The main priority of email marketing is the ability to keep in touch with the existing customers and encourage them to make more purchases from your online store. This traffic source requires the following three factors.

Sufficient Database Volume

This means that you should have an adequate number of users to whom you will send your emails to. You can either buy data or build it yourself. Buying data can be fast and easy, but it does not guarantee that users will react—after all, they don't know you, so you're likely to be marked as spam. Building your own email list may seem more reasonable, but it usually takes a good deal of time to attract enough customers, especially if you've just started your business. However, you can use organic ways to encourage visitors to share their email addresses with you. This includes creating visual incentives, for instance, that offer bargains on your items to subscribed users.

Frequent eMail Delivery

Any type of email marketing campaign suggests that you should provide a regular email delivery to your contact list users. However, this regularity should not exceed three letters a month, because frequent emailing will cause people, as well as email services, to consider you as a spammer. When a smart email service, such as Gmail, identifies you as a spammer, your emails are automatically sent to a spam folder, which prevents a recipient from even noticing it. Thus, you should be consistent but unobtrusive while gaining traffic.

Appropriate Quality of eMail Content

When it comes to building up content for your emails, use information that can only be found on your website. Goods and prices that don't exist on your Magento store will disappoint potential customers. Don't make your emails too long—write only about the most relevant things that will make people interested in what you are doing. It's often useful to combine textual content with catchy images to make it more user-friendly. For instance, you can write four or five sentences to describe your content and then support them with a relevant picture representing your offer. Apart from the things mentioned, I recommend adding corresponding links to your website.

Thus, you should manage email marketing during the first days of your website existence. Providing yourself with an opportunity to bring your customers back at any particular time can double your conversions and create friendly relationships between you and your customers. Although email marketing accounts for 10% to 30% of visitors, it won't work for acquiring new customers, because you are unlikely to interest people who have never purchased your products.

Apart from independent research and testing opportunities of your email marketing campaigns, you can also utilize the services of specialized email marketing providers. They can consult you (often for free) and give useful advice on how to get along with this source of traffic. The price for paid services varies, depending on whether you want to save your time and make the whole process run automatically or manage everything yourself. MailChimp is a service that combines a set of valuable ecommerce features at a reasonable price.

MailChimp

For a minimum of $10 per month, you can get high-end email content that will be appealing to your customers. Moreover, you can also take advantage of regular analytics reports that inform you about the current progress of your email campaign. With MailChimp's functionality, you will be able to easily improve your marketing performance by utilizing a set of its useful features, such as those described next.

Email Designer

Email Designer is an all-in-one editor that is based on drag-and-drop principle. It can be managed from a PC or a laptop, as well as from a tablet or a smartphone. Its built-in toolkit allows to do the following:

- Edit and resize images.

- Effectively interact with your team no matter where you are.

- Conduct a testing campaign before actually launching it.

- Store and retrieve your files in a specialized file manager.

- Automatically verify every link you submit to emails.

- Email templates.

MailChimp offers a smart collection of predesigned templates that you can use if you lack enough time or experience to create a good-looking design. So the only thing you have to do is submit the content and check how it looks with each particular template. If you intend to code your own email template, there is the Email Template Reference option that has a lot of useful information and recommendations on how to make a nice working template for a successful email marketing scheme.

Smart Reports

When your campaign is finally on the go, you can instantly start monitoring its performance through MailChimp's smart reports, which provide you with detailed data, such as the number of newly subscribed users, URL visits, and impressions.

Integration with eCommerce Platforms

If you want to reach various categories of customers with equal efficiency, you need to import all user data to your MailChimp account. Take into consideration that the service supports integration with Google Analytics, Magento, and Shopify.

There are three plans available for acquisition on MailChimp: Entrepreneur, Growing Business, and High Volume Sender.

The Entrepreneur package is free of charge and has no expiration date. You can send a fixed number of 12,000 emails to 2,000 users each month. Also, you can sort your customer list to manage email delivery to target groups of customers. The plan supports ecommerce integration and the access to the pack of ready-to-use email templates. The downside of this plan is in the lack of support for analytical tools for monitoring website traffic. The Entrepreneur package is intended for small businesses that don't have a large audience; this guarantees that every user will receive at least one email per month. If you acquire more than 2,000 users, you will need to subscribe for a paid plan, which widens the functionality of your account and allows you to send an unlimited number of messages. It will cost you only $10 per month.

The Growing Business plan supports unlimited monthly email delivery to 600,000 subscribers. You can use MailChimp[1] for calculating an actual amount of money required for a given number of users per month. For instance, a plan for up to 5,000 users will cost you $50, while a plan for 10,000 costs $75. The same pricing works for the High Volume Sender package as well. The plan supports customer list segmentation and integration with ecommerce platforms. Additionally, you get an opportunity to manage your teamwork by using Email Designer and you have a regularly available consulting team of experts to help you adapt the MailChimp system within your ecommerce store.

The High Volume Seller package suits large corporations with wide audiences (600,000 customers). It offers the ability to send billions of emails per month. You can automatically adjust your delivery due to provider responses and protect data with a two-factor authentication process, SOC II, and PCI DSS certifications and security alerts. There is also access to a full API, provided with detailed documentation and user guides. In addition, the package features multi-user accounts for agencies to manage their cooperative engagement and interaction with clients.

Organic Search Engine Results

These are results displayed to a user after he enters a search request. The first results usually contain the most relevant information, which is more likely to meet search requirements. That's why organic search results almost never include advertising links in the top results. Even Google tries to divide relevant result links from ads, putting the former in the first place and moving the latter down to the lower positions. This means that placing your website among the first positions requires high popularity among people, or original and rare products and services that won't create excessive competitiveness on the Internet. In addition to the things mentioned, you need an effective SEO strategy.

In general, organic search results bring from 10% to 30% of visitors on a regular basis.

Paid Search Results

Paid search results, if used properly, can provide you with up to 50% of visitors, which is the highest rate among all traffic drivers. This source of customers usually requires a sufficient number of resources to be spent, since advertising tends to become more and more complicated in attracting people's attention. In a perfect scenario, you should be able to invest in both offline and online stores to gain maximum profit from the paid search. Online marketing campaigns usually include the following methods: SEO, pay-per-click ads, and affiliate marketing.

---

[1]http://mailchimp.com/pricing/growing-business/.

Search Engine Optimization

This technique is considered to be the most popular for increasing website traffic because it cannot attain crazy numbers of visits. Please note that it usually takes months until SEO strategy shows its results, so you will need consistency and patience to gain the desired traffic flow to your website.

Although the main SEO optimizations are described in the first chapter of this book, I'd like to draw your attention to this complicated process once again. The main issue related to search engine optimization is content, which means that you have to work on the effectiveness of your texts and product listings. The whole procedure includes the following:

- **Check and improve your product categories**. Make sure that every product contains a sufficient amount of keywords (words and word-phrases that users are likely to type in when they search for these products on Google or any other search engine). Then, include these keywords in the most noticeable places of your website: headers, item descriptions, image names, internal links, and the body text itself.

- **Make your text authentic**. Work with professional writers that will make your descriptions, articles, and other text pieces readable and informative for potential customers. Your main aim is to put the most relevant information in the proper order.

- **Utilize landing pages**. Primarily, a landing page is a single website page that contains relevant and crucial data for a viewer. For instance, you can create a customer-specific link that will direct a person from a search results page or an ad toward a certain product page containing a description, characteristics, and price. This is likely to motivate a user to make a purchase.

- **Ask bloggers and other retailers to mention your store on their websites**. This part is the most difficult one, because further success of your marketing campaign becomes in some sense dependent on whether your website URL appears on other blogs or pages. It makes sense to be friendly in order to become successful.

- Submit your website to various directories. Google, Bing, and Business.com must be your primary candidates.

Pay-Per-Click Advertising

The pay-per-click ads are really good at increasing your website traffic faster than any other alternative solution. This technology allows you to buy visitors on the websites where you place your ads. Once users click your ad, they are instantly redirected to your website. As an advertiser, you have to pay website owners for every single click.

The most popular pay-per-click management service is Google AdWords, which can bring you about 70% of paid search visitors. But before using it, you should learn all the opportunities related to this pay-per-click solution. Note that the service is full of other retailers—many of who occupy the top positions in search results.

- Analyze the number of retailers that sell the same goods as you.

- Make the most powerful set of keywords for your product ads.

- Work on the appearance of your ads (design, colors, images, etc.)

- Adjust retargeting ads for your website. Retargeting ads are basically the same old ads but their aim is to track your website visitors' after they have left a website page. For instance, when a person goes to your website, nothing happens, but as soon as he or she proceeds to other websites, your ad will be displayed on each of these sites.

- Note that cost-per-click, or CPC, options are always better than cost-per-mille, or CPM, options. Don't pay for viewers—pay for their actions, especially if your goal is to capture leads.

- Your ads should have URLs with a unique tracking token. Thus, you will be able to test them and evaluate their effectiveness. Without this information, you will never optimize your ROI.

- The writing style of your landing page and an advertisement on social media should correspond to one another. At least, try to use the same language; otherwise, you'll confuse your customers.

- Provide high-quality content: avoid typos (if they are not a part of your creative campaign), make sure that every image has a proper size and check that every URL goes to the right landing pages.

- Use A/B testing and try out different types of ads. This will help you choose better options and get the most out of your PPC campaign.

It is also worth mentioning that pay-per-click management works in social network environments, including Twitter, YouTube, and Facebook. Even more surprising is that you can use pay-per-click ads on mobile devices.

Affiliate Marketing

Affiliate marketing includes interaction with third-party websites that will definitely come in handy when it comes to driving traffic to your store. Basically, these sites use the same methods about selling your products "on their territory," but it will require extra expenditures (about 10%) from every sale they make. The most reliable affiliate websites are Affiliate Window, Linkshare, and Webgain.

Unfortunately, dealing with affiliates involves additional investments into the development of specific data feeds obtained from your product database. These data feeds will be integrated into the affiliate's own database to enable ordering of your products on their website. Moreover, additional banners and newsletters that will be distinguishable from those you use on other advertising platforms are required. Keep in mind that you can track user activity on affiliate websites by using the Google Analytics platform.

The Best Magento Affiliate Modules

There is a set of Magento extensions aimed at simplifying the process of finding and cooperating with affiliates. Each affiliate module serves different purposes, so be sure to pick up the one that you really need. The full list is here: The Best Referral And Affiliate Marketing Magento Extensions[2].

Affiliate by Magestore is an extension that offers standard and platinum editions. Standard edition incorporates six various methods of friend referrals, four ways for your affiliate owners to pay their commissions, and the ability to fix commission amounts in currency or percentage rates. Platinum edition allows you to create multiple affiliate programs with different rates, provides a coupon scheme for affiliate websites, and gives regular reports based on results of a current program. The price for Standard Edition is $99, while Platinum Edition costs $229.

Affiliate by aheadWorks specializes in automatic advertising campaigns that turn customers into promoters. The price charged by your affiliates depends on your current conversion rates. And, you shouldn't forget that you have the right to pay only after you make sure that a purchase performed through their websites occurred according to previously defined rules. This pay-per-sale system seems to be quite reliable, especially if you cannot be sure about the loyalty of your companions. You can download this module for only $99.

The Auguria Sponsorship module is based on a sponsorship earning system that allows gaining special points that can be further sold or exchanged among your customers. The acquisition of points is possible through making purchases or after inviting a friend to your website. All the features of the module are easily adjustable, and you can get it for free.

Refer a Friend module by aheadWorks is also aimed at stimulating your customers to invite their friends to your Magento store. As a reward, they get discounts on further purchases, while you get additional traffic and better conversion rates. Unlike the previous module, this will cost you $99.

Reward Points by Magestore is a high-end reward-gaining alternative that allows your customers to earn in-store currency, not only for inviting friends, but for writing comments, using product hashtags, or subscribing to your social media blog. You can build your own loyalty program to effectively encourage customers to earn and spend their points. Although the extension's price reaches $99, you are guaranteed to get free lifetime updates and support.

---

[2]https://firebearstudio.com/blog/the-best-referral-and-affiliate-marketing-magento-extensions.html.

Reward Points by mirasvit[3]. This modulÃ'Æ' gives points for mentioning your store in social media networks, such as Facebook, Twitter, Pinterest, and so forth. Another interesting feature concerns those customers that haven't visited the website for a long period of time. Thus, the extension can automatically award them with free points; then you can send emails with an offer to spend these points on purchasing your products. You can also limit the possible amount of points that a customer may spend for purchasing a product. The module can be acquired for $149 on the developer's official website.

Sweet Tooth Loyalty and Reward Points. With the help of this extension, you can develop a profound loyalty program that can turn your visitors into customers, who in turn, will bring you more clients. This extension differs from others since it requires a monthly subscription of $59 per month.

Additionals Ways to Earn Your Rewards

Figure 2-1. *Sweet Tooth Loyalty and Reward Points*

Affiliate Pro Extension by MageWorld is designed for those who would like to create an efficient affiliate network based on multi-level marketing. You can utilize an easy-to-use sign-up form for your affiliates and help them receive their commissions on time. The module supports multiple payment methods and allows tracking all affiliates' transactions to evaluate the quality of their performance. The price of a full-featured module is $197.

---

[3]https://firebearstudio.com/blog/mirasvit-reward-points-referral-program-magento-2-and-1-review.html.

Affiliate by Magegiant. The extension contains a set of useful options intended for various purposes, and you can choose which of them to include in your personal pack. Each option costs $50. You can even purchase an expert module installation ($49.99). The extension offers diverse commission payment methods, including percentage rates and clean amounts, fixed ones, and tiered ones. It is also possible to let affiliates withdraw commissions independently or use their in-store credits for paid orders on your website.

J2T Reward Points + Referral program. For only $49.99, you can make in-store point reward calculation faster. The J2T Reward Points + Referral program module also allows appointing a specific amount of points for each product; therefore, a customer could not purchase a product solely by using obtained points. Moreover, you can adjust discounts to be available for products including or excluding tax and shipping fees.

ReferralCandy extension provides you with an opportunity to make discounts for each new customer on your website without any additional costs to your budget. You can utilize multi-use coupons, charity donations, free items, personalized messages and notifications, and much more with this module. In addition, your customers may become referrals of your website since the extension offers them personal referral links. The cheapest package costs $25 per month, but if your store requires additional attention and maintenance, there are Medium, Large, and Enterprise packages for a monthly fee of $65, $195, and $885, respectively.

Referral Bonus and Reward System is aimed at converting your loyal customers into dynamic traffic driving sources. You just need to give them points necessary for purchasing your goods. As effective referrals, your customers can invite their friends to your Magento store through various sources: social media, email, and even direct link sharing. The full-featured module is available for $99.

The Ambassador Magento extension focuses on the fast and easy building of high-end referral campaigns involving customers, team-members, and even cooperative companies. With the help of this module, you can track and analyze your current affiliate program metrics, make instant changes, and improve your performance in real time. A customizable reward system allows you to motivate your customers by introducing the most appropriate types of incentives. The extension has three diverse plans: Starter, Professional, and Enterprise, where the Starter plan costs about $200 per month and the Professional one is $800.

Other Useful Traffic-Driving Techniques...
...to Use on Your Website
Simplified Checkout

Approximately 50% of all abandoned check-out processes are caused by complex and unfriendly shopping experiences. The lengthier and more complex this process is, the less inclined customers are to make a purchase. To increase sales, try to simplify the checkout experience:

- Choose the most user-friendly template for your shopping cart options.

- Simplify a sign-in process for returning customers.

- Reduce overall checkout time by uniting closely related data in one checkout step.

Full Shipping Information

This concerns mostly information about shipping costs. When a customer literally bumps into a shipping price at the final step of his or her order completion, it often spoils a previously settled positive mood. The same happens when a shipping price is not exact, with a myriad of additional conditions and restrictions suggesting that the final sum is a subject to vary significantly. Therefore, complex shipping costs and conditions increase the number of failed checkout processes.

The most reliable solution in this case is to put shipping information at the first steps of your checkout procedure and make the price as low as possible to avoid discouraging positive expectations of customers.

Mobile-Friendly Environment

There is almost nobody who doesn't have access to a mobile device these days, and there is a huge number of people that spend much more time surfing the Internet from their smartphones and tablets than laptops or computers. This must call you for adapting the universal trend and optimizing your website for smartphones and tablets. Providing your customers with an intuitive mobile shopping experience will greatly increase your traffic and sales.

Giveaways

Everybody likes getting things for free, and you can use this tendency to attract attention of potential customers. It can be anything ranging from supporting mobile apps and extensions to handy accessories and packaging services.

Feedback Opportunities

About 80% of all customers tend to make their purchasing decisions based on reviews they read on retail websites. The most important thing is that reviews and recommendations can be used by consumers in order to provide additional information about your products to their colleagues and friends, making them even more valuable for retailers. Moreover, having reviews available makes your website generally more reliable in comparison with those that don't have this option. But in order to make it more effective, don't hesitate to ask your customers for a feedback—not everyone is apt to leave it after purchasing a product.

Although reviews can be positive and negative, you must be ready to see both types on your website. It's not always the case that your products or services must be bad, though. But the reason for bad feedback doesn't matter—think of it like of a factor that can help you boost your market performance and increase overall traffic to your website.

These techniques are also important when estimating the conversion rate of your website. Abandoned shopping carts, zero returns from email campaigns, and absence of feedback from your customers are the main factors affecting your conversion rate. Because this value plays the main part in determining how good your relationships with existing customers are, you will also have to be ready to take steps toward a conversion rate optimization strategy.

111

...to Use Outside of Your Website
Don't Give up on Traditional Advertising

Although we live in the age of computers, it doesn't mean that we cannot use old-school methods anymore. It also concerns advertising, however controversial this sphere may be. Traditional advertising is still actualized through magazines, newspapers, direct mail marketing, radio stations, TV, and even billboards. Moreover, it can also increase your website traffic!

Consider such giants as Zappos, Diapers.com, Bonobos, and Amazon. Although they are hugely popular on the Internet, these companies still rely on traditional advertising to keep their sales and website views high.

Entertain Your Customers

Using entertainment as a source of new traffic may seem an odd thing, but it really works. Try to turn on your imagination and think of content that could bring you more customers because it is funny. One of the most commonly used entertaining elements in the sphere of ecommerce is a viral video. Viral videos are made by many world-famous brands, and their efficiency is considered proven due to the enormous success they achieve afterward. Some brands even adjust themselves to YouTube and create official channels where they promote their products by introducing them in a row of funny or creative video series.

Take Part in Offline Events

This might be especially useful if you have only an online store that has been recently launched. Apart from using traditional ways of ecommerce marketing, you can simply attend various offline fairs and other sales events to get people acquainted with your products and services. Accompany your attendance with original and colorful leaflets and product samples—use all possible ways to make people visit your online store.

Expose Your Business to Other eCommerce Platforms

If you don't feel yet stable enough with traffic, don't hesitate to promote your products on bigger ecommerce platforms such as Amazon and eBay. Millions of people visit these sites every day, so it's likely that they will stumble upon your products for being original, cheap, or both.

Use Banner Ads

This is another efficient technique for driving traffic to your Magento website. Since it is quite complicated, I've decided to devote a separate part of this chapter to banner ads. You can read about it next.

Banner Ads

This type of advertisement must be familiar to every ecommerce retailer, but many of them do not consider it as effective as previously thought. First, because modern users are highly knowledgeable about computers and specifically the Internet, it's not that easy to attract their attention anymore. The only reaction people experience when seeing an ad is utter irritation, because their presence on a website is dictated by the need to read/watch something interesting or to communicate with somebody, not to click some crazy-colored suspicious banners. As a result, retailers develop more original approaches and switch to more complicated banners, but the strategy still crashes due to ad blocking software that is popular among users all over the world. In spite of these unpleasant facts about banner ads, there is still a green light for retailers to use them for driving traffic to their websites. Next, I tell you how to use them properly.

How to Use

Considering current problems related to banner ads, you will come to a conclusion that it's almost impossible to make a profit from using them. But here are the key conditions observe to make your banner ads work:

- Define a list of websites relevant to your audience. If you think that having an ad everywhere can improve your situation, you're highly mistaken.

- Spend more time making your ads creative. Creativity still attracts attention, as it can be beautiful, entertaining, smart, and eye-catching.

- Conduct some tests before submitting your banner ad. If it does not work properly or it cannot be monitored from tracking services, it's better to fix all these problems before investing in it.

- Contact potential banner ad publishers directly. Being able to communicate with website owners is a useful skill that provides the most favorable advertising conditions. You should sound natural and generous. These owners are basically the influencers of your products, so the more contacts you have, the more successful your banner ad campaign.

- Be aware of the F-shaped view pattern. This is a general page view pattern and a common feature for everyone browsing the Internet. According to it, users tend to look at the top of a page first, then explore the content itself starting from a left side, proceeding to a right side and then back, then go to the middle, do the same left-right manipulations, and so on. You can use the knowledge of the F-shaped pattern to find the best place for your banner ads. Accordingly, it will be either the top of the page or its left side. Unfortunately, when dealing with ad publishers, you will only have to rely on their own ad placement priorities.

- • Enhance your landing pages, since they are important for all kinds of online ads due to the ability to direct users to the most desirable places of your website, either already existing or newly created ones. The main purpose of a landing page is to incline users to buy your goods. Thus, it's up to you where you place the landing page on your Magento store.

Where to Buy

Basically, you have to choose among two kinds of banner ads sources—individual publishers or ad networks.

Individual Publishers

If you already have a list of potential banner ad publishers dealing with a similar market segment, contact with their owners or advertising operators. Learn their prices and subscription conditions, and decide how long you are going to work with them. Keep in mind that if you advertise on a particular website for a long time, you may become easily recognizable by its audience and therefore more trustful. Therefore, you can obtain a stable number of loyal customers. But it does not mean that you don't have to update your ads and their design regularly.

Ad Networks

Ad networks are not niche-specific banner ad resources, but can be considered as a competitive alternative to direct ad publishers. Ad networks are usually a third party that chooses the websites to publish your banner ads on. Thus, they can save you time by performing all the work instead of you. As for the down side, it is harder to drive traffic to your store, and you are not able to communicate with publishers directly. The most popular ad network is AdWords.

AdWords

AdWords is Google's official advertising program that is commonly used by businesses all over the world. It's the first thing you're advised to try in your never-ceasing attempts to get more traffic to your website. With the help of this program, you can manage your ads and choose the most appealing websites to place them on. The main advantage of the service is its relatively low cost and easy break-up procedure. In addition, you can adjust the program so that your ads are seen only by local users, especially when you tend to attract more customers to your physical store. You also can place your ad right on a Google results page; thus, users can go directly to the product page that they are interested in.

How It Functions

Keyword is a basic element of the AdWords toolkit that allows you to place your website ads near the first positions of a Google search results list. You should simply create a range of the most relevant keywords based on your business activity or products. Be specific when choosing the most important keywords and give priority to two-to-three word phrases rather than simple words.

It is also important to mention that AdWords can show your ads on other websites sharing Google-owned properties (like YouTube), as well as Google's partner sites (like NYTimes.com or Families.com). The place on the website used for showing your ad is called *placement*.

AdRank is an additional value of AdWords that is used to determine your ad's position on a website or among search results. It also determines whether your ad will be displayed at all. You should remember, though, that the main factors defining ad's location are the amount of bids you offer (the sum you're ready to spend) and the quality of your ad. As a result, the first and the most prominent positions in the list are given to the ads with highest bids and quality. What's even more interesting about AdRank is its ability to recalculate processing data and update positions of ads according to their current value.

As for bids and ad/website quality, their value varies depending on the kinds of ads you use, as well as the kind of website you have. Note that your actual bid is closely connected to your maximum cost-per-click bid, which is the maximum amount you could pay per one click. However, usually you're charged less—everything depends on the quality of your ad that is calculated according to the expected number of potential clicks, ad relevance, and landing page availability. An ad auction determines the maximum cost-per-click bid, which is required to keep your ad at a given position.

How to Fit into Your Budget

One of the main drawbacks of AdWords lies in its competitiveness—that is, the constant competition among retailers for getting the best ad positions. The more money you offer, the more chances you get to appear among the first positions, and accordingly, get more clicks to your website. Thus, a steadily developing retailer has to be able to invest at least $2,000 to $5,000 a month in an ordinary AdWords campaign. Nonetheless, buying website traffic consists of more than clicks. The better retailer that you are, the more bids you're required to offer. So before starting your cooperation with AdWords, take the following into account:

- How much money are you willing to spend on a single day of your advertising campaign? Days are more relevant than weeks or months because you cannot predict how long your ad will bring you enough profit.

- Will you vary your daily bid into parts by bidding in specific times of a day? This ad scheduling is very useful and cost-saving if you know when your website experiences its best-selling hours.

- Is your quality score high enough to be worth risking? If you're not sure about the relevancy of your keywords and the quality of your ad and landing page, it's better to invest into their improvement first.

How to Structure Your Ad Campaign

Depending on the kind of ads you have, your approaches to an AdWords campaign will vary. Product ads usually tend to work out, provided they are divided into definite categories; for instance, furniture products are better structured when categorized into beds, chairs, tables, and so on. Furthermore, you can specify each category by introducing single-size beds and double-size beds. That will make your ads more specific for potential customers and will clarify which products are more popular than others.

How to Manage Your Resources

Working with AdWords requires certain time expenditures as well. The more developed retailer that you are, the more profound ad campaign planning you should do. To buy Internet traffic simply by putting some money into it is never enough. Using text ads is indeed easier, but it's evident that for a range of products, you should work on its proper listing in AdWords webpages, manage regular updates of assortment and price, and automate submissions to Google Merchant Center. These hard tasks often require hiring corresponding specialists, but the results are definitely worth it.

How to Launch an AdWords Campaign

Next, I shed light on launching an ordinary AdWords campaign for your Magento website. Let's start with some basic aspects, such as your AdWords account.

Create an Account in AdWords

Take the following steps to create an AdWords account.

1. First, visit AdWords' main page and choose **Try AdWords Now**.

2. If you already have a Google account, then you can simply sign in with the existing login and password; otherwise, tick **I do not use these services** and enter your email address and a relatively strong password. Then solve a captcha and create an account.

3. Select your country, time zone, and the currency you'd like to deal with. Google's billing will highly depend on this information. Remember that after submitting this data, you will not be able to change it.

4. Click **Continue** and verify your account through the link sent to your email address.

Choose Your Ad Campaign

Each campaign can be run on the same or various AdWords settings—it's up to your tastes and the possibilities. There are three basic settings areas:

- Budget and bid amount

- Optional elements that can be adjusted to the main ad structure through ad extensions

- Specification of places where you want your ads to appear

Now, it's time to look through settings:

- **Campaign name**. This name will only be visible to you, but it would be great if you specify it according to your actual business goals. It's not recommended to use default Google names to find a particular campaign afterward.

- **Type**. Here you can specify what kind of ads you're going to create. For novices in advertising it's reasonable to select the "Search Network with Display Select" type of a campaign that allows you to gain access to the most popular ad placements. You can also choose a subtype of your campaign, which determines the range of settings you will use for making an ad. The Standard subtype is preferred when you're a newbie.

- **Networks**. You can choose either Google Search Network or Google Display Network to manage the appearance of your ad on other websites. The first option implies that your ads will be shown on Google-related websites, including YouTube and AOL. The second option enables your ads to be shown on other websites that have a partnership with Google.

- **Devices**. You can work on this option later when you decide to optimize your ads for tablets and mobile devices.

- **Locations and Languages**. Here you can choose an appropriate language for your ads, as well as a location that will provide only targeted location users with the ability to see your ads.

- **Bidding and budget**. You can insert bids manually or delegate them with the help of this option. Remember that your default bid represents the maximum amount you're ready to pay for your ads placement, while budget shows how much you really intend to spend for every day of your campaign.

- **Ad extensions**. This category contains additional settings, including the placement of links to your website, your local store address, or phone number.

- **Advanced Settings**. Here you will find optional settings aimed at displaying your ads on your customers' screens at the most appropriate time. This category features different schedules, such as your campaign program or the times that ads appear each day.

Create a New Campaign

Take the following steps to create a new campaign.

1. Click **Create your first campaign**.

2. You'll be directed to the **Select Campaign Settings** page, where you can set up all the previously mentioned categories.

3. At the end, don't forget to click **Save and Continue**. Later you'll be able to edit most of the settings.

Ad Groups

After you're done with settings, you will be automatically introduced to the "Create ad and keywords" page. It is possible to create an ad group here and use it as part of a more general ad campaign.

Each ad campaign includes one or multiple ad groups, depending on the type selected in Campaign Settings. Each group consists of an ad, a specialized keyword set, and bids for its placement. With certain keywords for every ad group, you enhance the relevance of your ads in a list of search results. Therefore, an ad group should correspond to a particular type of product you offer. After creating an ad group, you can proceed to managing the ads themselves.

Ads

There are different formats of ads available for your ad campaigns. Regardless of the format, it is required to create a separate range of keywords for each of them. The available ad formats vary from text and image ads to video and mobile ads.

Let's have a look at the simplest text ad.

1. Choose **Create an ad** and click **Text ad**.

2. Fill in the spaces by writing your headline, description, display URL (your homepage), and landing page. Note that both links have to belong to the same domain.

3. Type in your keywords in the appropriate section. The recommended minimum number of keywords is 10 to 20.

4. Click **Save and Continue to billing** to activate your campaign.

Billing Information

After you've created your first ad, you will be asked to fill in billing information. Follow these steps:

1. Select the country of your billing address. Then you will see additional settings available for your country. Input any additional information.

2. Choose your payment method: backup credit card for automated payments (after your ads have been displayed) or a manual payment method (before your ads have been displayed). Please note that there are some restrictions related to certain countries.

3. If you chose backup credit card payment, you don't have to perform any additional actions. Otherwise, you can pay for your first bid in **Settings ➤ Billing** by choosing **Make a payment**. Don't forget to choose the amount of a bid.

4. Now, you should provide additional payment information.

5. Save the input data.

Creating a Shopping Campaign

The format of an ad campaign is valuable when you have a store with various product items. Ads of such format usually include an image, name, description, price, and a landing page leading toward a product page on your website. To enable shopping campaigns for your AdWords account, submit your product information in Google Merchant Center. Consider that a shopping campaign is especially useful when you are targeting specific users.

Setup

Take the following steps to set up your campaign.

1. Click **Campaigns** and then **Campaign ➤ Shopping**.

2. You will be forwarded to the **Campaign Settings** page. Type the name of your campaign.

3. Select your country and add Merchant ID information.

4. In the **Country of Sale** field, select the country where your products are sold.

5. Then you can manage optional settings in **Shopping Settings (advanced)**:

- Choose a **Campaign priority** value when there are several shopping campaigns promoting the same product.

- **Inventory filter** allows you to limit the number of product items you'd like to advertise.

- You can also activate **Local Inventory Ads** for your Local Products feed to Merchant Center.

- In **Locations** you can choose countries to display your ads in.

- **Bid strategy** allows you to adjust bidding options. If you set bids manually, use default parameters. For conversion tracking, choose enhanced cost-per-click (ECPC).

6. Save these settings.

AdWords Conversion Pixel

AdWords provides its users with an opportunity to track their conversion rates based on customers' interaction with your Magento website. This includes the number of ad clicks, product page views, app downloads, order check-outs, and so forth. Conversion tracking also features all the necessary tools for maximizing profit from your ad campaigns and reducing overall expenses. In addition, it sheds light on how good your ads are. The key element of AdWords conversion tracking is the conversion pixel tool, which is basically a 1×1-pixel image placed on one or several website pages through a piece of code that you can copy and paste as a part of your primary ad campaign. This pixel effectively reacts on every activity on your website, including:

- Ad clicks from affiliate websites

- Checkout button clicks on a checkout confirmation page

- Clicks referral URL's leading from your store, which allows you tracking visitors even when they leave your page

Despite the fact that Magento does not support out-of-the-box AdWords conversion tracking, there are a lot of third-party possibilities for effective integration. For instance, here you can find a handy module written in JavaScript. Its primary role is tracking conversions from a checkout/success page of Magento stores. Alternatively, you can make use of the extensions described next.

Google AdWords and Facebook Ads Conversion Tracking and Remarketing

This Magento extension provides double-sided integration with Google AdWords and Facebook advertising campaigns. As a result, you get a high-end experience of conversion tracking process. The module is easy to set up, and after launch, its conversion tracking code is automatically stored on the Checkout Success page of your website. There is also a useful feature called Remarketing Integration, which enables ecommerce owners to capture data about what particular products your visitors are interested in. Thus, you will be able to follow your customers on other Internet resources with the aim to show them the most appropriate ads. Therefore, there will be more chances to see these customers on your store again. You can get the latest version of the extension for only $49.

Kulmage Google AdWords

This is another useful Magento extension for tracking your AdWords conversion rates. The extension's code is placed on the Magento Success page without any additional adjustments. Later on, you can easily manage its performance through your admin panel. The module is free and easy to use.

LUKA Google AdWords Conversion Tracking

This is a free-of-charge module for AdWords conversion tracking integration. The great advantage of this extension is that you can place conversion tracking pixels on any page of your website. If you find any bugs or inaccuracies with the module's performance, you can always inform its developers, and they will help you solve your problem. You should note that this module is compatible with Magento 1.5+.

Google AdWords Conversion Tracking

For only $31.45, you can easily connect your Magento website to AdWords conversion tracking. The module features the ability to update your stock information, manage conversion-related configurations from your Magento admin panel, supports both sub-domain and multi-domain pages, and can be effortlessly turned on and off at any particular moment.

Here is a list of other useful guides and articles that could help you boost your AdWords experience:

- Official Google AdWords Guide

- Pay for Google AdWords

- 5 Ecommerce AdWords Tips from an ex-Googler

- Search Advertising 101 - Your Guide to Google AdWords

- How to Start Your AdWords Well

- 12 Rules For Maximizing conversions from AdWords

Alternatives to Google AdWords

Many retailers are accustomed to think that Google AdWords is the most effective pay-per-click management service for driving more traffic to websites. However, it may not be that efficient, or it may be even harmful to your business, especially if you're a new entrepreneur. The problem is that you cannot realize the consequences until you invest in AdWords campaign. Thus, you are facing the following:

- **Rivalry**. Being especially popular among large and highly developed companies, the AdWords platform makes it impossible for small businesses to be competitive. You have to invest more and more just to be able to provide your ads with the best working keywords. With such cost-intensity, you're likely to burn out at the very beginning of your campaign.

- **Time-wasting**. As an ecommerce newcomer, you won't be really knowledgeable in all the specifics of AdWords, so you have to spend some time on getting acquainted with the toolkit. But such experiments are risky, because again, you spend your money on them and you don't know any end results.

- **Vague bidding system**. AdWords has a very intricate system of money distribution. Although you can control the amount of bids you submit for you campaign, and even invest as little or as much as you want, you will spend much time trying to find out where your money eventually goes. Moreover, if you fail to be attentive and forget to set a proper management over your bids, you're likely to lose everything.

This appears to be an uneven game where big corporations get the best advertising results and small businesses struggle uselessly for a more or less satisfying position in Google search results because they have a tighter budget.

In this situation, you have to think of other ad sources that could be more loyal and suitable for such a small business as yours.

ExactSeek

ExactSeek is a flexible advertising platform that allows retailers to attract many visitors to their online stores. It offers various programs from which you can choose the most appealing one.

- **Traffic Program**. This program requires a quarterly subscription update and seems to be very profitable due to the relatively low cost of advertising services. All ads provided by this program can bring you up to 3,000 visitors during every subscription period. ExactSeek's exclusive traffic gaining program targets users specifically from the United Kingdom, the United States, Canada, and Australia.

- **Featured Listings**. The program includes the Traffic Program combined with simple sidebar ads implemented in search engine result lists and directories. The Featured Listings tool offers low-cost investments and prevents you from tracking your ad performance, making additional bids, and inventing too complex advertising schemes.

Facebook Paid Ads

Facebook has its own advertising platform that helps new entrepreneurs address certain demographics and audiences within a billion-member social community. The principal aim here is to create a separate Facebook profile that represents your website inside the social media environment. From there, you can try various advertising schemes to gain the maximum website viewing results. The main advantage of Facebook Paid Ads is its simplicity and high efficiency.

Clicksor

Clicksor is another alternative to AdWords that targets certain market segments. It has extremely cheap bidding offers; therefore, you can start investing at just 5 cents a month. Clicksor relies on time and contextual and geo targeting to achieve the best advertising results.

Yahoo! Bing

The Yahoo! Bing advertising platform is the second most popular service after Google AdWords, which has a lot more to offer. If you decide to cooperate with Bing, you can forget about investing in other platforms, since apart from being advertised in Yahoo! Search results, you get an opportunity to access the service's ad partnership, which includes such giants as Amazon and Facebook. Bing is very popular in the United States, so you may already know what audience to target there. Moreover, bidding prices are significantly lower on Bing than AdWords.

Yahoo! Gemini Ads

This is an additional advertising tool in the Yahoo! search engine that helps you effectively encourage people to visit your website. Even if conversions remain low, you can be sure that your brand will become more popular than it is now. Gemini Ads works simply: you create an ad and then choose the most appropriate target audience. As always, add a couple of the most relevant keywords and bid for publishing your ad at specific resources.

BuySellAds

BuySellAds is not as popular as the ones already described, however, it is none the less effective. It has recently reached the milestone of selling over 6 billion ads a month; consequently, there are no reasons to omit it. First, BuySellAds is aimed at small businesses. It provides convenient ad monitoring conditions, as well as simple and transparent reports that show how your investments are spent. With BuySellAds, you can easily monitor your current advertising performance and even pause regular investments in the event of an unexpected money shortage.

BlogAds

The BlogAds service offers more suitable advertising conditions for certain segment retailers. In fact, with the help of this platform, you can advertise your products using a blog format with various types of ads, ranging from banners to custom skins. BlogAds actively cooperates with large blog websites and social networks that contain easily identifiable target audiences. You should note that monthly prices on BlogAds vary depending on ad placement—the lowest price is about $150 a month.

StumbleUpon Ads

The main advantage of this service is that you can advertise literally everything you want and still get nice visit rates. However, numerous visits won't necessarily bring you numerous customers, and StumbleUpon Ads is a place where you can become certain of this statement. Thus, the platform is more likely to be used for getting people acquainted with your brand rather than convert them into buyers.

Partner Promotion

Cooperation among individuals and companies can significantly influence your market presence. Thus, it is often enough to be mentioned in somebody's blog to receive a huge feedback and increase the amount of your sales. That's why you should always be sociable and head toward friendship with companies sharing your interest.

Social Media Advertising and SMM Campaigns

Social media is still widely used for advertising and sales boost, and it's hard to deny its efficiency in terms of ecommerce retail promotion. With millions of people surfing social network websites, the traffic source is worth investing in. Since different platforms unite people with various tastes and interests, you have lots of opportunities to reach your target audience. Unfortunately, social advertising is no longer free of charge. Sometimes, you even have to pay as much as you would spend on an AdWords campaign, but there are still lots of opportunities related to this kind of advertising. Start your SMM campaign with the following steps:

1. Clarify your campaign's objectives: increased traffic, engagement, clicks, and so forth.

2. Choose the right type for your campaign. You can use ads (boosted organic ads for everyone; specific promoted ads aimed at certain user group), share some brilliant content, or combine both approaches.

3. Define your target audience. Luckily, social media provides tons of information about users. Use this data wisely to find your customers and create an approach to uninterested ones.

4. Plan your budget. Set a total monthly budget and calculate a daily budget.

5. Design your ads. Note that different social networks have different requirements for the content of ads, such as image size and resolution, or the number of characters.

6. Always be on. Note that a quick response can turn your visitor into a buyer.

7. Work with shopping in mind. Socializing is the main reason for people to spend their time on social networks. Therefore, you should spend your attention on making shopping better with the help of these services. Sometimes it is enough to add social sharing buttons and enable customer reviews in order to gain maximum profit from social networks. At least, these are the core requirements for every ecommerce store. At the same time, you can incorporate a social media experience into every aspect of your Magento website, so don't hesitate to provide your customers with the ability to use their social network profiles everywhere from login to checkout.

8. Combine social media strategy with other marketing strategies. You can always enhance your email marketing template with the help of social sharing options. Moreover, think of utilizing your social media connections to multiply customer subscriptions to your mailing list. And don't forget about Google+ and its influence on search results.

9. Avoid being self-serving. Rely on an 80/20 ratio, where 20% is your promotional content and 80% is the content that engages your customers.

10. Use promoted posts. Usually, such posts don't include any advertising information, drawing users' attention by introducing some truly useful information like how-to guides, interesting facts, digests, photos, videos related to your activity, downloadable ebooks, and so forth.

11. Think of target ads. Using target ads helps you get to a specific social media audience, and as a result, increase website traffic.

12. Utilize specific social media for specific purposes. For example, business-to-business ecommerce advertising is more reasonable on LinkedIn. At the same time, women-related products can attract Pinterest users. Thus, you should figure out the demographic majority of the social network that you're going to use for online advertising.

13. Reward your social followers. Provide them with exclusive offers, bonuses, and discounts. Do you like feeling special? Of course you do. So why do you think your customers wouldn't like being treated the same way?

14. Use a social media marketing strategy and visual content.

    - Create eye-catching visual content.

    - Include infographics and video content in your social media campaign.

    - Run video ads with good CTAs.

15. Use SMM and SoLoMo (social-local-mobile technology).

    - Rely on real-time engagement to get loyal and highly active customers.

    - Utilize both offline and online marketing data to track individual and collaborative performance.

    - Reach people with the help of a mobile version of your ads (especially Facebook ads).

    - Use local awareness ads.

    - Try to increase conversions and decrease CPA. Get the lowest possible cost per acquisition.

    - Rely on advanced data insights and social media marketing analysis in combination with ROI-driven advertising.

16. Use new platforms.

   - Don't limit your SMM campaign to only Facebook and Twitter.

   - Explore your traffic in order to understand where your audience hangs out.

   - Learn the preferences and tastes of your target audience.

   - Don't try to conquer all social networking services.

   - Find new social ad channels.

   - Allocate your budget wisely and reduce wasted ad expenditures.

   - Try to avoid using outdated social media tactics.

   - Experiment with new platforms and approaches.

In any case, you should analyze the results of your campaign. Thus, you will be able to make vital improvements and fixes, and as a result, enhance its future productivity. It is extremely important to take all of your mistakes into account, as well as utilize all past practices. Always try to find answers to the following questions:

   - Did you get the expected results?

   - What is the ROI of your campaign?

   - How did a conversion rate change?

   - What are your mistakes?

   - How could you improve a future campaign?

Now let's take a look at various social media ecosystems and proven ways of advertising within these ecosystems.

Facebook

Facebook is the most powerful source of online advertising in a social media sphere. Since this network is surfed by all possible users, you can easily reach people who might be interested in the products that you are selling.

Start with creating your official store page on Facebook. You can do it even more easily by linking your personal page to it, as follows:

1. Go to **Options** and select **Create page**.

2. Choose the most appropriate business category (i.e., local business, company, brand, entertainment, etc.).

3. Specify the chosen category to fit your industry type.

4. Agree with the **Facebook Terms and Conditions** and click **Get Started**.

You then have to fill your new business page with content. The procedure is quite similar to personal page content management. You should necessarily include a description of your store, create a profile image (such as your company logo), and add this business page to your personal page's Favorites (to get an immediate access to it).

Of course, there are several helpful features aimed at increasing the performance of your Magento website on Facebook. The following describes the most reliable ones.

- **Custom Audiences** is a handy tool that allows you to monitor those users who come to your website from Facebook. Moreover, you can even identify which pages they have seen. It is possible with the conversion tracking pixel. With the help of the data gathered by this pixel, you get better understanding of your customers and their preferences.

- **Lookalike Audiences** is another useful Facebook tool that gathers information about the existing customers and utilizes it for searching new users that might be interested in your products.

- **Friend-to-friend Payments** is an additional payment method for your store. All Facebook users can now link their debit or credit cards directly to their personal pages and purchase any products right there. As a retailer, you can adjust this feature to eliminate the necessity for your customers to visit your Magento website and struggle through a standard checkout procedure.

- **Dynamic Product Ads** is a library of cool ad templates that considerably simplifies the process of creating ads on Facebook.

- **Multi-Product Ads** allows you to display several products in a single ad. It increases your chances to grab the interest of your target audience.

If you still have questions regarding Facebook advertising management, I recommend you to look at these profound video-lesson devoted to effective online advertising.

The Best Facebook Modules for Magento

Facebook covers a vast variety of demographic groups that can help you build a good stock of loyal audience that always looks for new items on your digital shelves. Utilizing Facebook's endless potential for attracting new customers will become even more effective when you connect your Magento store directly to the social network's features and functions, and choosing specialized Facebook modules for Magento. Since there are lots of various extensions available for Magento, next you will find only those that are really worth using.

Facebook Store Application

This extension offers a complete integration with Facebook as well as an opportunity to customize almost every feature. Developers from StoreYa provided their product with a set of tools that can import all of your website data to a corresponding Facebook page with just one click. Moreover, the module is easy to use, so you won't stop trying to enable or disable a specific feature. Facebook Store Application contains a flexible stats dashboard that allows you to monitor visitors coming from Facebook to your website, the number of clicks made to get there, and products that tend to be more popular than others. In addition, your Facebook store will be available in all languages and will accept transactions in all currencies. The extension is free and adjustable for sharing content across various social platforms.

Facebook by ORBA

With this module your website, customers get the ability to connect with their personal Facebook pages right on an ecommerce store. Basically, they can register and login to your website by entering their Facebook login and password, which means that you automatically get access to the audience of this social network. Moreover, your customers will always stay logged in on your site while being logged in on Facebook. The extension also contains a Like button that can be placed on all relevant pages, such as pages and categories. Note that the module is available for free.

Facebook Comments

Facebook Comments is a relatively new module that enables your users to use their Facebook accounts for leaving comments under blog posts or products. Comment fields and an interface look as they do on the social network itself, creating a more habitual atmosphere and encouraging users to leave comments. Another useful feature is presented by an offer to share comments with users' friends through personal pages. When these friends see those comments, they are more likely to become interested and click an attached link leading to your website page. This opens even more possibilities for driving additional traffic to your online store. The Facebook Comments module costs just $15.

Facebook Fanbox

This extension activates the Facebook Fanbox, which is basically a box that contains fan users' posts dedicated to your store or its content. A website visitor can "like" these posts and subscribe to all the following updates from the box. You can allocate the box either on left or right side of your website and set a desired size and width to suit the rest of its components. The module is free.

Facebook Wall

As the name suggests, this extension allows you to display a feed with the latest posts from your store's official Facebook page. The module costs $39, but it's worth it, considering that the extension runs on all major browsers and uses the latest graph API versions.

All4coding Facebook

This extension provides you with a full package of Facebook integratable features, including Fanbox, a Like button, a Send button, comments, sharing, and many more. With their help, you can easily monitor the activity of Facebook users on your website, as well as on your Facebook official page, in order to maximize the overall benefits from Magento-Facebook integration. You can try out a demo version of this module for free.

Facebook Referral Discount

The main purpose of this extension is to adjust your online store for promoting your products with the help of Facebook functions. In fact, you motivate your visitors to promote your goods and website when they recommend them to friends. They will do it in order to get discounts on the products they share on their Facebook friend list. The extension displays a link to a product, its name, picture, and a short description. The module can be purchased for $59.

Twitter

Since this social media network ranks second after Facebook in number of users, it is necessary to utilize it for promoting your business as well. Although Twitter shares many features typical for other social networks, it also has a certain amount of unique stuff that makes it more appealing for online advertising. Let's consider Twitter's unique features:

- **Promoted tweets** are basic types of ads that require using small input space to attract customers in the most concise way. Thus, you can promote the most relevant products of your website, the upcoming items of your company, and marketing events that you take part in by putting them into a neatly structured tweet.

- The **Promoted accounts** feature lets your brand account appear among the leading positions on the Who to Follow list. This will primarily gain more audience to your store and evoke extra interest in your current inventory.

- **Promoted hashtags** are available to the most successful merchants due to high cost. They are placed in the Trends widget to make users notice and discuss them in their feeds. Moreover, users often click hashtags to find all related tweets and discussions.

- **Liking product-related tweets**. It's a pretty smart promotion scheme that attracts Twitter users' attention to your brand. For instance, if your business concerns making furniture, you can use Twitter Search to look for users that have your keywords in their posts (like new bed, furniture store, nice wooden tables) and you can add their posts to Favorites.

- **Twitter** offers is an official Twitter feature that enables merchants to create card-linked promotions and share them with other Twitter inhabitants.

- **Quick Promote Ads**. To use this Twitter feature, you need an advertising account. According to it, your tweets will target those users that are interested in your current followers.

Twitter Modules for Magento

Of course, managing your Twitter profile apart from the website will not work unless you link it to your store page. Magento users can utilize one or several Twitter extensions (described next) for a successful integration with the Twitter environment that maximizes the amount of traffic coming from this popular social media.

Multi Twitter

This extension will display your latest tweets on the main page of your Magento website. Furthermore, you can display tweets of multiple Twitter users if they mention the name of your store in their posts: simply add necessary usernames to the extension's configuration field. It is also worth mentioning that Multi Twitter is compatible with the latest versions of all major browsers, including Chrome, Firefox, and IE. Another useful feature allows choosing a desired amount of tweets for displaying on your website page. Note that customers often read not more than three to five tweets per visit, so there's no need to display more than ten of them. After all, the main content on your store is products, not tweets. You can purchase the module for $39.

Latest Tweets from Twitter

With the help of this plugin, you can enhance your Magento website with the functionality of the previous solution for free. Since it provides regular and flawless updates of your Twitter box, your visitors won't miss any important announcements and offers regarding products and services from your store. Apart from major integration features, the module has a user-friendly interface and an easily configurable toolset. Due to the open-source nature of the extension, you can customize and improve its performance by adding new features and tools.

SM Twitter: Responsive Module

Unlike the previous modules, this one provides more a profound social experience for you and your visitors. It not only displays a timeline on your website, but it also provides you with the ability to interact with Twitter followers right from the store. This interaction includes such features as posting tweets, retweeting posts, adding tweets to favorites, and following. You can edit the size, placement, and design of the module's Twitter box anytime. The extension is available for free and is fully compatible with Magento 1.7.x.

Twitter "Tweet" Button

![Twitter 'Tweet' Button](images/Twitter 'Tweet' Button.png)
　　With the help of this extension, you can enable Tweet button on all pages of your store (on product pages and blog posts). Although the function of the Tweet button is quite straightforward, it still can be customized either by size or text type. In addition, you can set the most appropriate URL to be opened when somebody clicks the Tweet button. For instance, it's possible to shorten your link and add the name of your brand to make it more eye-catching. The module is completely free.

Creare Latest Tweets from Twitter

This free module is very popular due to the OAuth protocol and Twitter API 1.1 standard, which make it safe and reliable in terms of usage. It also offers a customizable Twitter box and a Tweet button for a full-range social interaction.

Instagram

Although Instagram is considered to be less adjusted for advertising, it still attempts to level up as a competitive social marketing platform. Merchants are now widely using Instagram for posting the photographs of their goods to attract attention of local users. There are more than 475 huge companies on Instagram. Such giants as Disney, Electronic Arts, The Gap, and Taco Bell implement their ad campaigns with the help of Instagram. This social networking service still lacks real advertising features, but there are already numerous methods created to boost your efficiency on Instagram:

- **Carousel ads** is a feature that has recently been launched within the network. It enables merchants to add multiple photographs into one post; images are simply swiped left, so there are no obstacles for you to grab users' attention. Such brands as Samsung, Banana Republic, and L'Oréal Paris have efficiently used this feature for their campaigns.

- A specific amount of **hashtag** adoption. According to recent stats, ecommerce merchants prefer using more hashtags than any other businesses that work on Instagram. The lack of keywords and links is the main reason of such behavior. So don't hesitate to utilize hashtags, but use them wisely.

- **Feedback** to your followers is the most powerful action on Instagram because it helps you get more trust and loyalty. An individual approach is likely to bring positive results from your interactions within this social media service.

Instagram Extensions for Magento

If you intend to make Instagram your primary social media traffic source, you will hardly achieve your goal without specialized Magento extensions developed for the best practices in interaction with Instagram users.

Instagram Extension by iKantam

This extension provides high-end integration with your account, allowing you to post Instagram images on your website. In addition, you can decide which pictures will be shown on your store and which are to be omitted. All the images can be easily filtered by appropriate hashtags or usernames to make your content more relevant. The module is available for only $39.

Instagram Connector

Instagram Connector is a module intended for creating an exclusive Instagram library of product images that can be displayed on your ecommerce shop. When a new image is uploaded to your Instagram account, it becomes visible on the website. The same action is possible after updating a gallery through the extension panel. All pictures in the gallery are instantly displayed in a slideshow manner, which prevents your visitors from the long and tiresome clicking on every image individually. The extension is very light and costs only $4.99.

Instagram Extension by eGrove Systems

This Magento module also extends website opportunities by displaying Instagram images at the right side of your homepage or blog section. You can also customize the order of their appearance depending on specific keywords used for a content description. The module also features a user-friendly interface and flexible configurations. You can acquire it for $69.

Instagram Widget

With this extension, you get the ability to display Instagram profile pictures anywhere on your online store starting from the homepage and ending with checkout for only $10. The module covers the whole range of previously mentioned features. In addition, it offers the count of pictures that are shown on your website, unique customizations for various pages, and an easy-to-use enable-disable option.

Pinterest

Pinterest is a visual content social media network that consists mostly of US users. Another useful demographic fact is the ratio between female and male users: women account for about 80% of all Pinterest users. Moreover, most of these women are in their forties; consequently, you get a sufficiently reduced target audience. But you still have all chances to get new customers here, so don't ignore this network.

So what should you do to drive more traffic to your Magento website?

- Create multiple company boards. Each board can be devoted to a specific type of your products. Additionally, try to utilize more creative, sensitive, and even touching images that are somehow related to your product.

- Provide short descriptions, direct links, and prices to your item images.

- Give preference to lighter, taller and no-face images. According to statistics, these tactics boosts the amount of repins to 23%.

- Place a pin button on your website to provide your customers with the ability to share your products with their followers.

- Use both rich pins and promoted pins features for your ad campaign. Although these features are not free, they are rather effective in Pinterest environment. Rich pins allow you to include additional information about your products including prices, sales, quantity, and brand. Promoted pins are designed to enlarge your audience.

- Utilize an effective hashtag since there is only one you're allowed to have on Pinterest.

Pinterest Extensions for Magento

Here, you can find all Magento extensions for integration with Pinterest.

Best Blogging Platforms Worth Using

If you haven't adapted a blog for your online store yet, take a look at the following descriptions of the most powerful blogging platforms. All the solutions mentioned next will provide you with a full set of features that allow you to maximize customer responsiveness and bring more traffic to your Magento store.

WordPress

WordPress is considered to be the best blogging platform that perfectly suits the needs of ecommerce businesses from any possible niche. The platform is built on PHP and MySQL and is totally open source, which allows you to implement further customizations to meet the specific needs of each user. The main functionality of this blogging solution is available for free, but if you intend to attract more customers to your store, you might acquire a special business plan for $299 per year. This plan includes unlimited storage space, the ability to create custom links, and an access to advanced plugins and additional blog themes.

Movable Type

This blogging solution is aimed at businesses looking for an advanced dashboard to manage their workflow, optimize the level of performed tasks, provide a high-end self-service support, and so forth. The main advantage of the platform is its ability to create original and outstanding content that is likely to interest your customers. The whole pack of tools and features can be purchased for $595.

Squarespace

This platform offers a unique blogging solution for ecommerce merchants by introducing a mixture of a blog and an online store where you can share information with your customers and at the same time sell your products and services. You can utilize Squarespace's free customizable domain together with paid plans (ranging from $8 to $24 per month). The most expensive plan allows merchants to sell an unlimited number of products through Squarespace platform.

Typepad

Typepad combines easy-to-use functionality and a set of useful analytics tools that can easily turn your blog into the second main source of traffic. For only $8.95 you will get all the necessary features aimed at the best blogging experience.

Tumblr

Being a smart combination of a micro-blog and a social network, Tumblr offers support for texts, images, and videos. With such content, you can create a perfect environment for merchant-customer interactions. Since it is possible to use all the platform's features for free, you're welcome to utilize all of Tumblr's potential for embodying your creative ideas.

Pen.io

Pen.io is an alternative blogging platform that can be used anonymously and absolutely for free. Thus, you don't have to register or pay for using any features. Moreover, you're allowed to use your own URLs without any additional domain submission. The platform is fast and user-friendly, so you won't have to waste time learning how to apply any particular feature.

Weebly

The Weebly platform is famous for its multipurpose functionality that allows you to create a blog, an online store, or a separate website. Blogging features include drag-and-drop mechanics, customizable themes, and progressive feedback opportunities. You can start your blog with a basic free plan or you can purchase a more advanced premium plan for $4 per month.

Anchor

Anchor is a useful open source platform that offers an opportunity to build custom blogging elements in HTML, JavaScript, and SCC. The only restriction is that it works with the latest browser versions, so don't hesitate to update your software. You can get full access to the platform's features for a single donation of $5.

You can find more information about other useful blogging solutions in this article. Also review the list of social media integration Magento extensions[4].

Best Magento Modules for Blogging

Despite the fact that blogging platforms significantly improve the performance of ecommerce projects, they still have one major disadvantage—blogs are detached from the primary online store, which makes it more difficult to interact with customers. That's why ecommerce developers are concerned with integrating blogging features into retail websites. Magento platform also has a wide range of free blogging solutions that you can use along with your website.

Blog - Community Edition by aheadWorks[5]

This blog module for Magento will allow you to create regular news posts and special offer announcements to keep your customers loyal to your products and services. Furthermore, the extension can generate SEO-effective text links to improve your

---

[4]https://firebearstudio.com/blog/the-best-social-media-integration-magento-extensions.html.
[5]https://firebearstudio.com/blog/aheadworks-blog-for-magento-2-and-1.html.

rankings and bring more visitors to your website. Also, you can switch on a commenting feature that provides your visitors with an opportunity to leave comments under your posts. Thus, you can easily see their opinions on your articles.

nBlog - Blog extension by Neotheme

The nBlog Magento module includes all the typical blogging features and at the same time offers something unique. For instance, a pack of cool predesigned layouts can be used for making a custom template if you don't possess any serious programming skills. These predesigned layouts can be applied to various categories of your blog to make it look original.[6] Other useful features include delayed posting, blog RSS integration, and Facebook commenting.

Blog Pro

This extension concentrates on making your blog responsive. In addition, you can make it even more attractive by adding thumbnails, images and videos. There is even a social media sharing feature that allows users to share your blog posts with their friends on all major social platforms, including Facebook, Twitter, Pinterest, VK, and so forth.

Magento WordPress Extension by FishPig

If you've already created a blog on such a popular blogging platform as WordPress and would like to integrate it with your Magento store, I recommend that you pay attention to a specialized extension developed by the FishPig team. This is a multilingual module available for all Magento editions. It offers a complete WordPress integration and supports all major plugins, original URL addresses, and shortcodes. You can also associate your blog posts with Magento products and apply a Magento theme for your blog to make it look a part of your native environment.

If you would like to find out more about how to integrate your ecommerce project into online social environment, don't hesitate to read this profound social guide[7] from the Firebear team.

Real-Time Social Experience with Periscope and Meerkat

Periscope and Meerkat are two new social services designed for real-time streaming. Both solutions can be utilized within any ecommerce business. Here, I describe their features, core differences, and ecommerce opportunities.

---

[6]https://firebearstudio.com/blog/the-best-free-blogging-extensions-for-magento.html.
[7]https://firebearstudio.com/blog/a-complete-guide-to-the-use-of-social-media-in-e-commerce.html.

Both Periscope and Meerkat produce live streams, which is a core common feature. Another aspect is integration with Twitter; sharing is optional with Periscope links, whereas Meerkat tweets all content automatically. Thus, Periscope users can easily control their audience.

Another difference consists in the availability of recorded content after the end of your stream; Periscope keeps videos for 24 hours, whereas Meerkat doesn't provide any storing capabilities, which leads to a broken user experience. In addition, Periscope provides tighter integration with Twitter; you get access to your followers from within the app.

Periscope is currently used by such giants as Pepsi's Mountain Dew, Spotify, and DKNY. Starbucks and MasterCard are among Meerkat's prominent users. When it comes to the number of users, Periscope also holds the leading position. But what about ecommerce opportunities?

Since videos have always helped merchants become transparent with customers, live streams play a prominent role in this process. You can easily inform your target audience about any latest offer or product by using social streaming services.

There is also an opportunity to show your business from inside, since you already have lots of customers interested in this information. Moreover, this will help you to get new ones. Note that a live stream is a great tool for establishing credibility among your target audience. You can even stream live demos of your products, which will make your ecommerce business even more attractive. Thus, by providing live lessons related to the products you sell, sharing some interesting facts, or offering any other engaging content, you will utilize the ecommerce opportunities of Periscope and Meerkat:

- **Place your customers in the middle of flash sales**. You can easily engage your customers with the help of Periscope or Meerkat by placing them at the center of a flash sale. You just need to start a live broadcast of your event and make customers communicate with you. This should look like a TV show. Your customers are not only situated on your ecommerce website—they're live on the air with you.

- **Introduce your ecommerce business with the help of a Q&A session**. There are probably dozens of customers willing to ask questions about your business. Don't send them to the FAQ section of your website, because there is a better decision. You can gain their confidence with the help of question-and-answer sessions. You just need a Periscope or a Meerkat live stream. Don't be afraid to show yourself to your customers; by being relatable, you will push your ecommerce business to a new level.

- **Build product awareness and grow your sales**. Ask your customers to add their real-life examples while you broadcast product information. This will not only help with building product awareness, but also increase consumer confidence, and as a result, sales.

- **Provide the customer with a better user experience**. You can utilize live streaming for your customer support needs. Thus, you will be able to provide help not only to a particular customer, but to your whole audience of buyers.

- **Get real-time feedback**. Ask buyers to leave real-time feedback about your goods and services. You can call them, or even them invite to broadcasting events. If someone famous is using your products, ask this person to take part in the streaming.

- **Turn all of your offline events into online ones**. With the help of both Periscope and Meerkat, you can easily turn all of your offline events into online real-time translations. Since you have customers who are not able to take part in your events, you will provide them with such opportunity.

The following tips will help you maximize the effectiveness of your Periscope or Meerkat campaigns:

- **Think about personalization**. Greet your viewer by nickname or name. Remain polite. Don't be afraid to say a name every time you answer a question or address a user.

- **Announce your live streams a few days before you go live**. You should do this on all possible platforms, as well as on your website. You can also use eye-catching banners to attract more attention.

- **Never omit questions**. It's always better to say that you don't know the answer.

- **Use only portrait mode**. In landscape mode, Periscope still displays messages from your customers in portrait mode, making a stream inconvenient for viewers. That's why you should use it in portrait mode only.

- **Use hashtags**. Both Meerkat and Periscope are tightly connected to Twitter. You should always remember this nuance when creating a title for a new broadcast. Use the following hashtags to increase your findability on this social network: #periscope; #werelive; #livestream; #livebroadcast.

Social Influencers for Promoting Your Products Online

One of the most up-to-date methods of gaining some traffic to your website is dealing with famous people on the Internet. They include media personalities, bloggers, vloggers, and even social media accounts run by different people all over the world. All of them are perfect as marketing channels to boost sales on your website. This marketing technique might be particularly interesting for those who have recently launched their business, but now suffer from the shortage of traffic.

Get to Know Some Instagram Influencers

Instagram is now very popular among younger audiences. It may become crucially tempting to attract new customers from such a crowded place. Moreover, it was found that Instagram is the platform giving 25% more customers to those brands that integrate their products with the local influencers than any other social media networks.

So, if you intend to find influencers for promoting your online store on Instagram, start looking for primarily those accounts that specialize in activities that might be directly or indirectly connected with your goods or services. The common mistake in this case is to look for the most popular users with a high number of followers; but it's more likely that you will tap into a community that has nothing to do with your website at all.

To make your search even more productive, use a handy website called WEBSTA that keeps all the popular Instagram hashtags and user information in its database. Users with an impressive amount of followers usually don't limit themselves by having only an Instagram page. They probably have their own websites and blogs; meanwhile, Instagram plays the role of an additional promoting source. Once you have found several potential candidates, don't forget to look at their bio or contact page—website links and email addresses are the main indicators that they don't mind cooperating with ecommerce businesses.

Another way to target influencers on Instagram is through the official mobile app. You can basically browse "the popular page" (with thousands of the most popular photos) in search of those that somehow relate to your business. Through them you can reach the owners of those photos and contact them through email (if possible).

The final thing is to write to the chosen Instagram account holders to attract their attention to your website and its products. You basically have to write a letter, which must be as neutral and loyal as possible, telling the person that you're a fan of his or her posts, and you've just launched your own website dedicated to the things you're selling. Further, you should kindly ask the person to try a sample of one of your products and share it with his or her followers. At the end, you can attach one or two images of your product. Alternatively, you can just leave a link to your website page.

Look for Popular YouTube Vloggers, Bloggers, and Press

Like Instagram, YouTube is full of popular users. What is more important, they don't mind promoting stuff that is not only a part of their target subject and also stuff that is not related to their subject at all. To reach out to the appropriate vloggers, you can use the native search engine of the website by typing keywords that describe your business interest. The same traffic-gaining strategy applies to bloggers, but can be realized through the Google main page. It's worth noting that targeting bloggers with fewer followers is often more profitable than targeting those with thousands of them since a small audience is usually more loyal to its blogger and his content and advertisements.

As for the press, you might pay more attention to local news sites rather than global ones. Here, however, you have a chance to promote your products only by writing about them in the most original way and presenting it as a good pitch: laconic and interesting to read. So if you want to grab the attention of the press, make your story concise and valuable.

Do Some Smart Advertising on Reddit

This platform is very useful in terms of its mechanics, which allows you to get involved with an appropriate user category through a corresponding thread called a *subreddit*. There are thousands of subreddits devoted to all possible subjects, so you're likely to find what fits you the best. But the thread that must be of the utmost importance to you is always in the "/r/entrepreneur" subreddit. There you will find a lot of useful discussions concerning business and ways to improve. "/r/smallbusiness" is another option for new entrepreneurs.

If you managed to find a subreddit dedicated to your website content, you can post unobtrusive little sentences there containing a nice and catchy offer to purchase your products for satisfying user needs. However, if you exaggerate with this offer, you'll probably be banned, which will bring you no actual profit. Therefore, read general and/or local Reddit rules first.

Convert Your Family and Friends into Customers Through Facebook

Making advertising posts on your Facebook page seems legit, and also important, free. Moreover, this way of attracting customers is one of the first free online advertising methods being adopted by thousands of businesses all over the world. It might not bring you much profit in the end, but you shouldn't lose the opportunity of making a few customers out of the people you know. You can even give them a 50% discount. Allowing your friends and family to be special customers can make them become loyal buyers.

Extend Your Website to Twitter

It's also a good idea to create a separate Twitter profile for your website, but it's certainly not enough for getting more traffic to your website.

The initial strategy in this case is the same: use appropriate keywords and find people posting tweets about content related to your website.

The next step is to follow those people, as they might become interested in what you're doing.

Take part in events related to your products, such as fairs or presentations; make sure that you post a tweet with cool photos.

Inform your followers about new stuff coming out—keep their interest warm.

Mention Your Potential Influencers in a Profound Blog Post

This method might become one of the most effective ones, as it's probably going to get through to target influencers' hearts. The only thing you need to do is to write a blog post about their activities, combining all the information you have under a unified title and catchy introduction. When writing about their blogs, don't forget to mention their names, because this is what will make your website better.

Amazon Product Advertising

There is nothing more reasonable than advertising on Amazon since it is the biggest and the most popular ecommerce platform that ever existed. It's no surprise that the company works hard on allowing merchants to fulfill their marketing ambitions in the easiest way. However, if you want to turn your website into the primary destination for Amazon users, then Amazon Product Ads is what you really need to utilize.

In general, Amazon Product Ads is a program for external businesses selling their products outside the Amazon platform which plays the role of a product promoter that attracts more customers. How to start using it?

1. Create an Amazon Product Ads account here. If you already have an account, simply sign in on the same page.

2. Go to the **Settings** bar and select **User Permissions**. Here, you will get a long list of product, advertising, reports, and other settings that you have to either check or uncheck, depending on your preferences. Save the changed permissions.

   Complete your account information. Go to **Settings** ➤ **Account Info**. Set a daily budget by clicking the corresponding category on the **Advertising** bar. The daily budget setting page is rather straightforward, which means that you can set only one price for all of your ads on Amazon.

3. Then you're able to upload a product list file by selecting **Add Products via Upload**. In the new window, click **Download Template**. You have to choose the most convenient template format here.

4. Amazon Product Ads requires using the following attributes: category, title, link, SKU (stock keeping unit), and price. Thus, you should be ready to edit your uploaded product feed according to the requirements.

5. After you have uploaded your product feed, wait while it is processed. You should also check the status report for errors.

6. Later, when you decide to change the bidding amount or update your inventory, you will have to upload a new product feed to Amazon Product Ads. Seems tough, but if you find Amazon helpful, it's the only way to get the maximum from the marketplace, since there are no alternate solutions.

Conclusion

Keep in mind that every SMM campaign is unique. Try to figure out all the particular proprieties of your ecommerce business in order to create the most effective social media strategy. You can rely on third-party social media companies, hire a social media marketer, or do everything with the help of existing specialists—it's up to you, but the core principles of successful campaign will always be the same.

CHAPTER 3

■ ■ ■

Growth

This chapter is about ecommerce growth, covering such topics as business expansion. The chapter is also closely related to the previous one, but it shades light on more advanced topics, such as conversion rate optimization, trusted shops, cart abandonment, referral and affiliate marketing, promotions, discounts, customer support, A/B testing, advanced analytics, and extended admin, tax, invoices, shipping, and order management.

Conversion Rate Optimization

Conversion rate optimization (CRO) is a system of methods aimed at increasing the percentage of website visitors, who eventually become customers or take a desired action in your Magento store. It is also often called *conversion optimization*.

Since conversion rate optimization is about turning your visitors into buyers, it is a key factor of your business growth and success. Unfortunately, young entrepreneurs and ecommerce startups make one common mistake: they spend too many resources on CRO without gaining traffic. This leads to a failure when a Magento store is optimized for a high conversion rate, but the number of users is not enough for the sustainable development of a company. There is often the lack of investment required for other vital enhancements.

Therefore, you should start your conversion rate optimization with free tools, investing money into driving traffic to your Magento store first (this topic is covered in the previous chapter). Robust CRO solutions are relevant only when you have a constant daily flaw of visitors.

© Viktor Khliupko 2016
V. Khliupko, *Magento 1 DIY*, DOI 10.1007/978-1-4842-2457-1_3

How to Increase Your eCommerce Conversion Rates

Increase the performance of your Magento website and implement proper search engine optimizations. These are two of the most important CRO steps you should start with. Higher performance makes your customers more loyal and decreases your bounce rate. Proper SEO not only generates more traffic, but also helps your potential buyers to find exactly what they are looking for. When your content does not match search queries, conversion optimizations and performance improvements are useless. You can read more about performance and SEO in the first chapter of this book.

Make your store as simple as possible; people don't like irrelevant content or overly complicated websites; some features are often useless and you should remove them, but don't get carried away with simplification.

Pay more attention to the most important content. Place it above the fold—the area on every website that is visible without scrolling. And don't forget to proofread everything, because your website will lose credibility if there are spelling or grammatical errors.

Use CTA buttons. Combined with a great offer, they can work as important conversion rate optimizers for your Magento store. Pay attention to their placement, color, size, and text.

Use A/B testing. This will help you avoid ineffective enhancements and get better results from trusted CRO solutions.

Optimize landing pages for your audience. I've already mentioned the importance of this step in the previous chapter. Tailor the rest of your store to suit the customer's needs. Take into account that the different technological competence of your potential buyers requires certain design improvements. Younger visitors like sleek, efficient, and straightforward websites, while older ones prefer easy-to-read text.

Listen to your customers and satisfy their propositions. By adding a rating system and a comment section to your store, you will turn your customers into participants of conversion rate optimization. Use their reviews, comments, and social network activities to turn new visitors into buyers. You can also use a "Thank you" page. And don't forget that the design of your brand should be everywhere on your Magento website.

Think about top-notch customer support. You should implement a live chat and other helpdesk solutions, as well as ensure that all of your emails have correct text, attractive design, and are readable without downloading images. This step is explained later in this chapter.

Simplify the checkout process. Since it lies in the core of the entire shopping experience and is the main exit page of every ecommerce store, you can drastically improve the conversion rate of your website by using one page checkout. You can find out more about this improvement in the next section of this chapter.

Use a competitive pricing model. Online buyers always compare prices on different ecommerce stores. Thus, you can easily enhance your conversion rates by showing that your prices are the cheapest. You just need to display your competitor's prices on your website.

Reward loyalty bonuses to all returning customers. Note that repeat sales (sales from returning customers) not only increase your conversion rate, but help you get viral word-of-mouth publicity as well. Thus, by offering discounts and sending gift cards, you will not only improve the conversion rate of your store, but also gain more visitors.

Set expectations by displaying accurate shipping times and inventory status. This will help you avoid cancellations, which provide a negative impact on your conversion rate.

Enhance your Magento store with improved navigation. There are dozens of reliable solutions aimed at making the navigation of your store more user-friendly. Of course, such improvements will positively influence your transformation of visitors-into-buyers. I explain how to implement this enhancement shortly.

Invest in product photography. Due to the inability to see your products in real life, online buyers prefer ecommerce stores with high-quality visual content, because it is often the only way to check the quality of the desired goods. Keep in mind that the better things look, the more likely they are to be purchased.

Assure security across your store. There are enough bottlenecks in default Magento, so you should remove them as fast as possible. The security improvements are covered in the first chapter of this book.

Always use analytics reports in CRO. Keep in mind that you should utilize all your past experience in order to get a maximum effect for your conversion rate optimizations. Pay attention to various analytics reports and you will be able to optimize your conversion in the best possible way. Read this article for a detailed description of this process.

Always check real-world examples. You can find 13 ecommerce case studies here: https://goo.gl/dukCUh.

Magento Extensions for Conversion Rate Optimization

I've already described the best Magento extensions. All of them are aimed at increasing your CRO to some extent. Now, I'm going to draw your attention to specific modules developed for conversion rate optimization. Let's start with one page checkout.

One Page Checkout

One page checkout is among the most important improvements for out-of-the-box Magento. Both Enterprise and Community Editions incorporate a complicated checkout procedure divided into several steps. Of course, such checkout implementation provides a negative impact on conversion rate, but you can fix this issue thanks to an appropriate "one step/page checkout" solution. With its help, customers will see all the fields required for placing an order in a single block. As a result, the new checkout process becomes easier and faster, improving the conversion rate of your store. The full list of improved checkouts is available here: The Best One Step / Page Checkout Extensions For Magento[1].

The IWD Magento extension does the following: reduces the checkout process from six steps to one; provides your customers with the ability to save their contact information for future purchases; supports multiple languages; and integrates with PayPal and Braintree. Also, there is an enterprise version of One Step/Page Checkout by IWD. You can review both solutions here: https://goo.gl/72qrA8.

---

[1]https://firebearstudio.com/blog/the-best-one-step-page-checkout-extensions-for-magento.html.

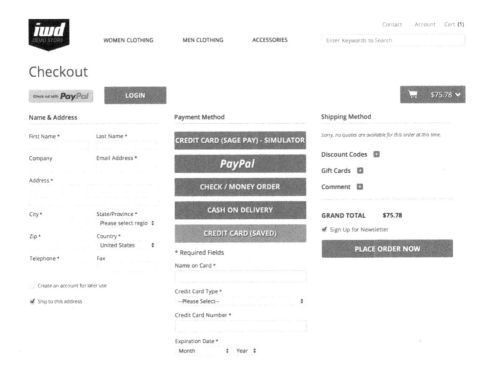

Figure 3-1. *One Step Page Checkout by IWD*

The most popular paid one step checkout extension on Magento Connect is One Step Checkout v4. It is fully responsive and compatible with smartphones and tablets, which is extremely important nowadays. Unlike the aforementioned module, it allows customers to enter a coupon code directly in the checkout page and offers lots of other useful features. The extension costs $245. You can find additional information here: http://goo.gl/AhGomx.

Improved Navigation

Navigation is another bottleneck of default Magento. Luckily, there are lots of third-party solutions designed for improvement of the issue. For instance, there is an opportunity to use filters. With the proper configurations, they enable users to narrow down a website's selection of products to just a few items. Unfortunately, a lackluster filtering experience prevails among ecommerce websites. According to *Smashing* magazine, only 16% of online stores provide worthwhile options: 42% lack category-specific filters; 20% have problems with thematic filters; and 32% don't provide compatibility filters.

The problem often lies in the way merchants promote filtering options. Since there are certain highly important filters beneficial for your users, you should display them separately from traditional ones. Otherwise, there is a risk of overlooking these options or incomprehension of their importance. Only 16% of ecommerce websites actively promote important filtering options. Thus, they improve their conversion rates by offering a better user experience. If you would also like to spend money on improved navigation, I recommend you check out the following free Magento extensions:

Sidebar Navigation Menu Professional adds vertical category navigation into the sidebar columns of your store. The extension offers powerful configurations and intelligent design, which looks good with custom themes. The module works with anchor and non-anchor categories, as well as flat and non-flat categories. You can download Sidebar Navigation Menu Professional here: `http://goo.gl/stZIZP`.

Another reliable solution is Multiple Select In Layered Navigation. This extension adds the ability to apply several values of the same filter criteria at the same time. For instance, your customers can simultaneously browse for black and yellow boots. Unfortunately, there are no admin configurations related to the module, but it works as expected. You can grab the Multiple Select In Layered Navigation extension from Magento Connect: `http://goo.gl/XvXt9`.

The Improved Magento layered navigation extension by caciobany is likewise worth paying attention to. It is based on Ajax navigation, uses history pushState/popState, offers price slider with a submit button, supports SEO-friendly URLs, as well as multiple filters for the same attribute. All of these features can be easily enabled/disabled from the back end. You can download this extension on GitHub: `https://goo.gl/OEvKYL`.

The best paid solution is Improved Layered Navigation by Amasty. It supports lots of features typical on different modules. SEO layered navigation, shop by brand, Ajax layered navigation, layered navigation filters, advanced categories, a layered navigation, and a price slider are key options available with Amasty's extension. The module costs $139, but it absolutely pays off. You can find additional information here: `http://goo.gl/OOPJwB`.

More tools are described in this article: Improved Catalog Layer Navigation Magento Extensions[2].

---

[2]`https://firebearstudio.com/blog/the-best-improved-catalog-layer-navigation-magento-extensions.html`.

Improved Catalog Search

Every ecommerce site needs a great searching tool. By installing the correct extension or using an ecommerce search engine, you provide your visitors the ability to easily find the content that they are looking for. Improved catalog search is a great addition to the enhanced navigation. Add a fast and friendly solution and turn your customers into buyers, as they will rapidly find desired goods, avoiding navigation and filters.

The best improved catalog search option is offered by Elasticsearch, which is one of the most popular search engines, used by the best ecommerce sites. Being based on Lucene, Elasticsearch offers multitenant search capabilities. It utilizes schema-free JSON documents and a RESTful web interface. As an ecommerce search engine, Elasticsearch provides real-time search. Moreover, the system is highly scalable, so you just need to add a few more nodes to provide cluster with the ability to take advantage of additional hardware as your business grows. And you will be surprised with the Elasticsearch performance, because it is one of the fastest tools for ecommerce site search. Last but not least, it is a price. Elasticsearch is open source, so you can download and use it for free. You have the ability to implement it on your Magento website with the help of the following extensions:

The Smile Magento Elasticsearch module is designed to integrate your Magento store with Elasticsearch for free. The extension offers such features as full-text search improvement, rich autocomplete, highly tunable scoring, and so forth. The module is free and you can download it from GitHub: `https://goo.gl/QiOqMk`.

Extension for Elasticsearch by BubbleShop is the best paid option. It costs $99 and supports "Did you mean?" and autocomplete features, smart correction for misspelled text queries, product attribute search, ultra-fast indexation, and tons of other ecommerce opportunities. A full list of features is at `https://goo.gl/dHdnSc`.

If your server does not support Elasticsearch, you can improve the default Magento search option with the aid of the Catalog Search Refinement module. By installing this extension, you will provide your customers with more relevant search results. Note that you can download it for free from Magento Connect: `http://goo.gl/ibGfrC`. Additionally, I recommend that you to review the list of the best ecommerce search engines here: `http://goo.gl/dkBhGu`. A digest on the best extensions for improved catalog search is here: `http://goo.gl/jbpPj2`.

Social Login

According to ConversionXL, 86% of users are bothered by the necessity of creating new accounts on websites. Moreover, 92% of average visitors will likely leave your ecommerce store instead of resetting their login information. Fortunately, you can easily improve a broken user experience by using a social login feature. At least, 77% of users think so. Facebook, Google+, Twitter, and other accounts are widely used for logging into various ecommerce websites and platforms. You can see the examples of social login on BlaBlaCar, AirBNB, as well as on thousands of other popular websites. But why is this feature so popular?

First, social login reduces the headache of typing out personal information during registration. Furthermore, it minimizes the time required to register to a few seconds. The next major reason is control over data: most social login accounts allow users to review sites that have access to their information and delete those that they don't need any longer. The third important aspect for using social login is the accuracy of information. Since users utilize their social networks for logging into a system, they have to use relevant data, but only if they've used it previously.

As you can see, social login improves user experience and fixes a long and boring login procedure, providing a positive impact on conversion. Nowadays, everyone has several accounts in various social networking services, so don't hesitate to implement social login on your Magento store. I recommend that you use one of the following extensions.

The best free option is Inchoo Social Connect. With this module, you will add Google, Facebook, and Twitter buttons to your Magento website. As a result, your visitors will be able to login or register with the aid of their social media accounts. Note that the buttons are available not only for creating an account page, but also during checkout. You can download the extension on Inchoo: `http://goo.gl/63iQrs;` or on GitHub: `https://goo.gl/OpB1aY`.

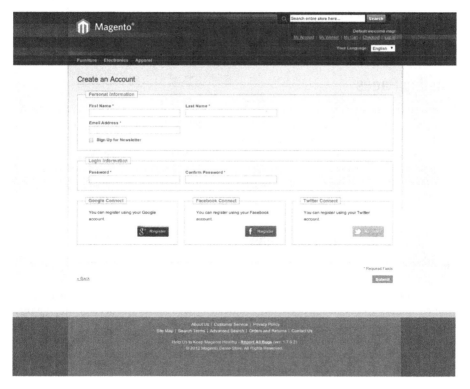

Figure 3-2. *Social Connect*

The best paid extension is Social Login by MageStore. The module supports up to 18 networks with Facebook, Google, Yahoo!, Twitter, and LinkedIn among them. Having entered the system, your customers have the ability to change their passwords. Social Login by MageStore costs $99. You can download it here: http://goo.gl/pCvMQG.

Also pay attention to AheadWorks Social Login[3].

How to Optimize Each Page of Your Magento Store

This section lists the steps required for the optimization of your conversion rate. All the improvements are divided into groups related to certain web pages.

Home Page

Since lots of visitors land on your home page, it should be informative and show the variety of products that they might be looking for. And don't forget about CTA buttons that will encourage visitors to explore your store further. Use high-quality visual content and show top-selling, featured, and recommended products on your home page. You can see the best home page examples here: http://goo.gl/Q9lio.

Landing Pages

Landing pages are often used for specific promotional campaigns, such as AdWords PPC. They provide a higher conversion rate than a home page. That's why you should set a headline, banner image, intro text, and product selection there. Note that this content should be highly adapted according to the conditions of your promotional campaign. It is a good idea to add testimonials and badges to your landing pages, as this will reduce customer anxiety. The last but not the least improvement is CTA: your landing pages should incorporate "Add to cart" or "Begin shopping" call-to-action buttons.

Product Listings and Catalogs

These pages appear after your customer has selected a category or performed a product search. A listing page for a particular category needs a dedicated introduction and an overview of available products. Stock and availability are also a must, since you will help your customers avoid clicking each product to check its availability. For returning visitors, display offers based on their previous views and purchases.

Another important improvement for default product listings and catalogs are the sorting and filtering options described earlier. Pay attention to small details, such as the number of products that match certain criteria.

---

[3]https://firebearstudio.com/blog/aheadworks-social-login-for-magento-2-and-1.html.

Note that categories such as "Customer favorites" and "Best sellers" matter to customers and are often helpful for converting casual visitors. Another useful optimization is an infinite scroll or a "View all" link, since it simplifies navigation and improves the user experience.

A powerful search capability is a reliable CRO feature on your Magento website. It should provide such options as suggestive search or promoted goods. I covered this earlier.

Individual Product Pages

For individual product pages, make the "Buy" buttons stand out from other content. At the same time, wish lists and "Save for later" buttons should be not as prominent. Using collaborative filtering on product pages is a good idea too. If you don't know how this option looks like, this is an example: "Other customers that bought A also bought B" is the most popular implementation of collaborative filtering.

Now it's time to talk about content. Take into account that long rambling descriptions are unlikely to be read. Thus, you should keep product description texts concise. With lengthy posts, use a "View more" link. Keep in mind that your descriptions should answer seller's potential questions. If there are a lot of product details, it is better to tabulate them.

To increase your conversion rate by making your ecommerce experience more similar to real-world shopping, pay extra attention to images of product pages. Your photographs should show a variety of angles, as well as lifestyle shots, and support a product zoom feature. Additionally, you can include videos, as there is a tendency that interesting and creative videos are often shared. Thus, you will get a chance to turn your visitors into promoters of your brand.

Reviews from past customers are a proven way of conversion rate optimization. Positive feedback from other buyers persuades new visitors that your Magento store is a reliable place for online purchases. If you are a reseller, you can even use reviews from other sources.

Clearly inform your customers about your stock levels and returns policy. The same goes for trust seals, supplier logos, payment methods, estimated delivery times, and prices.

Use sharing buttons in addition to social login to improve conversion and promote your store on various social networks. It is necessary to provide product titles and descriptions with relevant keywords as well.

Shopping Cart

Don't upset your customers by showing hidden fees only at checkout, since it is the number-one reason for cart abandonment. You should provide them with this information through a shopping cart. It is also a place for displaying stock levels, specification details, user-selected options, estimated delivery time, suggested products, and so forth.

Provide a convenient way for removing products and updating their quantities right in a cart. Additionally, it is important to take care of a coupon code field. Your customers like discounts, which is a good opportunity to improve conversion. The same goes for various shipping options, such as free or same-day shipping.

The Checkout

One step checkout is the main requirement for CRO on this page. Keep it free from unnecessary items and navigation, reduce everything to a single page, offer social login, and provide access to real-time support. Depending on your products and audience, you can add a gift wrapping option to checkout.

Don't forget to implement several payment options, since different customers have different preferences. Note that by offering free return shipping, you will easily convert doubters.

Trusted Shops

A trusted shops badge will never improve any of your existing Magento store features, but it can easily increase a conversion rate by providing your customers with confidence that they will receive a top-notch user experience while shopping on your ecommerce website. Both Google Trusted Stores and Trusted Shops for Europe offer seller ratings and customer reviews. Moreover, the integration of your website with these platforms is extremely easy, so there are no reasons to avoid a badge. Read the full Google Trusted Stores and Trusted Shops for Magento[4] article.

Install Google Trusted Stores for Magento. You can read its review here: Wyomind Google Trusted Stores[5]. Create a Google Trusted Stores profile, submit your shipment and cancellation feeds, and put the Google Trusted Stores badge on your Magento store. Now your customers will be informed that your website is a good place for shopping.

Integration with Trusted Shops is a little more complicated. You can go to the Trusted Shops with Trustbadge Magento extension here: `http://goo.gl/3D97kR`. After downloading and installing it, go to your Magento back-end system, choose Configuration, and open Trusted Shops. Enter your Trusted Shops ID (you can get it here: `http://goo.gl/Q2Z5Ci`). Follow the link to Trusted Shops, where you can generate your personal integration code. Copy the code and paste it into the appropriate field in your Magento back end. Save changes and you're ready!

Now you know how to persuade your visitors that your Magento store is trustworthy.

---

[4]`https://firebearstudio.com/blog/google-trusted-stores-and-trusted-shops-for-magento.html`.
[5]`https://firebearstudio.com/blog/wyomind-google-trusted-stores-for-magento-2-and-1.html`.

Cart Abandonment

Abandonment of virtual shopping carts happens quite commonly. The abandonment rate for ecommerce retailers varies between 60% and 80%, and an average index is 67.91%. To find the shopping cart abandonment rate, you have to compare the number of abandoned shopping carts to their total number. For example, there were 50,000 attempts to buy something from your Magento store during a particular month, but only 10,000 transactions had been made. Thus, 40,000 carts had been abandoned. The abandonment rate is (40,000 ÷ 50,000) × 100% = 80%. Why is it so high?

First, it's because of shopping carts alternate usage. Customers utilize them as a tool for determining the total price or looking for hidden costs. And, shopping carts can play the role of wish lists. At the same time, there are many reasons for leaving shopping carts:

- Unexpected costs

- Better price elsewhere

- Too expensive overall price

- Too complicated website navigation or too long checkout process

- Website crashes

- Expensive payment security checks

- Concerns about payment security

- Unsuitable delivery options

- Price in foreign currencies

Some visitors of ecommerce websites are just killing time, so don't expect that they are going to buy something, but you can always try to incentivize the purchase. Improve the situation by using wish lists. Clear information about prices and additional costs also decrease abandonment rate. Shopping cart abandonment reminder emails are useful too—at least 50% of all consumers think so. You can even make a shopping cart more flexible to reduce your current abandonment rate. Don't forget about Magento extensions designed to solve this problem. You can see a full list on the Firebear blog: Magento Shopping Cart Abandonment Extensions[6].

I recommend that you take a look at Abandoned Cart Alerts Pro by Aitoc. This module informs your visitors about their abandoned carts and failed orders. It sends emails with discounts encouraging your potential customers to buy in your store. The extension can send up to three follow-ups. Moreover, it offers the ability to restore a cart within one click. Abandoned Cart Alerts Pro costs $99. You can get it here: http://goo.gl/rhdow7.

If you are interested in a more robust cart abandonment solution, take a look at these cloud services: Granify, Barilliance, and WebEngage. All of them offer appropriate features aimed at reducing abandonment rates.

---

[6]https://firebearstudio.com/blog/magento-shopping-cart-abandonment.html.

Granify (http://goo.gl/sWM2he) analyzes a shopper's behavior. By monitoring over 400 attributes per second, the system predicts further steps. If a potential buyer is going to leave your ecommerce store and abandon his cart, Granify tries to prevent this while he is still on your site. Barilliance (http://goo.gl/Ixh8lz) relies on emails, informing customers about abandoned carts, and WebEngage (http://goo.gl/Mox7lg) utilizes personalized offers.

I must also mention MageMail, an amazing cart abandonment tool by members of Real Magento Community. With this application, you will easily get your customers back to your website. In addition to cart abandonment features, the tool also offers a great opportunity to recommend various products to your customers based on their past purchases. Other important features include wish list reminders, A/B testing, birthday emails, review requests, one-click discounts, and so forth. For further information, visit http://magemail.co/.

Referral and Affiliate Marketing, and Promotions and Discounts

Both referral and affiliate marketing, as well as promotions and discounts, are inevitable in your ecommerce essence if you are going to spread influence on new customers and markets. Next, I'll show you the best Magento solutions related to these marketing areas.

Referral and Affiliate Marketing

Adding new customers to your Magento webstore by running referral and affiliate marketing campaigns is extremely easy. Long gone are the days when referral and affiliate marketing was the advantage of big businesses. Nowadays, there are tons of reliable solutions available for companies of all types and sizes. But what is the difference between referral and affiliate relations?

Affiliate marketing relationships are always financially driven while ones in referral marketing are personal. By choosing affiliate marketing, you motivate your customers to promote your ecommerce store for a financial reward. As a result, they often work with people they don't know. As for referral marketing, it is based on altruism underpinned by a discount or some other incentives. Thus, customers recommend you to someone they know quite well.

As you can see, by implementing both referral and affiliate marketing campaigns, you can get new visitors and potential buyers to boost your sales. As mentioned, you can do it with appropriate Magento extensions. The best solutions are described in this article on the Firebear blog: The Best Referral and Affiliate Marketing Magento Extensions[7].

---

[7]https://firebearstudio.com/blog/the-best-referral-and-affiliate-marketing-magento-extensions.html.

Sweet Tooth Loyalty and Reward Points is one of the most reliable referral solutions. With this extension, you can create successful loyalty and reward programs that convert your visitors into first-time buyers and subsequently into profitable customers and brand advocates. The Sweet Tooth Loyalty and Reward Points Magento module is highly customizable, so you can set different conditions for earning and spending points. You can reward any customer action with this extension. You can get additional information here: http://goo.gl/OSaiul. The module costs $59.

Additionals Ways to Earn Your Rewards

There's more than just buying, here are other ways to earn rewards:

Figure 3-3. Sweet Tooth Loyalty and Reward Points

Other honorable mentions include J2T Reward Points + Referral program (http://goo.gl/AeGSQ7) and Refer a Friend by aheadWorks (http://goo.gl/BIsNm). The first module costs $49.99 and the second module is $99.

You should check out Affiliate by aheadWorks (http://goo.gl/jN44Mr). Using this module, you are able to build a strong team of sales reps, which use their opt-in lists and visitors to promote your ecommerce store and products. Take into consideration that you have to pay them only if they make a profit for you. The extension costs $99.

Another important module is Affiliate Pro Extension by MageWorld (http://goo.gl/bh6zWo). It offers all the features required for building a strong and reliable affiliate network.

The module has the ability to sign up affiliates and manage their accounts within your admin. Your customers can easily refer their friends with the help of email, IM, banners, and social networks. The module supports different affiliate programs aimed to promote specific products, categories, or brands. You can purchase the extension for $197.

Promotions and Discounts

Get your customers involved in the marketing process by adding an advanced discount system to your Magento store. Create different rules and motivate your visitors to perform certain actions by installing the appropriate modules. Extended discounts and promotion rules extensions will easily enhance your existing marketing capabilities. To find the best tools and toolsets, I recommend that you check out the blog post The Best Magento Extensions for Extended Discounts and Promotion Rules[8]. Or, you can read about the following modules instead.

Special Promotions Pro Magento Extension allows you to use customers' account information to get a better insight into your customers' wishes. By installing the module on your store, you'll be able to create special offers based on order history, and rules based on both customer attributes and order subselection. The extension allows you to sell the most expensive products by giving discounts to additional cross-sell products, and excludes specially priced products in your discount programs. You can examine Special Promotions Pro by Amasty here: Amasty Special Promotions[9]. There is also a light version of this module: `https://goo.gl/ZSX3Cz`.

Another essential tool is Auto Add Promo Items (`https://goo.gl/Dlj7mp`). With its aid, you can automatically add free promo products to a cart. Little surprise gifts will make your customers loyal, so they won't hesitate about returning to your Magento website.

Customer Support

Providing top-notch customer services is an important step in your ecommerce business growth. It can be used in different situations: as a marketing strategy, a way to raise your brand awareness, or a customer retention technique. Keep in mind that you should not only offer a reliable support, but charm your customers as well.

Provide services timely and in a professional manner in order to increase the success of your ecommerce business. Please note that it is just as crucial as defining your brand, and the best customer support solution is multichannel one. It is a strategic way to manage customer related questions within all possible platforms: email, phone, social media, and even your own website with live chats and helpdesk services. Not all of these are necessary for a small online store, but when growing a company, it is important to know what options are available.

---

[8]`https://firebearstudio.com/blog/the-best-magento-extensions-for-extended-discounts-and-promotion-rules.html`.
[9]`https://firebearstudio.com/blog/amasty-special-promotions-for-magento-2-and-1.html`.

By using all possible customer support channels, you will be able to deliver a first-rate experience to all your customers and impress them in hopes that they will return and become repeat buyers, or at least share their experience with others. Here are five tips that could work to your advantage:

- Provide your customers with email support, as it is the easiest and the most common way to communicate.

- Don't ignore social media as a reliable support tool.

- Integrate a live chat within your ecommerce store; it is one of the fastest ways to get information.

- Use helpdesk services to offer rapid customer support.

- Don't forget about inbound phone support; it is also appreciated by your customers.

Take into account that there are customers requiring support even before purchasing something on your Magento website. Often, they simply go to another store to find the desired information or find other sources of help, rather than wait for your email. Customer services therefore should be visible and timely. If you are interested in how to treat customers, read this article: https://goo.gl/Uh15WY. Next, I shed light on live chat and helpdesk services.

Live Chat

You will probably lose potential customers if they don't receive answers to their questions in real time. But you can change this situation dramatically by adding live chat support. With an online chat system, your customers get immediate help. Keep in mind that this solution reduces waiting time, which is often much less than that for phone support. At the same time, a live chat is a more cost-effective solution than call support, as it leads to lowering average interaction costs and reduces the need to hire more employees.

By installing live chat on your Magento store, you will increase conversion rates, reduce costs, and get more loyal customers. But what solution should you choose? In the The Best Live Chat Magento Extensions[10] blog post, you find the following extensions: Official Zopim Live Chat (http://goo.gl/Oln73H), LiveChat live chat software (http://goo.gl/bz7BKy), Olark Live Chat (http://goo.gl/9tL7Gl), LiveAgent – Live chat & Helpdesk (http://goo.gl/ojs690), and Casengo Live Chat Widget (http://goo.gl/XIeRND).

---

[10]https://firebearstudio.com/blog/the-best-live-chat-magento-extensions.html.

Helpdesk Services

Helpdesk services and tools are used for offering support related to products and services. They are usually aimed at all possible kinds of troubleshooting, but it is not mandatory, since helpdesk software can be utilized for providing customers with information about their future purchases, for instance. As you might have guessed, this type of services provides a significant impact on overall customer experience; therefore, it is hard to imagine a successful ecommerce company lacking such solutions. Nowadays, there are tons of different helpdesk companies that provide unique customer support. Some of them focus on cards, live chats, emails, or phone calls, while others offer several channels of support. Kayako (http://goo.gl/zDeln), Kana (http://goo.gl/Dnu9G), Zendesk (https://goo.gl/zNYueN), and other reliable companies are described in this post on our blog: Top Helpdesk Services and Tools[11]. I recommend that you collect customer feedback and use it for future improvements. You can even rely on A/B testing to find out what solutions are the most suitable for your ecommerce store.

A/B Testing

A/B testing is a randomized experiment with A and B variants, which are the control and the treatment in the testing. Variant A (the control) is the currently used version, while Variant B (the treatment) is a modified one. The goal of A/B testing is to identify changes in your Magento store that lead to better results. Note that you can use this technique to test almost everything on your website, but there are five important things to start with.

The first one is a product title, as it is the most important content part of every selling page. The second vital thing you should test is the area of product images. Product descriptions are also in this list since they should make your customers click the "Add to Cart" button, which is also a candidate for testing, as well as other call-to-action buttons. The fifth place goes to stock availability notes.

When you know what to test, it is time to talk about the best A/B testing solution. According to my experience, the most robust and reliable set of tools is offered by Optimizely (https://goo.gl/RvCPm). Having implemented this solution, you will be able to A/B test all vital elements of your Magento store. The company provides a wide range of services and offers different pricing plans, so you can start using Optimizely without any unnecessary expenditures. A/B Testing for Magento is fully described here[12].

Extended Admin Management

Unfortunately, Magento admin is not a subject of A/B testing, but you can always enhance it by installing appropriate extensions. By optimizing this part of your ecommerce store, you will reduce tons of routine processes. Therefore, you will be able to cut some costs (if you have administrators) and concentrate on more important aspects of your business development.

---

[11]https://firebearstudio.com/blog/top-helpdesk-services-and-tools.html.
[12]https://firebearstudio.com/blog/ab-testing-for-magento.html.

Always pay attention to the Magento Community Edition User Guide (http://goo.gl/VpV5dm) since it covers all possible nuances related to the platform. With the knowledge of theory, you will avoid common mistakes, and as a result, save a huge amount of time. In addition to the official user guide, you can get an advanced admin with proper Magento modules.

Enhanced Admin Product Grid, for instance, provides the ability to add some useful features and extra customizations to an admin product management grid. New features include Full Product Search, Grid Row Highlighter, Catalog Grid Thumbnails, Mass Product Refresh, and Quick Export. The module is free, so don't hesitate to download it. Use this link: http://goo.gl/5NhzL.

Pulse Storm Launcher is a fast and free productivity tool that brings the power of launcher applications to your Magento admin. The extension offers one-click access to the most used pages of your back end, as well as global search results. It saves you time and makes routine processes fun. You can download the Pulse Storm Launcher Magento extension for free on Magento Connect: http://goo.gl/iaSdQL.

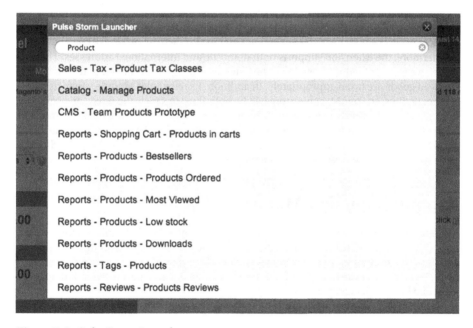

Figure 3-4. Pulse Storm Launcher

Admin Logger logs all changes made on your back end. It helps with monitoring actions around products, categories, and taxes. Since the extension gathers user-related data, you always know which of your admins performed certain changes. The module costs $80 and you can get it here: http://goo.gl/D5KR2O.

See our post on the Firebear blog for more extensions: How To Get An Advanced Magento Admin[13].

Magento Tax Management

Tax management is among the trickiest aspects of the Magento setup. You can use the official guide for implementing basic settings, but for more advanced improvements, extensions are required. You can see a full list of the best modules aimed at improved tax management here: Best Magento Extensions for Improved Tax Management[14].

For example, you have the ability to outsource your sales tax management to experts with AvaTax integration. The Sales Tax Extension for Avalara's AvaTax module not only calculates sales tax, but also manages exemption certificates and file returns. It is also able to remit payments between different tax regions. AvaTax is based on more than 100,000 taxability rules in over 11,000 taxing jurisdictions, applying them to all transactions within your Magento store. You can download the module for free from Magento Connect: http://goo.gl/KZMHYQ.

Exactor Sales and Use Tax Module is also worth mentioning. It provides the ability to calculate sales tax by a zip code or the street address where an order will be sent. Furthermore, the extension supports both domestic and international addresses. There is even a support of reduced or exempt tax rates, as well as an automated option that checks if goods are taxed appropriately. In addition, Exactor Sales Module supports tax-exempt entities, so your Magento store will be optimized to satisfy the needs of resellers, hospitals, schools, governments, and so forth. Another important feature of this extension is its integration with a shopping cart: all sales tax rates are displayed there. You can get all of these features for free here: http://goo.gl/FhYPTi. And don't forget to check other modules from the aforementioned blog post.

Extended Invoice Management

Although it is extremely easy to create invoices in Magento, the platform's default opportunities are a little limited. Luckily, there is a huge community of both professionals and enthusiasts always trying to improve the out-of-the-box Magento experience. Their work results in thousands of modules developed for all possible purposes, including extended invoice management.

PDF Invoice for Magento allows you to customize invoice templates with additional fields. With this module, you can print your documentation with ease. It includes a lot of useful features, which turns invoice creation into a flawless process, and offers free lifetime support. The extension costs $99. You can get it here: http://goo.gl/ndUXpx.

---

[13]https://firebearstudio.com/blog/how-to-get-an-advanced-magento-admin.html.
[14]https://firebearstudio.com/blog/best-magento-extensions-for-improved-tax-management.html

PDF Invoice Pro is a tool for PDF customization that allows you to change the look of PDF invoices by using HTML/CSS. The extension supports multiple PDF layouts and languages, as well as QR codes and barcodes. It works with orders, shipment, invoices, and credit memo PDF templates. You can purchase PDF Invoice Pro for $99. Get the module here: http://goo.gl/LRGQ2a.

Another popular solution developed for extended invoice management is the AdvancedInvoiceLayout extension. By offering highly optimized, configurable PDF layouts for invoices, credit memos, and shipments, it allows you to make your customer correspondence nicer and cleaner. The pre-configured layout offered by the module requires only your address and logo. AdvancedInvoiceLayout costs $53.55. Visit the Magento Connect web page for additional information: http://goo.gl/SAJGOn.

You can find other extensions for invoice and PDF management here: http://goo.gl/OJBA6e.

Advanced Shipping Management

Shipping management is another crucial facet of growth. When you've decided the carrier that you plan to work with, it's time to install an appropriate extension. Note that all major shipping providers, such as DHL, UPS, and USPS, offer official tools for Magento integration. In addition, you can look for third-party solutions on Magento Connect.

Magento Community Edition User Guide (http://goo.gl/soQt5i) is also useful for configuring settings related to shipping. After installing an extension, you should perform additional tune-ups, as described in the official documentation.

You can always enhance the default shipping options with special Magento modules. By installing the WebShopApps MatrixRate extension, for instance, you will provide your customers with multiple shipping options based on their locations. The extension offers different shipping rates according to such parameters as zip code, country, shipping method, price, weight, and quantity. There are both free and premium editions of the MatrixRate extension. You can see the free edition here: http://goo.gl/NhQUQv.

Figure 3-5. *WebShopApps MatrixRate*

As for shipping labels, Community Edition has a high level of integration with major shipping carriers, so you can easily set up and create shipping labels within your store. Just check the user guide: `http://goo.gl/8BLnH1`. This guide is also helpful: Top Magento Extensions For Custom Shipping Methods And Rules[15].

Order Management

As a routine process, order management consumes a lot of time, but you can easily improve the default workflow with the aid of proper Magento modules. Since there are more than ten pages of order management tools on Magento Connect (`http://goo.gl/UzSeZ2`), I recommend that you get acquainted with Order Manager by Fooman.

This is the only order management extension officially verified by Magento. It is aimed at managing your orders in bulk with just one click. Since such an approach saves hours of time, you can focus on more important things than processing every order manually.

---

[15]`https://firebearstudio.com/blog/top-magento-extensions-for-custom-shipping-methods-and-rules.html`.

Order Manager by Fooman provides you with the ability to invoice and mark all orders as shipped, right from the Order Overview Screen. You don't even have to worry about native invoices or shipments because they are automatically created. The extension sends configured sales emails automatically. If you are interested in scalability, Order Manager also deserves your attention, since the module is suitable for the largest ecommerce stores. You can get the Fooman Order Manager extension for $99 on Magento Connect: http://goo.gl/djv2FY.

More solutions are described at 25 Best Magento Extensions for Advanced Order Management[16].

Extended Analytics Extensions

Google Analytics and default Magento reports are not enough for a rapidly growing ecommerce business. When you need information about your sales, products, customers, or any other vital metrics, you should try extended analytics solutions, such as Advanced Reports by aheadWorks.

With this extension, you get a new source of information related to your store. This Magento plugin offers 22 different business reports that provide a clear picture of your ecommerce development. The dashboard of this extension shows all key sales metrics within a user-friendly interface. At the same time, all the reports can be sent by email. Since Advanced Reports by aheadWorks provides such features as profit calculation, abandoned cart monitoring, and "stock vs. sold" comparison, it can offer much more than default solutions do. The module costs $149. You can review it here: AheadWorks Advanced Reports[17].

---

[16]https://firebearstudio.com/blog/25-best-magento-extensions-for-advanced-order-management.html.

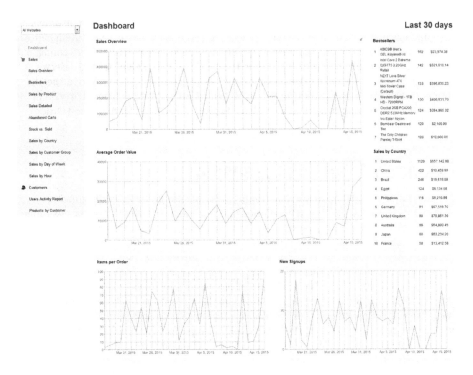

Figure 3-6. *Advanced Reports by aheadWorks*

You can also try the following services:

- **RJMetrics** (https://goo.gl/6hDfcp): This tool is designed to identify the best customers.

- **GoSquared** (https://goo.gl/3Z6LW): An advanced ecommerce analytics solution with simple integration.

- **Kissmetrics** (https://goo.gl/V3Ges): A platform that delivers data necessary for turning visitors into customers.

- **Jirafe** (https://goo.gl/oOEGwZ): An advanced tool for getting data related to marketing and merchandising optimizations.

- **Extended Analytics and Reporting Solutions for Magen**to (http://goo.gl/wQTUaU) on our on Firebear blog.

---

[17]https://firebearstudio.com/blog/aheadworks-advanced-reports-for-magento-2-and-1.html.

How to Keep Your Magento Website Clean and Healthy

In addition to installing extensions and optimizing settings, it is extremely important to keep your ecommerce store in good shape. Therefore, I recommend that you follow the advice described here:

- Always upgrade both Magento and installed extensions to a recent version. That way you will be able to fix all bugs and remove bottlenecks related to older software.

- Check community updates. Open source and open minds offer you access to the latest features and vital improvements. The community around Magento is strong, so you can always rely on it.

- Clean up Magento logs and temp files. Read this article on Nexcess: https://goo.gl/oq6Wml. It describes an entire clean-up procedure in detail.

- Track your server/hosting free space, as this will save you from unexpected trouble.

Migration to Magento 2

Although official support for Magento 1.x will remain over the next few years, you should already think about the migration to Magento 2[18], since the platform already offers a lot of new ecommerce features, better performance, scalability, and SEO. Later, I cover some important nuances of Magento 2 and provide information on migration to Magento 2.

Magento 2 introduces some vital improvements to scalability, performance, and security. These three areas caused a lot of trouble and inconvenience among users of the previous platform version; therefore, you see a lot of extensions and services aimed at solving various performance and security problems.

How much has the situation changed after the release of Magento 2? A lot, but it doesn't mean that there is no room for improvement. There are already some robust Magento 2 modules designed to enhance the existing capabilities of the platform, but even without installing them, Magento 2 shows better ecommerce results than Magento 1.

Since Magento 2 relies on a modern technology stack and a revamped code base, it offers such advantages as easier and (at the same time) unlimited customization, faster time to market, and higher deployment flexibility when it comes to cloud environments.

Magento 2 introduces an absolutely new approach to adding product lines, exploring new channels, and integrating additional ecommerce capabilities. When compared to 1.x, your daily routine is now much simpler and faster. In addition, you get rapid testing, advanced omnichannel features, and world-class business metrics management. Next, I explain these benefits in detail.

---

[18]https://firebearstudio.com/blog/migration-to-magento-2-plans-updates-tools-extensions-tutorials.html.

Architecture and Technology Stack

Since Magento 2 offers both a more modular code base and rebuild service contracts, you get a platform with an environment that is more open to new ecommerce ideas and to customizing default features. With extensive APIs and automated testing, Magento 2 introduces faster and higher-quality integration, and deployment with other ecommerce solutions and tools. Furthermore, a plethora of additional technologies that were unavailable in Magento 1.x are used to improve the performance of Magento 2. Deep integration with various third-party solutions also brings a lot of benefits.

With the aid of modern tooling and approaches, Magento 2 provides developers a better working environment that shows an absolutely new level of flexibility and ensures compatibility among its components. Thus, the new architecture and the revamped technology stack lead to a decrease in server response time and an increase in the rendering speed on the browser side. Just look at the following image by Session Digital, which illustrates the throughput measurements of Magento 2 compared to Magento 1.

Although this Magento 2 vs. Magento 1 picture illustrates the great difference between two versions of the platform, it is only the beginning of our comparisons.

Performance and Scalability

Being clumsy and resource-hungry, Magento 1 works at full power only with large enterprises, which is a sufficient drawback; but with the new release, the situation has changed dramatically. Magento 2 not only offers higher performance capabilities, it also offers them to the smallest merchants. Visitors can forget about delays when accessing a Magento 2 website. Furthermore, large order volumes and Enterprise-level site traffic are easily handled by 2.0, as illustrated in Figure 3-7.

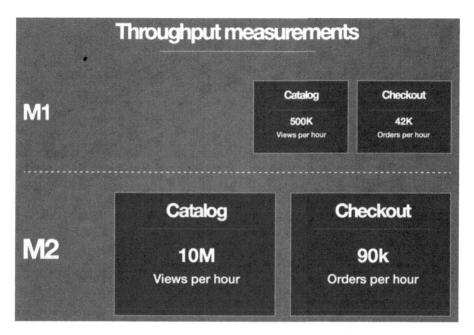

Figure 3-7. *Throughput Measurements of Magento 2*

As for scalability, Magento 2 no longer relies on a monolithic structure using a number of independent components. Figure 3-8 is an image by Session Digital that illustrates the scalability opportunities introduced in Magento 2.

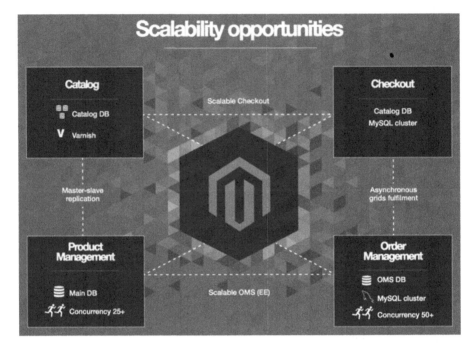

Figure 3-8. Magento 2 scalability opportunities

As a result, you get a completely revamped shopping experience.

New Shopping Experiences

Magento 2 offers fast and easy checkout, better responsive design options, enhanced personalization, and simpler product discovery.

The two-step checkout process is lightning fast in Magento 2. It not only reduces the number of overall steps, but also minimizes the amount of required information. Every customer can now create an account with just one click and without any need to interrupt the transaction.

As for personalization, Magento 2 relies on data-influenced content in promotions, product recommendations, and other processes, making the available ecommerce experience much more user-oriented than it is in 1.x.

Easier shopping in Magento 2 is also possible due to better search capabilities and layered navigation. Customers can find exactly what they are looking for without any headaches.

Productivity Features

Productivity features introduced in Magento 2 include a new more user-friendly admin panel, guided product onboarding, which is also quite convenient. Faster import/export (you can make it even better with our The Improved Import / Export Magento 2 Extension[19]) and customized views are also among the benefits introduced in Magento 2. As a merchant, you can manage various data types more efficiently, selling the right goods to the right customers at the right time.

Customization

Major layout manipulations are now available to everyone. While Magento 1 requires technical knowledge for the implementation of layout changes, Magento 2 relies on the Visual Design Editor with a drag-and-drop interface. Consequently, every merchant can easily modify blocks and containers within a website.

File Structure

As a developer, you can feel the benefits of Magento 2 with a new file structure. Major working files are now reorganized and moved under the "app" file. The only exception is the config.xml file. All of your templates, layouts, and CSS/JS files are situated under the "View" file of each module. And that is true for both the front end and the back end. Magento 2 offers a single code pool for both custom and core modules.

Migration

After the launch of Magento 2, it is vital to understand how to migrate from Magento 1 to Magento 2. Since the migration is a complex process with lots of aspects, you should know what to do with themes, extensions, data, and custom features. In this chapter, I've gathered all information about Magento 2 migration. Next, you will find useful migration tips as well as reliable Magento 2 migration tools.

Requirements

Migration elapse time is among key requirements. Although critical for big projects, it is less important for small sites. For a big website, migration could take from several hours to a few days. Keep in mind that it shouldn't be necessary to take the site offline for too long. The problem is in performing a full bulk copy of the database, which lasts a long time. A variation of the catch-up phase is also required. This phase occurs after the main bulk copy and requires an offline phase.

---

[19]https://firebearstudio.com/blog/the-improved-import-export-magento-2-extension-by-firebear.html.

It is important to place restrictions on operations that should not be performed during the migration. For instance, it is possible to place orders, but all the changes done by administrators are prohibited. It is also expected that developers are going to provide migration support for their extensions. There are two possible approaches to data migration for extensions. First, developers can provide the necessary documentation with the detailed tutorials about migration. There is also the possibility of a more flexible and pluggable framework that can automate the migration.

Current Conditions

Exporting database contents and importing into Magento 2 are both too slow. The current design relies on a direct database-to-database data transfer.

A configuration file specifies which content should be copied from the Magento 1 database to the Magento 2 database. The official support went only to the recent Magento 1 releases. Earlier versions require the appropriate adjustment of the configuration file.

In addition to simple table copies, PHP code can be plugged into the process. It is required to perform more complicated data migration.

To capture changes to selected tables during the bulk copy, database triggers are used. All of these changes are saved in a table for the later use. To reduce the number of triggers, you should limit the administrator actions.

The migration tool also works with product images. Sites that do not rely on the default image storage may require some additional actions.

The Migration Procedure

The following are the steps in the database migration procedure.

1. Create database triggers, which are necessary to capture increment changes.

2. Run the data bulk copy.

3. Stop all changes and take the old site offline.

4. Perform catchup changes.

5. Delete all triggers from the old database.

6. Turn the new Magento 2 site online.

More tips on migration to Magento 2[20]

---

[20]http://karenbaker.me/2015/09/14/1-x-magento-2-quick-migration-tips/.

Magento 2 Migration Tools

In this section, you will find the most robust tools designed to make Magento 2 migration seamless. Official and third-party software solutions are described.

Code Migration Toolkit

A new tool that simplifies migration to Magento 2 has been developed. As members of the Magento community, we've been waiting for a new migration instrument aimed at modules since the first announcement of Magento 2—and finally, we've got it. Dubbed the Magento Code Migration Toolkit, the software solution will essentially change the way you work with custom Magento extensions while trying to port them from 1.x to 2.0.

With the Magento Code Migration Toolkit, you get scripts that streamline the conversion of custom 1.x modules to Magento 2 by automating time-consuming processes. The software solution automatically converts such important things as module directory structure, as well as PHP, config.xml, and layout.xml files.

Please note that the Magento Code Migration Toolkit requires that some manual operations be performed. For instance, conversion scripts must be run in a specified order. Also, it is necessary to manually edit some files in the installation.

The following are the prerequisites:

- PHP 5.5.x+

- Composer package management software

- A designated source (Magento 1.x)

- Target Magento 2 directories

The installation procedure and module migration process are described on the Magento Code Migration Toolkit page on GitHub.

Get Magento Code Migration Toolkit[21]

Official Magento CE Data Migration Tool

Painless migration from Magento 1.x to Magento 2 is possible with the Magento CE Data Migration Tool. Currently, the extension supports the following components: data, themes, extensions, and customizations.

The Magento 2 Data Migration Tool provides the ability to move store configurations, promotions, customers, products, and order data from Magento 1.x to Magento 2.

Please note that code is not ported due to its inability to be automated.

Still, there is no particular information about porting extensions. Check GitHub for the additional data. Developers are working hard with the community to provide the ability to port Magento modules. Magento 2 relies on an innovative approach to themes and customization. Thus, merchants and developers will need to change the existing

---

[21]https://github.com/magento/code-migration.

products in order to get all the abilities of new shopping experiences. Don't forget to check official documentations for themes[22], layouts[23], and customizations[24].

The Magento CE Data Migration Tool works with Community Edition 1.9.1.0. Support for CE 1.6.x, CE 1.7.x, CE 1.8.x, and CE 1.9.x is expected.

It's important to comply with these requirements:

- Set up your Magento 2.0 to these system requirements[25].

- Set up the topology and design of a new system with your existing Magento 1.x system in mind.

- Please note that Magento 2.0 cron jobs are prohibited.

- Back up your Magento 2 database after installation. Do this as soon as possible. You can also dump[26] it.

- The Magento CE Data Migration Tool should have a network connection to the databases of both Magento 1.x and Magento 2.

- The ports in your firewall should be opened. Provide your databases and the migration tool with the ability to communicate with each other.

- You can replicate your Magento 1.x database to provide redundancy in the event of unexpected issues.

- Migrate the existing 1.x custom code and extension to Magento 2.0.

- Ask the providers of your extension if you've ported them successfully.

Download Magento CE Data Migration Tool[27]
Testing Magento 2 Data Migration Tool
There is a good blog post about Magento 2 Data Migration Tool on Inchoo. The author describes current opportunities and limitations introduced in the tool. Unfortunately, the solution for data migration to Magento 2 is far from being perfect. It still does not provide support for themes and customizations, for instance. Therefore, get ready for tons of manual work while migrating to Magento 2. Firebear members believe that one day this process will be seamless, but not today. You can read more about testing the Magento 2 Data Migration Tool here[28].

---

[22]http://devdocs.magento.com/guides/v1.0/frontend-dev-guide/themes/theme-general.html.
[23]http://devdocs.magento.com/guides/v1.0/frontend-dev-guide/layouts/layout-overview.html.
[24]http://devdocs.magento.com/guides/v1.0/frontend-dev-guide/layouts/xml-manage.html.
[25]https://firebearstudio.com/blog/magento-2-system-requirements.html.
[26]https://dev.mysql.com/doc/refman/5.1/en/mysqldump.html.
[27]https://github.com/magento/data-migration-tool-ce.
[28]http://inchoo.net/magento-2/magento2-data-migration-tool/.

Magento 2 DB Migration

This script is designed to migrate a database from Magento 1.8 or 1.9 to Magento 2 beta5. Keep in mind that this tool comes with no warranty. In addition, this module should be adapted for each new version of Magento 2.

Pay attention to the fact that Magento 2 provides a lot of changes to the code. As a result, more internal refactoring will be necessary in the future.

Magento 2 DB Migration on GitHub[29]

Magento 2 Data Migration Tool by Ubertheme

The Magento 2 Data Migration Tool by Ubertheme is another solution designed to help you migrate to Magento 2. The process is described at GitHub. You can also find there all the necessary requirements.

Magento 2 Data Migration Tool on GitHub[30]

And don't forget to read this article on Inchoo: Magento 1 vs Magento 2 – should I stay or should I go?[31]. The author thinks that performance issues are the core reason to migrate to Magento 2. If your Magento 1 store works well, you can wait until there are more extensions available. Migration tools cope with all kinds of data, such as various customizations.

Conclusion

With the materials described in this chapter, you can easily extend your store to new levels of business complexity. Don't hesitate to implement improvements on your website, since they are a key to your ecommerce success. When you know how to get more traffic, convert your visitors into buyers, and keep your online store growing, it's time to talk about Enterprise-level solutions.

---

[29]https://github.com/SchumacherFM/Magento2-Data-Migration.
[30]https://github.com/ubertheme/magento2_data_migration.
[31]http://inchoo.net/ecommerce/moving-from-magento-1-to-magento-2/.

CHAPTER 4

Enterprise

This chapter begins with a detailed guide to getting all Magento EE features on the Community platform. Later, I share other features that are useful for reaching new ecommerce levels.

Turning Magento Community Edition into Magento Enterprise Edition (How to get all Magento EE features on the Community Platform)

Although the Magento Enterprise Edition offers many more opportunities than the Community Edition does, you can always make your CE online store much more robust. In this chapter, I share my experience with turning a Magento Community website into a Magento Enterprise–class ecommerce solution.

First, I should tell you about the advantages of Magento Enterprise over Magento Community. The platform is better optimized for a large number of products. It includes full-page caching by default. There are integrated rollback and backup systems in the Enterprise Edition. The platform is highly scalable and it has an out-of-the-box enhanced tax calculation system. There is also a faster checkout, as well as tons of advanced admin features, such as the ability to easily manage customer attributes. I must mention that a gift-wrapping option is built into Magento EE. Furthermore, the Enterprise Edition offers advanced marketing and segmentation, as well as private sales.

© Viktor Khliupko 2016

V. Khliupko, *Magento 1 DIY*, DOI 10.1007/978-1-4842-2457-1_4

The features in Magento EE include PCI compliance; gift registries, points, and cards; a return management authorization system; Solr Search; automated email; multiple custom landing pages; cross-sell, upsell, and recommended products; and customer-assigned shopping. Another important advantage of the platform is 24/7 developer support. In addition, all patches are pre-installed, which makes your store more secure. Luckily, you can get all of these features within your CE website.

But what are the drawbacks of Enterprise Edition? The platform costs $12,000 per installation per year, which is a lot for small and mid-sized businesses. In fact, Enterprise Edition is nothing more than Community Edition with several additional modules: CE consists of 65 modules, whereas EE includes 41 more extensions. Note that these additional modules can be installed with the help of third-party extensions. Some of the modules are bug fixes. Some of them are considered useless. You will probably never need all the features exclusively offered by EE, but they are mandatorily pre-installed. Enterprise Edition is heavier and slower than the Community Edition, as it includes a lot of additional software, which decreases website performance.

If the lack of support in CE seems to be a problem, install paid extensions. You will not only get the missing features, but also receive support from extension developers who will help you install, manage, and update purchased modules. Please note that you only have to pay once, whereas EE payments are annual.

Take a look at these blog posts for additional information: http://goo.gl/GUpa8R and http://goo.gl/fqF2gd. You can also watch this video: https://goo.gl/Lwcn3M.

The total price of all paid (unfortunately, there are no free alternatives for every module) extensions is $722. Since a basic hosting price is $20 a month (https://goo.gl/8NeYTe) and the average price of a good Theme Forest template is $100 (http://goo.gl/AQ14oI), you can run an Enterprise-level Magento Community based online website for less than $1,000!

Order Archiving

"Increase store performance and provide efficiencies in store management through an order archiving module, enabling merchants to archive orders after a configurable time. Orders are still available to both administrators and customers, providing increased performance by storing historical orders in an archive."

The following two extensions significantly extend Magento order management and provide the order archiving feature for the Magento Community Edition: http://goo.gl/4FM9eF and http://goo.gl/qlUKxj.

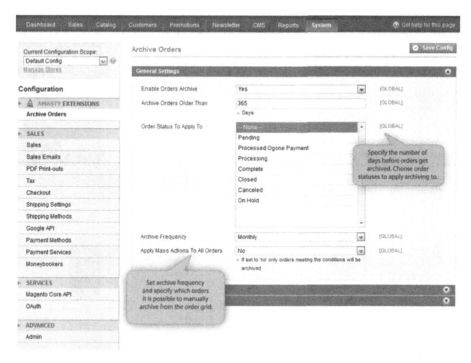

Figure 4-1. *Order Archive by Amasty*

Solr Search

"An alternative to the standard Magento search, Solr Search offers site-search options and enhancements to the speed, quality, and relevancy of search results provided to customers. Performance and search quality are improved with layered navigation and features like spelling/ synonyms/stopwords and weighted attributes."

Solr Search is not the only way to improve the Community Edition's default search option. You can check the most reliable solutions on the Firebear blog here: http://goo.gl/jbpPj2. I recommend that you pay attention to the Elasticsearch and Sphinx engines as alternative solutions to the default Magento CE search, or you can still use the Solr engine offered by Magento EE. There is even a free module designed for running Solr Search on Community Edition. You can download it from GitHub (https://goo.gl/cZTjoc) or Magento Connect (http://goo.gl/H6SEzE).

Solr Bridge Search is a paid solution. It provides Enterprise-level support and cloud-based features. You can get Solr Bridge Search for your Community Edition store here: http://goo.gl/85n6Tp. There is also an appropriate page on Magento Connect: http://goo.gl/FA297. Additionally, you can see the extension's demo here: http://goo.gl/4zCw6S.

Figure 4-2. *Solr Search*

Full Page Caching

"Enhance performance with caching of primary pages, including category, product and CMS pages for all users, including session users (excludes personal information). Caching of pages generally improves server response times and reduces load."

There are tons of amazing Full Page Cache extensions for Magento Community websites. All of these modules are designed to improve your store performance and make it faster than any Magento Enterprise site is. The best free open source Full Page Cache extension is Lesti FPC: https://goo.gl/NHxxDs. It's a good basic solution that can be replaced at any time with more robust software.

Another important aspect of full-page caching in the Community Edition is cache storage. I recommend that you use Redis, since all FPC extensions support both its free and paid versions. Thanks to a huge and productive community, we have a free way to implement on CE: `https://goo.gl/ADmnV4`.

The best paid Enterprise-level Magento Full Page Cache extension is Extendware Page Cache: Full Page Cache (`http://goo.gl/s4DeLH`). I've used it with many high-load Magento Community projects and it always shows amazing performance. Dozens of flexible settings, smooth integration with Magento templates, the "hole punches" system for handling dynamic Ajax blocks, partial cache flushing for specific entities—all of these features are available in the Community Edition. Please note that the default Magento Enterprise FPC system provides narrower opportunities.

See a full list of The Best Magento Full Page Cache Extensions[1].

In addition to Full Page Cache, it's important to get a full-page cache warmer—an extension that allows you to pre-generate FPC for every page of your website. A crawler/warmer visits every page of a website by performing a cron job, or you can do everything manually. As a result, your visitors get cached pages with amazing speed, which significantly decreases the bounce rate among first-time visitors. The best free open source solution is Magento Full Page Cache Crawler by Maveric (`https://goo.gl/3pJOdw`). It provides the ability to crawl pages manually or by performing cron from a command line and Magento admin.

The best Enterprise-level solution that supports multiple store views and currencies, and crawls all kinds of custom pages and modules, is Extendware's Cache Crawler: Cache Warmer (`http://goo.gl/cyXZy7`). The module leads to a significant performance boost if used along with the Extendware Full Page Cache extension. Together, they provide unique opportunities related to cache logging—extensions collect the most visited custom URLs (as well as any kind of URL—filters, search results, sorting, etc.) and then crawls them. As a result, you get bounce rate reduction, since visitors always get cached pages at lightning-fast speed. Although Magento Enterprise Edition provides FPC, it doesn't have a built-in cache warmer.

---

[1]`https://firebearstudio.com/blog/the-best-magento-full-page-cache-extensions.html`

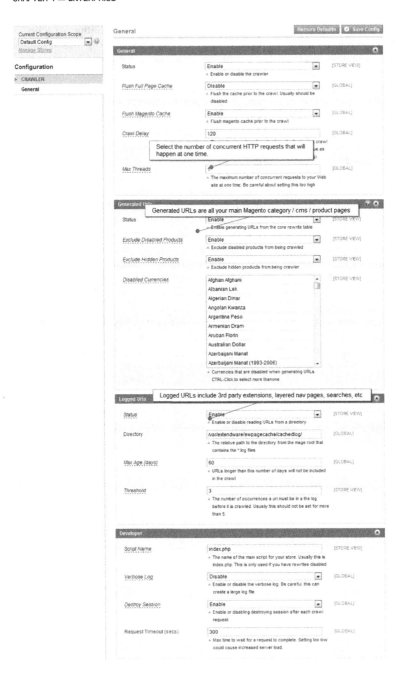

Using only Full Page Cache, you will not optimize your performance. Keep in mind that it is also necessary to take care of server-side improvements. By only using Nginx, the latest PHP version, alternative MySQL engines like MariaDB, and a proper cache strategy, you can make your Magento Community Edition faster than EE. (I shed light on these improvements in Chapter 1.) Also pay attention to The Best Full Page Cache Warmers/ Crawlers for Magento[2].

Optimized Indexing

"Optimized indexing enables significantly faster indexing with limited to no impact to the customer's shopping experience. This makes it easier to add and update products more frequently while ensuring URLs, promotions, navigational menus and product search tools are always up to date while never slowing down site performance. Incremental indexing reduces the need to perform a full re-index and offer most indexing operations are automated."

Indexing is one of the biggest performance issues on both CE and EE. Product quantity increase always leads to a rising demand of time and resources. Fortunately, a Magento Community website can be optimized with the help of appropriate extensions, which are described next. All of these extensions significantly reduce the time required for the process of indexing, and run reindexing in the background.

A free, open source, community-driven solution is FastIndexer (`https://goo.gl/ PNfT5l`). Another tool for speeding up catalog search reindexing is Sonassi Fast Search Index (`http://goo.gl/mnfZa2`).

Another Enterprise-level paid extension is Fast Asynchronous Re-indexing (`http://goo.gl/vO3pvs`).

---

[2]`https://firebearstudio.com/blog/the-best-full-page-cache-warmerscrawlers-for-magento.html`

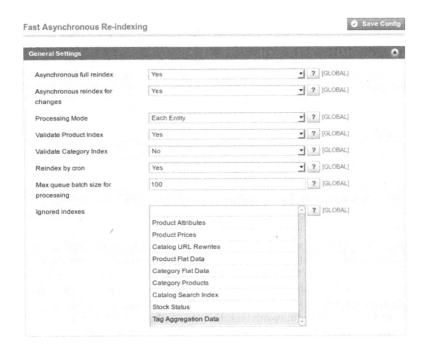

Figure 4-3. *Fast Asynchronous Re-indexing*

Configurable Order Tracking Widget

With this widget, customers can track the status of existing orders and returns without any need to log in to their accounts. There is a free community extension called Track Order (`http://goo.gl/jLFygF`). The best paid solutions are Mobile Order Tracking (`http://goo.gl/Og8veK`) and Advanced Order Status[3].

---

[3]`https://firebearstudio.com/blog/xtento-advanced-order-status-for-magento-2-and-1.html`

Figure 4-4. *Advanced Order Status*

Support for Alternate Media Storage: CDN and Database

Media files can be stored within the database or CDN (content delivery network) on a Community Edition store due to CloudFlare (https://goo.gl/hEiO). Being the best free CDN solution, the platform can be integrated with your website without any extensions; it just requires several manual changes. As a result, you get lots of additional security and performance features. When using your own servers as CDN, utilize the following extension: ImageCDN (http://goo.gl/prcjWt). There is also a CloudFront CDN (http://goo.gl/OXgECi), if you don't like CloudFlare.

AWS Service Charges		$11.27
⊟ Amazon CloudFront		$11.27
Download Usage Report »		
United States		
$0.120 per GB - first 10 TB / month data transfer out	51.811 GB	6.22
$0.0100 per 10,000 HTTPS Requests	2,314,996 Requests	2.31
$0.0075 per 10,000 HTTP Requests	3,391,088 Requests	2.54
$0.000 per URL - first 1,000 URLs / month.	67 URL	0.00
		11.07
Europe		
$0.120 per GB - first 10 TB / month data transfer out	0.369 GB	0.04
$0.0120 per 10,000 HTTPS Requests	18,153 Requests	0.02
$0.0090 per 10,000 HTTP Requests	20,252 Requests	0.02
		0.08
Asia Pacific (Tokyo) Region		
$0.201 per GB - first 10 TB / month data transfer out (includes consumption tax).	0.041 GB	0.01
$0.0130 per 10,000 HTTPS Requests (includes consumption tax)	2,785 Requests	0.01
$0.0095 per 10,000 HTTP Requests (includes consumption tax).	2,646 Requests	0.01
		0.03
Asia Pacific (Singapore) Region		
$0.190 per GB - first 10 TB / month data transfer out	0.068 GB	0.01
$0.012 per 10,000 HTTPS Requests	2,364 Requests	0.01
$0.0090 per 10,000 HTTP Requests	4,427 Requests	0.01
		0.03
South America		
$0.250 per GB - first 10 TB / month data transfer out	0.017 GB	0.01
$0.0220 per 10,000 HTTPS Requests	888 Requests	0.01
$0.0160 per 10,000 HTTP Requests	684 Requests	0.01
		0.03
Australia *(GST may be collected)		
$0.190 per GB - first 10 TB / month data transfer out	0.015 GB	0.01
$0.0125 per 10,000 HTTPS Requests	767 Requests	0.01
$0.0090 per 10,000 HTTP Requests	568 Requests	0.01
		0.03

Figure 4-5. *CloudFront CDN*

PA-DSS Certification/Payment Bridge Magento

"Secure Payment Bridge is a PA-DSS (Payment Application Data Security Standard) Certified payment application, enabling merchants to efficiently attain PCI compliance with minimum cost and effort. Customers will also be able to securely save their credit card information for future transactions. "

There are several ways to make your Magento website PCI compliant. Bear in mind that Magento CE is regarded as PCI compliant as long as you aren't storing credit card data, since there are no requirements for the encryption of other information. Thus, for making your Community Edition store compliant, you should eliminate the use of sensitive information within your website by redirecting customers to third-party payment platforms.

The second method requires using PCI-compliant gateways, such as PayPal or Authorize.net (http://goo.gl/cNBKFC). Check our list of payment gateways here: Best Payment Gateways for Modern eCommerce[4]. There are lots of PCI-compliant solutions described in the blog post.

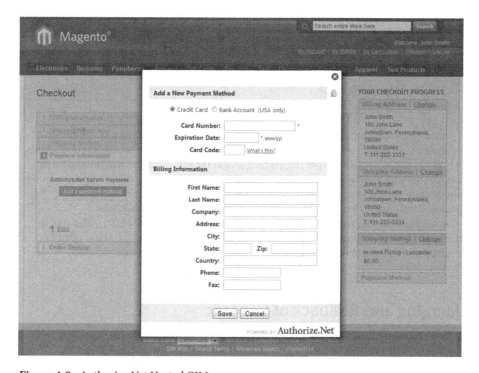

Figure 4-6. *Authorize.Net Hosted CIM*

Strong Data Encryption, Hashing, and Key Management

"Strong data encryption based on AES-256 and strong hashing based on SHA-256. Database keys are easily managed and updated."

The Magento Community also has an encryption key feature (http://goo.gl/cNBKFC), but it is not very useful, so I recommend that you to check the Magento Security guide mentioned in Chapter 1.

---

[4]https://firebearstudio.com/blog/best-payment-gateways-for-modern-ecommerce.html

Backup and Rollback

"Manage and schedule a variety of backup operations with the option to rollback the changes to reverse any modifications. This feature is particularly useful when testing new modules or customizations, or when upgrading to a new version of Magento. You can review specific customizations and their impact on the new code. (I do not recommend using this feature in your production environment.) There are three types of backup supported:

- System backup
- Database backup
- Database and media backup staging

Database backup could be performed in CE, but it is not the best way to back up your store, because it is not consistent and it cannot be restored in some situations. Thus, it is better to use Sypex Dumper (https://goo.gl/Imndik), which is a lightweight open source tool with a simple web interface. Sypex Dumper allows you to back up and rapidly compress a MySQL database, making it stable. Additionally, it provides support for broken databases, as well as different types of import and export strategies.

Another reliable solution is PhpMyAdmin (https://goo.gl/Ab4ZO5). This tool is useful for direct database management, including base URL changing. If you want to back up your Magento data to the Amazon S3 cloud, use cop_magento_backup (https://goo.gl/cL3T31).

Merging and Rollback of Content

"Create a staging site to test new categories, product information, promotions etc. Content can be merged to the live site after approval, either on-demand or per a schedule. Supports on-demand, scheduled merges and rollbacks of content."

Merging and rollback of content in the Community Edition is available with MageFlow (http://goo.gl/w9PkPC). It is an Enterprise-level service for Magento content migration. firegento-contentsync (https://goo.gl/iD9eKM) is a free open source community-driven solution for content synchronization. Genmato (https://goo.gl/vcAXSe) is a paid solution for CMS content and configuration migration.

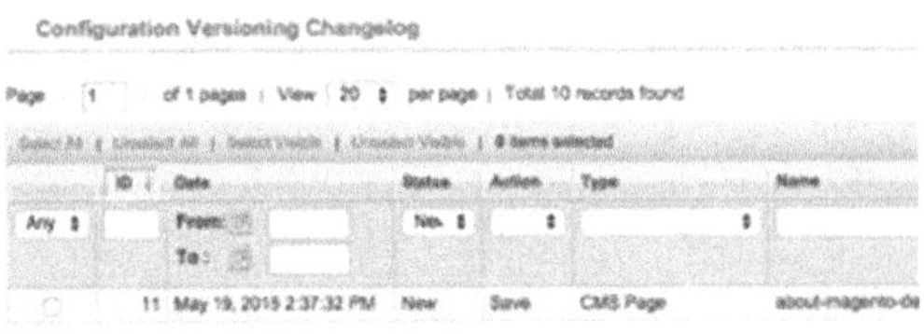

Figure 4-7. *Merging and rollback of content*

Customer Attribute Management

"Improve sales and marketing efforts with advanced attribute management. Customer account and address attributes are managed by the Magento Administrator interface and then used to create customized marketing campaigns and customer profiles."

Since an individual approach to customers is essential, an additional customer attribute is helpful. Unfortunately, Magento Community does not allow you to manage customer attributes at all. You can easily change the situation by applying a free module that offers customer information collection using Customer Attributes (`http://goo.gl/AnnZjU`). With the aid of this module, you will be able to use new custom attributes promotions, export, other extensions, and so forth. There is also a paid solution by the Amasty team called Customer Attributes[5].

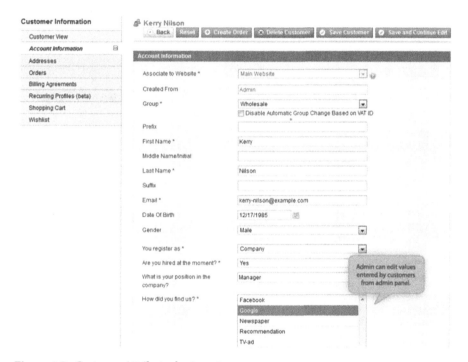

Figure 4-8. *Customer Attributes by Amasty*

---

[5]`https://firebearstudio.com/blog/amasty-customer-attributes-magento-extension.html`

Administrator Permission Roles on Website and Store Levels: Price and Promotion Permission

"Restrict access roles so that staff can view only the data to the stores relevant to them. Merchants can create and control multiple admin roles for reading and editing prices and promotions."

A free community-driven extension for advanced admin permissions and roles control is AdvancedAcl (https://goo.gl/9RS4cH). The best Enterprise-level module is Advanced Permissions by Aitoc (http://goo.gl/ejMDOT).

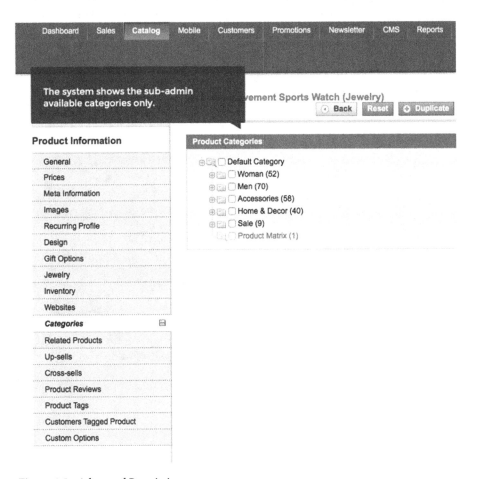

Figure 4-9. *Advanced Permissions*

Logging of Administrator Actions

"Track and review all actions taken by administrator users, with the ability to see views, edits and deletions of information. Logs are associated to specific administrator users, with the ability to see the action taken, when it was made, and more."

FireGento_AdminMonitoring is a free, open source solution for recording and viewing Magento admin actions on Community Edition. Admin Logger is a feature-rich commercial module.

Customer Administrator History

With the help of the Admin Logger extension you will be able to see admin actions with customers.

To see the Customer Administrator History, go to the **Customer → Manage Customers** backend page.

Choose the customer you need and navigate to the *Administrator History* tab.

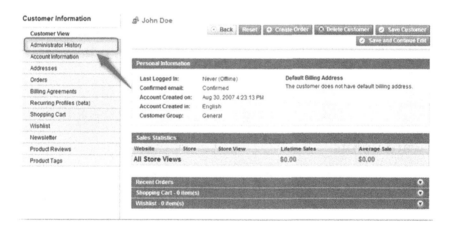

Figure 4-10. *Admin Logger*

Category View and Purchase Permissions per Customer Group (Limited Catalog Access)

"Manage viewing or purchasing items access by customer group. Access can be controlled globally or by specific category."

This feature is a must-have for almost any B2B Magento shop. You can use a great, free, open source solution by Magento master Vinai Kopp called Groups Catalog 2 (https://goo.gl/iwWJzG), as well as a more advanced paid tool by aheadWorks called

Catalog Permissions to provide a Community Edition website with the Category View and Purchase Permissions per Customer Group feature.

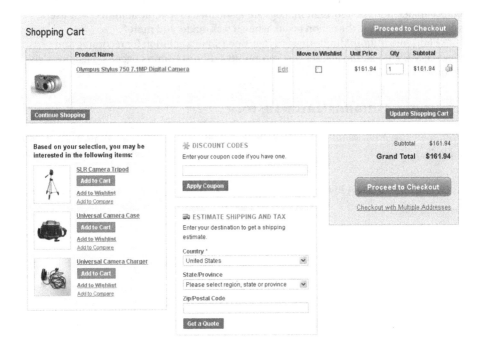

Figure 4-11. *Catalog Permissions*

Reward Points

"Enables merchants to implement programs that provide incentives to frequent shoppers, increasing customer loyalty. Points can be awarded based on a wide range of transactions and customers. Redemption rules can be controlled by merchants based on a variety of parameters including balances, expiration, customer history, conversion rate and more."

Unfortunately, there are only paid modules designed to provide Magento CE with the Reward Points feature. The most popular paid extension is the J2T Reward Points + Referral program (http://goo.gl/AeGSQ7). It costs only $50. An advanced Enterprise-level solution is Sweet Tooth (https://goo.gl/yNa7xC). It provides perfect integration with the Magento platform (http://goo.gl/0Sa1ul) and high scalability. You'll never need to change the solution because it grows along with your business.

Additionals Ways to Earn Your Rewards

There's more than just buying, here are other ways to earn rewards:

Figure 4-12. Sweet Tooth Loyalty and Reward Points

Store Credits

"Store credits can be created and tied to customer accounts. Orders can also be refunded with store credit or virtual gift cards which can be redeemed to make future purchases."

There is no free store credits solution for the Community Edition yet, but you can choose between two reliable paid modules from leading Magento extension developers. The first one is Customer Credits by Mageworx. The second module is Store Credit & Refund by Mirasvit[6]. Both cost $150. You can review the full list of The Best Store Credit Magento Extensions[7].

---

[6]https://firebearstudio.com/blog/mirasvit-store-credit-refund-magento-2-over-view.html

[7]https://firebearstudio.com/blog/the-best-store-credit-magento-extensions.html

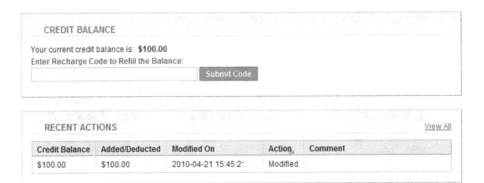

Figure 4-13. *Customer Credits*

Multiple Wish Lists

"Customers can save products to multiple wish lists and copy or move items from list to list. They can make their wish lists public so they're searchable by anyone. And merchants can review them to learn about their customers' wants and needs."

MultiWishlist (`https://goo.gl/brHT75`) is a free open source solution that allows customers to create multiple wish lists on Magento CE.

Add to Cart by SKU (Stockkeeping Unit)

"Streamline the ordering process, especially for B2B customers, by enabling them to enter a list of SKUs without having to go into product pages. This simplifies large orders, recurring orders and ordering based on offline catalogs."

Quick or fast-order capabilities are possible on Community Edition due to a wide variety of specific extensions. I'd like to draw your attention to QuickOrders (`https://goo.gl/IKG97i`). Discover more paid solutions in our blog post on Firebear: Best Magento Extensions for Quick / Fast Order[8]. As you can see, there are a lot of opportunities to implement the Add to Cart by SKU feature on CE.

Return Management Authorization (RMA)

"Enables of customer and merchant administration of returns with support for partial order and individual item returns, customer notifications, shipping methods and more."

There are no good free RMA solutions for Magento, but I know at least two reliable commercial extensions: RMA by aheadWorks[9] and RMA by Mirasvit[10].

---

[8]`https://firebearstudio.com/blog/best-magento-extensions-for-quick-fast-order.html`
[9]`https://firebearstudio.com/blog/aheadworks-rma-for-magento-2-and-1.html`
[10]`https://firebearstudio.com/blog/mirasvit-rma-magento-2-extension-review.html`

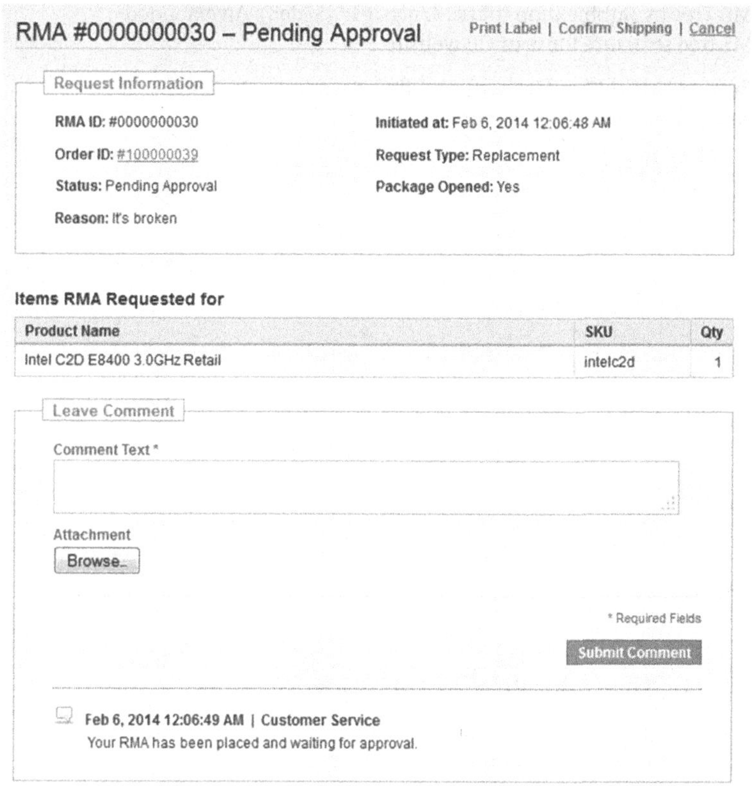

RMA #0000000030 – Pending Approval   Print Label | Confirm Shipping | Cancel

---

Request Information

RMA ID: #0000000030   **Initiated at:** Feb 6, 2014 12:06:48 AM

Order ID: #100000039   **Request Type:** Replacement

Status: Pending Approval   **Package Opened:** Yes

Reason: It's broken

Items RMA Requested for

Product Name	SKU	Qty
Intel C2D E8400 3.0GHz Retail	intelc2d	1

Leave Comment

Comment Text *

Attachment
Browse...

* Required Fields

Submit Comment

Feb 6, 2014 12:06:49 AM | Customer Service
Your RMA has been placed and waiting for approval.

Figure 4-14. *RMA by aheadWorks*

Content Management System

"Magento's CMS uses a WYSIWYG editor with support for rich content. Build complex content pages, create multiple versions of a page, restrict publishing privileges, and create menus. Easily add CMS pages to the navigation menu and create, copy or delete different CMS hierarchy trees for each website and store view individually or en masse."

Content is vital in every ecommerce business, since it is responsible for free organic traffic from search engines, and targets visitors ready to purchase from your website. Thus, you need a convenient CMS to simplify routine processes related to content. The default Magento CMS system looks very limited; that's why you should improve it. The following are the most reliable extensions.

- FireGento_FlexCms (https://goo.gl/Y2dSOv): A free open source solution for improving content management within your CMS.

- Mage Markdown Module (https://goo.gl/U7wGek): A text-to-HTML editor.

- CMS Tree by BubbleShop (http://goo.gl/jSEdqB): An extended CMS tree structure for your CE website.

- Advance CMS (http://goo.gl/XrI3PM): An advanced content management system for Community Edition.

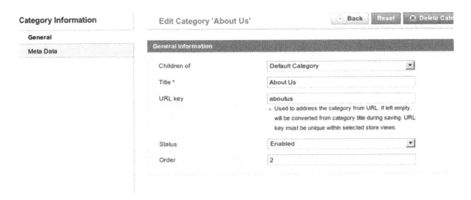

Figure 4-15. *Advance CMS*

Scheduled Import/Export Functionality

"Import and export product catalog data either locally or from remote FTP servers. Merchants can configure for error handling, status reporting and backup."

Ho_Import (https://goo.gl/AmvhV4) is a free import extension with a cron feature. The best paid modules are at http://goo.gl/1joJd and http://goo.gl/Qz8jfE. You can also read about other solutions here: The Best Improved Import/Export Extensions for Magento[11].

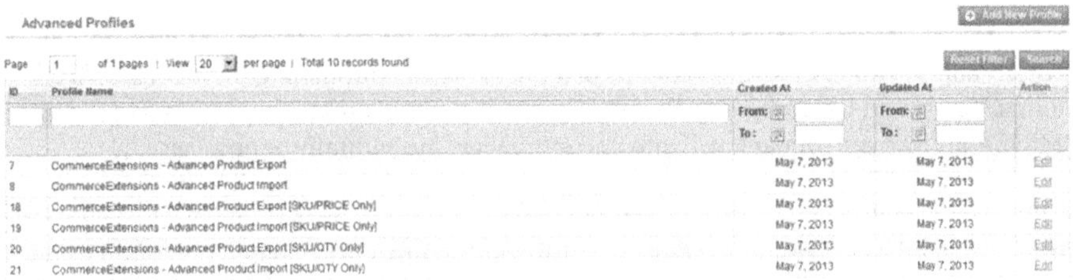

Figure 4-16. *Custom Bulk Product Import and Export*

---

[11]https://firebearstudio.com/blog/the-best-improved-importexport-extensions-for-magento.html

Customer Segmentation, Targeted Promotions, and Merchandising

"Segment customers into groups and optimize marketing initiatives by identifying specific customer groups using specific characteristics (address, gender, etc.) and/or value (purchase history, on-site browsing, etc.). Advanced segmentation capabilities include the ability to identify unknown site visitors. Whether they're new visitors or returning customers who have not logged in, you're able to identify and target them with special promotions to convert browsers into buyers."

Although customer segmentation is an Enterprise-exclusive feature, you can easily get it on your CE webstore after installing one of the following extensions. Both are paid, but they are the most reliable solutions available on the market. Also, check the part about customer attributes and limited catalog access; there are useful extensions for building a proper customer-oriented strategy.

- Market Segmentation Suite (http://goo.gl/GGgzu)

- Advanced Customer Segments by Amasty (http://goo.gl/Fw7ObF)

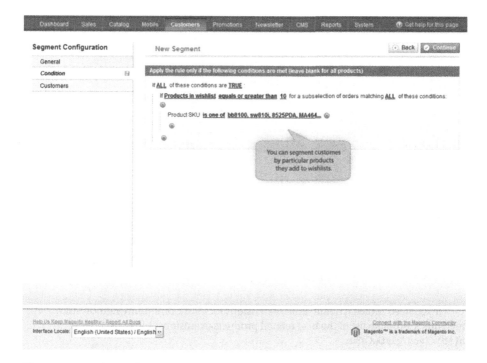

Figure 4-17. *Advanced Customer Segments by Amastycustomers*

Dynamic Rules

"Based Product Relations Dynamically target customers to present up-sells, cross-sells, and related products based on their specific product selections. Rules are easily administered through a condition based tool, allowing marketers to easily manage specific product suggestions, shopping cart price rules and banners to any customer segment to encourage additional purchases."

- Related Products Manager: A free extension for autogenerating related, cross-sell, and upsells products.

- iWeb Auto Related Products: Free autorelated products). The extension assigns products from the same category.

- FireGento_DynamicCategory: Automated category assigning by product attributes.

- Automatic Related Products by aheadWorks[12]: A paid extension with Enterprise-level features.

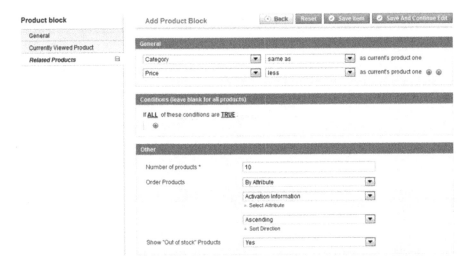

Figure 4-18. *Automatic Related Products by aheadWorks*

If you need more Dynamic Rules extensions for your Community Edition store, read our "Complete list of the best related products extensions" blog post here: http://goo.gl/UwCu8u.

---

[12]https://firebearstudio.com/blog/aheadworks-automatic-related-products-magento-2-review.html

Persistent Shopping

"Customers are able to shop and maintain items of interest in their shopping cart, wish lists, recently viewed and recently compared items between browsing sessions and from device to device. Once a customer logs in to a site, a long-term cookie is established for that browser/device combination and the customer can now view the contents of their shopping cart in subsequent sessions without logging in again."

You can easily implement this feature on your CE website with the help of the Persistent Guest Cart (http://goo.gl/XQPhka) and the "Checkout persistence remember data" (http://goo.gl/clk9VB) extensions.

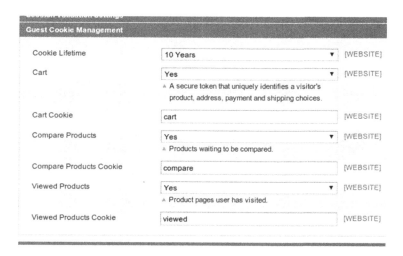

Figure 4-19. *Persistent Guest Cart*

Automated Email Marketing Reminder

"Increase customer retention by automating email reminders to customers with abandoned shopping carts and wish lists. Email reminder campaigns are configurable and customizable for a variety of parameters including frequency, cart value, quantity and more."

The best paid Enterprise-level extension designed to provide your store with this feature is Abandoned Cart Alerts Pro (http://goo.gl/rhdow7). The same functionality is also possible with MailChimp/Mandrill integration, a subscription-based service with limited free access (http://goo.gl/aRXMm5).

Autoresponder Emails

Figure 4-20. *MageMonkey*

Private Sales

"Restrict your catalog to specific customers. Create invitations and events for limited time sales to select customers and allow customer-initiated invitations. "

groupscatalog2 (https://goo.gl/iwWJzG) is a free and open way to restrict access by customer groups. Private Sales (http://goo.gl/XV8kQZ) is a free extension for private sales.

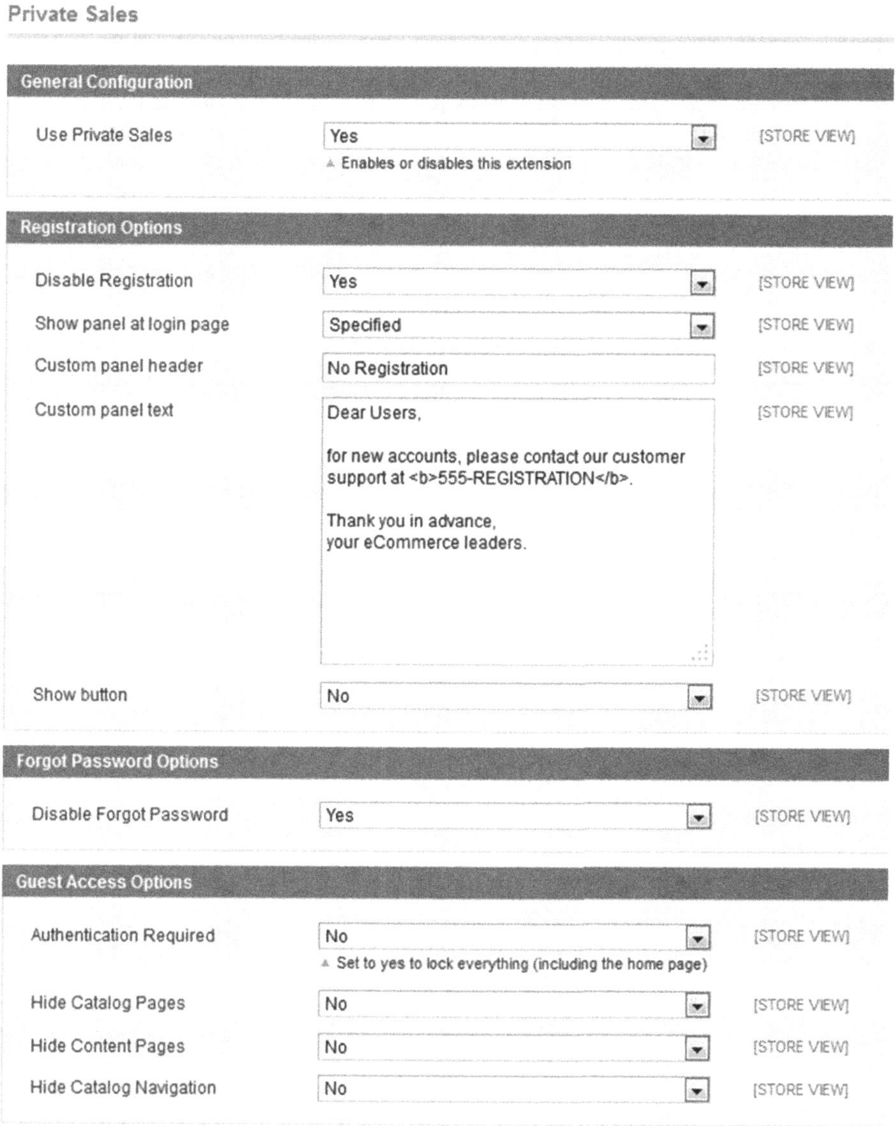

Private Sales

General Configuration			
Use Private Sales	Yes ▾		[STORE VIEW]
	▲ Enables or disables this extension		

Registration Options			
Disable Registration	Yes ▾		[STORE VIEW]
Show panel at login page	Specified ▾		[STORE VIEW]
Custom panel header	No Registration		[STORE VIEW]
Custom panel text	Dear Users, for new accounts, please contact our customer support at 555-REGISTRATION. Thank you in advance, your eCommerce leaders.		[STORE VIEW]
Show button	No ▾		[STORE VIEW]

Forgot Password Options			
Disable Forgot Password	Yes ▾		[STORE VIEW]

Guest Access Options			
Authentication Required	No ▾		[STORE VIEW]
	▲ Set to yes to lock everything (including the home page)		
Hide Catalog Pages	No ▾		[STORE VIEW]
Hide Content Pages	No ▾		[STORE VIEW]
Hide Catalog Navigation	No ▾		[STORE VIEW]

Figure 4-21. *Private Sales*

Gift Registry

"Increase revenue and capture valuable customer data with the Gift Registry feature. Those purchasing gifts can search for the registry by owner's name, email, or gift registry ID. Privacy settings are included. Gifting Options Allow customers to purchase physical and virtual gift certificates/cards for your store. Increase the average order value with gift wrapping and gift messaging options to individual products or complete orders before checkout. Applicable pricing and taxes for gift wrapping options are easily configured by administrators."

I'd like to draw your attention to Gift Registry by Aitoc and Unirgy_Giftcert. Both are paid extensions designed to provide your Community Edition store with gift registry features.

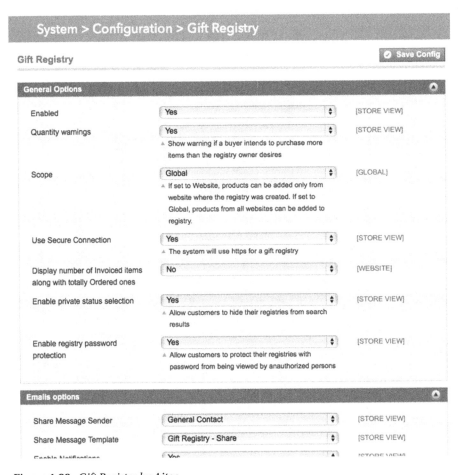

Figure 4-22. Gift Registry by Aitoc

Best Gift Registry Magento Extensions[13]

As you can see, there are lots of free and paid extensions to turn your Magento Community Edition website into an Enterprise-level solution. I should also note that security patches are available for both EE and CE. There are free community patches aimed at fixing bugs. Thus, you can easily get all Enterprise Edition features for a significantly lower price.

---

[13]https://firebearstudio.com/blog/best-gift-registry-magento-extensions.html

Multichannel Marketing

Multichannel marketing relies on different channels to reach customers. Such channels include retail stores, websites, mail order catalogs, and direct personal communication by emails, letters, text messages, or phone calls. Customers are involved in browsing, buying, returning, and pre- and post-sale services.

The objective of this marketing type is to simplify shopping from the perspective of a buyer. As a result, companies providing multichannel marketing increase customer loyalty, attract new target audiences, and gain more revenues.

Being a relatively new trend, multichannel marketing in ecommerce is already represented with various multichannel sale services and extensions. It relies on the same principles as multichannel marketing in brick-and-mortar retail, but has a limited number of instruments represented by different marketplaces and online stores.

I'm not insisting you create a brick-and-mortar store in addition to your ecommerce store, but I highly recommend that you implement core principles of multichannel marketing by integrating with core marketplaces. Luckily, you don't have to perform everything manually, as there is M2E Pro (http://goo.gl/K8ujr).

With this extension, your products are listed on eBay, Amazon, and Rakuten in just 10 minutes. Configure the module after its installation, select the products that you'd like to see on these marketplaces, and you are done. Moreover, you'll get a user-friendly interface for managing your sales channels from Magento admin. The following are other M2E Pro features:

- Full control over your inventory

- Centralized data management

- Unlimited accounts

- Scalability

- Task automation

- Order management

- Listing tools support

The integration of all three marketplaces is absolutely free. Furthermore, there are free support options offered by M2E Pro.

Other Magento solutions and extensions for implementing multiple channel sales strategies include M.O.M. (http://goo.gl/dyOh1u), StoreFeeder (http://goo.gl/PTk62F), and Blueclaw (http://goo.gl/1Z7Xd4). Explore a full list of multichannel extensions and services at Magento Multichannel Sales Services & Extensions[14].

---

[14]https://firebearstudio.com/blog/magento-multichannel-sales-services-extensions-ebay-amazon-integration.html

PIM

Product information management (PIM) software generates a set of product data that is up-to-date output for different media systems, such as ERP. PIM tools can be used for the integration of web sites with offline business. Moreover, they are aimed at producing data required for print catalogs or their digital equivalents.

Information management, implemented with the help of a PIM system, provides support for multiple locations and languages, making diverse partners or affiliates much more connected. All the members of such a system get a centralized interface, where they can modify product information in a cost-effective and consistently accurate manner.

Since modern retail involves numerous product data channels, brick-and-mortar stores are usually complemented by websites, mobile applications, print catalogs, and different digital feeds. Thus, PIM software becomes a tool designed for the organization and structuralization of data from different departments, systems, and people.

A PIM system utilizes a centralized and media-independent approach to data maintenance. As a result, a whole enterprise gets a simplified system for purchasing, production, and communication, as well as a new data flow suitable for repeated use in multiple systems. Moreover, foreign languages are no longer an obstacle.

Five Reasons to Use PIM in eCommerce

The following explains five reasons to use PIM in ecommerce.

- With a PIM system, you are able to structure your information without spending too much time on this process. The appropriate software helps you understand how your products should be classified; the number of attributes required for your ecommerce store; core principles of navigation on your website; major data sources with their priority and influences; a required level of data quality, and so forth.

- Product information management software is often used for information enrichment. Spreadsheets and ERPs never provide the most comprehensive data offered by PIM platforms. In addition, you are able to avoid different headaches, such as poor product pages or manual form filling.

- Since the work of recommendation engines and search tools is based on product data, you need to provide these tools with the most comprehensive information about your products in order to satisfy visitors with the most relevant results. Such information is generated by PIM systems.

- Multichannel support is another reason to use PIM. You can always connect your ecommerce website with a brick-and-mortar store or a mobile app using product information management software. Note that it is always easier to connect your Magento store with new channels through PIM than to make customizations directly to the website.

- It's more profitable to add PIM system to your enterprise right now, because with the growth of your digital store, the costs required for the integration will increase as well.

Visit the Best PIM Systems for Your E-Commerce website[15].

Asim (http://goo.gl/4uRCvg), Salsify (http://goo.gl/Q7rZRq), inRiver (http://goo.gl/NgbQXi), and Hybris software (https://goo.gl/fOvDTP) are examples of PIM systems widely used in ecommerce. A full list of services with short descriptions and all necessary links is here: http://goo.gl/bH5A29.

ERP

An *enterprise resource planning* (ERP) system is a set of software tools for business management. Usually, it is a suite of integrated applications that an enterprise or a company can utilize for data gathering, storage, management, and interpretation. ERP covers core business processes, tracking such business resources as raw materials, cash, production capacity, and stocks in real time. It also monitors the status of business commitments: payrolls, orders, and purchase orders. With an ERP system, you can turn your Magento store into a more robust and profitable business unit. To achieve this goal, you need a proper extension. Therefore, I am going to describe the most popular solutions next.

The first one is Embedded ERP. This extension is developed to help you with fulfilling orders and purchases, managing stocks, and performing other operations. Contrary to other similar solutions, Embedded ERP was developed especially for ecommerce businesses, so it fits perfectly with the Magento platform.

The extension covers four areas: stock management, purchasing, order preparation, product availability, and order planning. It supports multiple warehouses, stock level alerts, barcodes, inventory tracking, and sales history. Moreover, Embedded ERP lets you manage supply needs, purchase orders, and suppliers. The solution provides control over mass order fulfillment, printing, picking, and shipping labels. Advanced product availability options and order forecasts are also among the extension's strong points.

The tool is 100% open source and highly customizable; it costs $649. You can get additional information here: http://goo.gl/DHoxVH.

---

[15]https://firebearstudio.com/blog/best-pim-product-information-management-systems-for-your-e-commerce-website.html

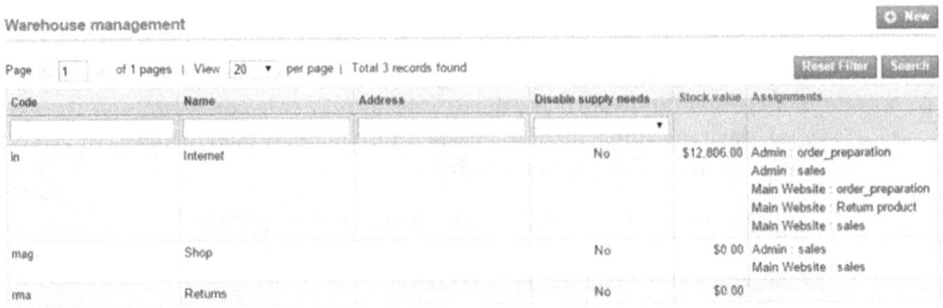

Code	Name	Address	Disable supply needs	Stock value	Assignments
in	Internet		No	$12,806.00	Admin : order_preparation Admin : sales Main Website : order_preparation Main Website : Return product Main Website : sales
mag	Shop		No	$0.00	Admin : sales Main Website : sales
rma	Returns		No	$0.00	

Figure 4-23. *Embedded ERP*

There are also different apps for Odoo suite integration (formerly known as OpenERP). Odoo is a bunch of open-source business apps used by 2 million users worldwide. The suite fits both small and big businesses. Odoo includes 260 core modules and more than 4,000 community modules. To integrate this solution with your Magento store, you can use Odoo Magento Connector (`http://goo.gl/bv7djd`), Open ERP Connector by Openlabs (`http://goo.gl/nFYSM`), or OpenERP Bridge by Webkul (`http://goo.gl/dohjkK`).

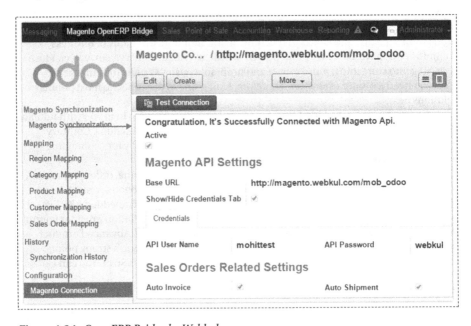

Figure 4-24. *OpenERP Bridge by Webkul*

eBridge Connections Accounting & ERP Integration can help you with the integration of your Magento website with 40+ ERPs. Microsoft Dynamics GP, Epicor Enterprise, Sage Peachtree, SAP Business One, Exact Macola, Intuit Quickbooks, and NetSuite are among the available solutions. eBridge costs $7,000. You can get it here: http://goo.gl/YaOvPu.

Enterprise resource planning (ERP) System Magento Integration[16]

CRM

Customer relationship management (CRM) software creates a system aimed at managing a company's interactions with both current and future customers. CRM's spheres of influence include marketing, sales, customer services, and technical support. Customer relationship management involves using different technologies and techniques to organize, synchronize, and automate all the aforementioned activities.

You can easily integrate your Magento store with any CRM system by installing appropriate extensions. The most reliable modules are represented next. Note that all of them work with certain CRM platforms.

Thus, SugarCRM Bridge helps with connecting your offline store to an online one by synchronizing information about your business activities. Having installed this extension, you connect your Magento store with SugarCRM as well. Accordingly, the module synchronizes purchases and site users with customers, opportunities, and cases from CRM's database. SugarCRM Bridge costs $299 and you can purchase it here: http://goo.gl/gBaH8I.

OroCRM Bridge represents open source CRM tools for ecommerce. The extension includes different built-in customer service and sales performance improvement tools. It also provides dashboards and out-of-the-box reports to better understand your customers. You can download the OroCRM Bridge extension for free: http://goo.gl/01PSQ1.

By installing OneSaas Connect, you will be able to integrate Magento with OneSaas CRM. As a result, the extension will synchronize your sales, contact, accounting, and billing data between the store and the customer relationship management system on an hourly or a daily basis. Although the OneSaas Connect extension is free, you have to pay for the different plans offered by the CRM. Get more information here: http://goo.gl/WHbdos.

If you are looking for salesforce integration, pay attention to eCS CloudGento. The module works with customer, inventory, order, and shipping information from your Magento store, and integrates it with the service, which is among the leaders of on-demand cloud-based CRM solutions. Take into consideration that the extension unites all data from Magento, Amazon, eBay, Volusion, and other platforms in one place. You can purchase eCS CloudGento for $99 here: http://goo.gl/wGRWVu.

---

[16]https://firebearstudio.com/blog/enterprise-resource-planning-erp-system-magento-integration.html

Figure 4-25. *eCS CloudGento*

Another useful tool is VtigerCRM because it allows you to synchronize data between your Magento store and the Vtiger CRM system. The extension works with information about customers, carts, products, orders, invoices, and so forth. You can purchase it for $299: `http://goo.gl/VSUhIE`.

Customer relationship management Magento integration[17]

SAP

SAP is a company that develops software for enterprises in all industries. The acronym stands for *systems, applications, and products* (in data processing). SAP ERP is an enterprise resource planning system developed by the company. There is also a solution stack of the company's technology products known as SAP NetWeaver. It consists of such building blocks as Portal, BI, Visual Composer, AutoID Infrastructure, Composite Application Framework, Development Infrastructure, Identity Management, Single Sign-On, and so forth.

Another important set of products is represented with industry-specific software. Tools for small enterprises and midsize companies include SAP Business One and SAP Business ByDesign.

The basic idea behind SAP is to provide users with the ability to work within a corporate database accessible from a range of business apps with all necessary management features.

With the appearance of mySAP.com, the company added business applications for customer relationship, supply chain, and other kinds of management. SAP's portfolio includes mobile business apps as well.

---

[17]`https://firebearstudio.com/blog/customer-relationship-management-crm-magento-integration.html`

As you can see, there are a lot of different software products developed by the company. But what are the benefits? Let's discuss some core SAP ecommerce opportunities.

- Your warehouse, store, and website are tightly connected with SAP: a stock level is updated in real time; you always know when it is time to reorder; your online customers can see a current availability of goods.

- You get a database of your online customers: this data streamlines ordering and shipping processes; the appropriate areas of the supply chain get all necessary information on time; customers enter their information only once and have the ability to track their purchases.

- SAP ERP integration optimizes the work of your administrators: they get all data in one central point with real-time automated processes; all manual store data updates are eliminated; and admin time is minimized.

Holding the leading position among all ERP providers, SAP offers dozens of useful features, which are especially important for big businesses. SAP ERP supports such aspects of ecommerce as multiple locations, international operations, enhances analytics, and so forth.

Furthermore, a standalone ERP solution by SAP is constantly updated. Since there is a whole suite of business products that you can add to the main platform, the solution offers extra flexibility and an advanced level of customization.

Note that there are a lot of Magento extensions for connecting your ecommerce store with SAP ERP. Unfortunately, they are all different, so you should choose the one that suits the needs of your business.

It is also necessary to understand that after installing a module, you should perform a lot of configurations, because both Magento and SAP ERP are complex systems. Luckily, there is the SAP Integration and Certification Center (http://goo.gl/EC3xXj), as well as several Magento companies that work with SAP ERP integration. For instance, you can rely on InSync (http://goo.gl/hZFGoA), eBridge Connections (http://goo.gl/8UBLMX), Speed 4 Trade (https://goo.gl/ybk2r3), and Netresearch (http://goo.gl/s7dFaH).

Please note that extensions aimed at SAP/Magento integration are not as effective as solutions offered by the aforementioned companies. That's why I don't describe them in this book; but you can always check our Firebear blog post related to SAP integration: Systems Applications Products integration with Magento[18]. There you will find additional information on Magento extensions and integration.

---

[18]https://firebearstudio.com/blog/systems-applications-products-sap-integration-with-magento.html

Dropshipping

Dropshipping is a special retail fulfillment method that eliminates the necessity to keep goods in stock. Instead, a retailer transfers customer orders to a wholesaler or manufacturer, who ships goods directly to customers. Thus, an ecommerce merchant never handles a product.

Dropshipping is easy to get started and requires much less capital than other retail methods. Other benefits include low overhead expenses, a wide selection of products, reduced risks, location independence, and high scalability. You can put products in front of an audience and start selling without getting stuck with unsold inventory or spending a lot up front.

If you are really interested in dropshipping, check out the uDropship extension and Doba platform. These are the most reliable solutions, preferred by thousands of ecommerce merchants worldwide.

As you might have guessed, the uDropship Magento extension streamlines communication between dropshippers and online stores. As a result, you, as an ecommerce merchant, get the ability to track shipments and orders handled by your dropship company or vendors. uDropship by Unirgy has a user-friendly interface and features necessary for gaining the most out of dropshipping. The extension costs $950 and offers a seamless upgrade to the uMarketplace solution. You can download uDropship here: `https://goo.gl/uIh78k`.

Doba (`https://goo.gl/eQb2DO`) is a platform that empowers retailers and wholesale suppliers to connect to do business. As a retailer, you get instant access to more than 2 million wholesale products from a growing supplier base. Thus, rather than working out relationships with new suppliers, you can access all of them through a single interface. Moreover, having installed the Doba Dropshipper Integration extension, you simplify the integration of your Magento store with this platform. The module costs $129 and provides the ability to automatically import products from Doba into your ecommerce store. You can get the extension here: `http://goo.gl/1FhBTN`.

The Best Drop Shipping Extensions for Magento[19]

B2B

Business-to-business is a complex of commerce transactions that occur among companies. The most common examples of B2B relations are transactions between manufacturers and wholesalers, or wholesalers and retailers.

B2B and B2C businesses have a lot of common features, but there is one fundamental difference: the target audience. B2B companies work with other businesses, while B2C companies are aimed at the end user. The audience of a B2B company can include only one consumer, while such a situation is impossible with B2C. B2B customers always buy with their heads, not their hearts. Their decisions are cold and logical. In the B2C world, the situation is often the opposite.

---

[19]`https://firebearstudio.com/blog/the-best-drop-shipping-extensions-for-magento.html`

It's very important to understand how this affects ecommerce websites. Due to intense competition, B2C ecommerce websites are forced to stand out from a crowd to be noticed, but it doesn't mean that B2B websites should have a less noticeable design or don't need any stunning features.

Furthermore, B2C websites have many more visitors, but a lower conversion rate. Thus, end customer–related merchants spend lots of resources on increasing this index. In business-to-business relations, these goals are not of the highest priority. Instead, B2B entrepreneurs focus on different business problems, such as providing real-time information and necessary connections.

It is also worth mentioning that B2B ecommerce websites use complicated customer logins, while B2C sites often rely on unobtrusive guest checkouts. B2B customers prefer long-term collaboration; they might have schedules, specific deals, and setups that are impossible to manage on a website with a guest checkout. At the same time, B2C customers are looking for new unobtrusive purchases without any registrations or logins.

Product information on both types of sites is also different. B2B ecommerce is impossible without explainer videos, spec sheets, how-to's, webinars, and tutorials. All of these materials can be used on B2C sites as well, but less often and in smaller quantities.

The checkout process is another distinctive feature of these relation types. On B2C websites, it must be as short as possible. On B2B stores, a better devised approach is required, since B2B purchases are more unique and complex.

Fortunately, you can easily upgrade your Magento website according to B2B requirements. You just need to spend a few hours installing special extensions. The most important tools are listed on the Firebear blog here: Magento B2B extensions and solutions[20]. Additionally, you can check the appropriate section on Magento Connect: http://goo.gl/BdF7n.

And let's not forget the Magento B2B Program. Although Magento was a B2B-friendly platform out of the box, there still were a lot of vital improvements required for those merchants whose businesses were aimed at other companies. Having installed extensions, they were able to turn their Magento websites into contemporary B2B platforms. Unfortunately, it was not the most convenient way to get a proper B2B experience, but it was the only one available. Since the Magento team is always trying to improve the existing platform, a new program was recently.

While B2B buying is becoming more B2C-like, the segment has a lot of new requirements. If an ecommerce website does not offer a dynamically changing set of features, customers will easily move on to competitors who provide this experience. Luckily, you can prevent your business from losing clients with the Magento B2B Program.

---

[20]https://firebearstudio.com/blog/magento-business-to-business-b2b-extensions-and-solutions.html

The platform now offers a consumer-like B2B experiences combined with flexibility and stability, so you can change any aspect of your work flow according to unique requirements of your clients or company. Moreover, there is a robust set of APIs designed for easy integration with all possible external systems widely used in a B2B segment. With the Magento B2B Program, you will be able to do the following:

- Provide a consumerized self-serve shopping experience

- Improve operational efficiency by getting higher-value data

- Get an Enterprise-level platform with top-notch functionality, performance, extensibility, and flexibility

Magento B2B features include advanced account management, quick bulk orders, inventory tracking across multiple locations, negotiated pricing terms for each client, ERP integration, and mobile support.

As you can see, Magento offers a lot for making your B2B store even more user friendly, but this doesn't mean that you can ignore the modules mentioned. Utilize the new opportunity along with existing solutions to get the highest possible business results. You can find more information about the Magento B2B program here[21].

Magento B2B

This one is an internal management system for ecommerce that connects an online shopping system, an accounting system to a logistics system, and an inventory tracking system. With this extension, your business runs faster and more accurately, saving you much in costs.

Magento B2B[22]

Magento Extensions for Quick/Fast Order

You can also utilize Magento Extensions for Quick/Fast Order in your B2B business. The best modules are gathered here: Magento Extensions for Quick/Fast Order[23].

Customer Activation

This Magento extension provides additional control over customers by making it impossible to log in until the account has been activated by the admin. It is a very useful feature, especially if you operate a big enterprise and want to avoid problems related to incorrect information posted by your customers.

Customer Activation[24]

---

[21]https://magento.com/solutions/b2b/overview
[22]https://github.com/helin16/magento-b2b
[23]https://firebearstudio.com/blog/best-magento-extensions-for-quick-fast-order.html
[24]https://github.com/Vinai/customer-activation

Multivendor Marketplace

Another Enterprise-level feature provided by Magento is a multivendor marketplace. You can utilize the platform for running this type of ecommerce business. The core difference between a multivendor marketplace and an ordinary ecommerce shop lies in the approach to traffic generation and SEO. In a marketplace, you always need to split your marketing and SEO strategies into two separate branches: one at aimed at vendors and sellers, the other at buyers. The same is about the construction of your website. As an ecommerce store owner, you won't need to sell on your own, as you will get interest from what your vendors are selling.

If this idea seems expedient, you can utilize the uMarketplace extension by Unirgy, since it is the best available solution. The module will transform your ecommerce store into a powerful online shopping mall. All your vendors will be able to sell their products through specific microsites, but within a centralized product catalog. In addition, uMarketplace provides all the tools necessary for configuring and automating a dropshipping workflow on your store. Other useful features include multiple ways to integrate with vendors, different shipping options, advanced order and shipment management, commission rates, various promotions, and fully configurable and controllable customer/vendor interactions. The uMarketplace extension costs $1,650. You can get it here: `http://goo.gl/vb2Nhd`. Don't forget about support and assistance, since Unirgy offers these options for its clients. The company has an amazing team that is always ready to help.

I should also mention that every Magento template from ThemeForest can be adapted to uMarketplace. The same for extensions: most high-quality modules can be configured according to the requirements of a multiple-vendor marketplace. In both cases you can rely on extensions and a template developer, or on the Unirgy team.

The situation with payment systems is more complicated. Not all providers offer multivendor features, so I recommend that you check PayPal Marketplace Payouts: `https://goo.gl/yWyJ2S`. For a full list of solutions, go here: Best Magento extensions for building Magento based multi vendor marketplace[25].

Dynamic Pricing

Due to its flexible pricing strategy, dynamic pricing is widely used across different industries, but it is relatively new to ecommerce. Among all pricing strategies, it is the most relevant to the needs of electronic commerce.

To create a successful dynamic pricing strategy, you need tons of information about the market. For various industries, it requires a lot of time and effort to collect necessary data, but ecommerce is an exception. In the age of big data, online retailers can easily get all information related to pricing of major competitors, key market trends, or sales volume for a certain period. With such abilities, ecommerce creates a perfect environment for the implementation of dynamic pricing, which is no longer a privilege of giant companies. It has become an effective way to boost sales and revenues—even for the smallest retailers.

---

[25]`https://firebearstudio.com/blog/best-magento-extensions-for-build-magento-based-multi-vendor-marketplace.html`

At first blush, dynamic pricing seems to be all about price changes, but it is not true. Its second major purpose is surveillance of competitor pricing. Keep in mind that your price matters only in relation to what your competitors offer. You don't need to provide the lowest possible price to become successful; instead, you should rely on relative pricing. And all your relative prices should be flexible in order to stay effective. Therefore, dynamic pricing is the best possible ecommerce pricing strategy. You can implement it within your Magento store with the aid of the following platforms: Wiser, Ventata, or Boomerang Commerce. See our full list of DPO solutions here: Best Dynamic Pricing Optimization (DPO) Services for eCommerce[26].

For example, Wiser's portfolio consists of multiple products designed to provide retailers with the ability to stay competitive and profitable. WisePricer is a flagship solution of the company. It is a dynamic pricing engine, which works in real time. WisePricer monitors market situation, analyzes data, and automatically sets new prices according to received information. It provides ecommerce merchants with the ability to boost profit margins, get better revenue, and implement more advanced merchandising due to a right pricing strategy. Another company's solution is WiseMapper. It is a MAP monitoring tool for manufacturers, which helps with pricing protection. Visit the official website here: http://goo.gl/tKg5eS.

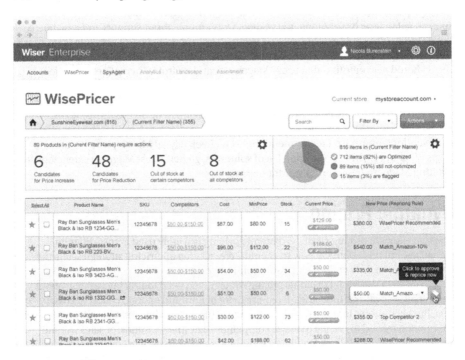

Figure 4-26. Wiser

---

[26]https://firebearstudio.com/blog/best-dynamic-pricing-optimization-dpo-services-for-the-e-commerce.html

Ventata is another provider of software for dynamic pricing optimization. Working with all major ecommerce platforms, it analyzes historical orders and determines sales velocity, curves of supply and demand, and repricing intervals, and it offers past-price testing. All of this information is displayed on a convenient control panel, where you can mix and match pricing strategies for all of your products. Get more information here: https://goo.gl/yo8kP.

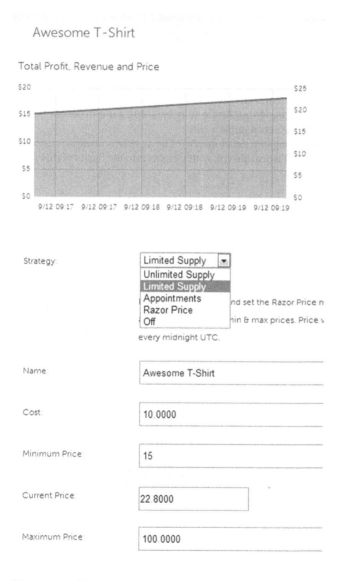

Figure 4-27. *Ventata*

Boomerang Commerce provides software for real-time data analytics, optimization, and machine learning, which brings dynamic price optimization to ecommerce. It tracks fixed and variable costs at different levels to measure true profitability of every online store. The platform provides rule-based automated price optimization, A/B testing, "What-if" analysis, and other useful features within a single dashboard. The official website is here: `http://goo.gl/nHZpVW`.

Conclusion

Congratulations! You've just become an advanced ecommerce merchant. Now, you know how to turn your CE store into an EE store. Multichannel enterprise is no longer a problem. PIM, ERP, CRM, and SAP are much more than just acronyms. You know how to sell goods without even seeing them. B2B ecommerce is not an obstacle anymore. Dynamic pricing optimization is among your future strategies. And a multivendor marketplace is a type of store that you can implement.

What's the next step in your Magento development? The answer is obvious: custom development. In the next chapter, I'll provide you with insights into the basics of this sophisticated topic.

CHAPTER 5

Custom Magento Development

You don't need to become a coder to get involved in custom Magento development. While there is always a necessity for making your store more competitive, default extensions are no longer helpful, since they are available to everyone. Therefore, if you are going to offer a unique customer experience, custom development is a must. In this chapter, I explain how to utilize this phenomenon if you are an ecommerce merchant.

Use the power of community: StackExchange, various forums, and open source projects are extremely useful if you've chosen the path of custom development. You can always find something suitable, as the Internet is full of unique solutions and custom projects related to the Magento platform. Before hiring developers and reinventing the wheel, try to look for existing but unknown solutions. This will prevent you from unnecessary expenditures of time and money.

Don't forget about support offered by extension developers. Since every paid—and even some free—extensions usually have a good team of experts behind them, you can always contact them to get some help. This often works when problems occur during an installation or maintenance, but you can always contact developers to share your ideas on customization. You can even ask them to implement certain features before buying a product. Such an approach will help you save money and get desired options at a regular price.

If these solutions don't work and you've decided to hire a team of developers, I recommend checking the following platforms.

© Viktor Khliupko 2016
V. Khliupko, *Magento 1 DIY*, DOI 10.1007/978-1-4842-2457-1_5

Upwork (oDesk)

Upwork, formerly known as oDesk, is a global online work platform for businesses and independent professionals. They connect and collaborate remotely through the website. As an ecommerce merchant interested in custom Magento development, you can interview and hire freelancers through the platform. Job posting is free, as well as bidding on jobs, but Upwork charges 10% of all payments. The site is entirely in English and utilizes payments only in U.S. dollars. The platform has been operating since 2003; its founders are Odysseas Tsatalos and Stratis Karamanlakis. As of December 2012, there were 2.7 million freelancers and 540,000 clients. You can hire Magento developers on Upwork here: https://goo.gl/6vmc7T.

Elance

Like Upwork, Elance allows its clients to post jobs and search for freelancers. The platform charges an 8.75% fee, which is paid by a client through the website's system. Elance was launched in 1999. As of February 2013, there were about 500 businesses and 2 million registered freelancers. Use this link for hiring Magento developers on Elance: https://goo.gl/L4ZwOS.

Toptal

Toptal is a new and rapidly growing network where you can find the most talented engineers from all over the world. Toptal's main goal is to connect a network of specialists with leading tech companies. The platform focuses on finding talented engineers and creating dynamic teams aimed at solving your unique problems. Find Magento developers on Toptal: http://goo.gl/6wE29e.

Freelancer

Freelancer is another global outsourcing marketplace where you can find qualified Magento developers. The platform was founded in 2009. Today it includes more than 11 million users. The fee is 10% of all payments. You can find Magento specialists on Freelancer here: https://goo.gl/6CNQ9A.

PeoplePerHour

On the market since 2007, PeoplePerHour consists of 250,000 active users; 72% are freelancers. The platform is popular among small companies that don't need full-time specialists. Hire Magento Developers on PeoplePerHour at http://goo.gl/DaK9Fq.

Guru

High-tech workers have been interested in Guru since 1998. The company allows employers to find freelancers for commissioned work worldwide. Founded by Inder Guglani, Guru was acquired twice: by Unicru and by eMoonlighter.com. In addition to Magento freelancers, the platform lists freelancers from 160 different fields. Use the following link to hire Magento developers on Guru: `http://goo.gl/lcewCN`.

Before hiring someone, check previous reviews and their portfolio. You can even offer a test task to see if your future employee is a qualified specialist.

Magento Community Events

If you are a Magento merchant, developer, or marketer, you should be interested in attending or at least monitoring core Magento events. We've already written about the impact of the Real Magento Community on the platform, covering such important topics as Hackathon Magento extensions, so now it is time to discuss key Magento community events. Next, you will find a list with some useful links.

First, we'd like to draw your attention to the official Magento website. If you do not want to miss any Magento gathering, check the official list of events here: Magento Events. Currently, there are three pages of various Magento meetings, including MagentoLive Australia.

As you will see, almost the entire year is filled with various events. As for the official website, you can choose among three categories of events: Industry Events, Magento Events, and Partner and Community Events. There is also an archive of past events and a Magento Event Listing Request Form.

Meet Magento Events

Leading Magento community events are represented by the Meet Magento Association, which provide a great opportunity to get in touch with members of the Real Magento Community, including merchants, developers, and agencies. Additionally, you can get the latest Magento news and extend your Magento and ecommerce projects during Meet Magento.

The first event organized by Meet Magento Association was held in 2008 in Leipzig, Germany. Over the last few years, the conference has become a successful international event series with events in Europe, America, and Asia. For further information about Meet Magento Association and Events, follow this link: Meet Magento[1].

---

[1]`http://meet-magento.com/events/`

Imagine Commerce

Another premier Magento community event is Imagine Commerce. The event gathers more than 2,500 experts, including merchants, technology providers, and agencies from more than 45 countries. It is a perfect environment for collaborating without borders and sharing the power of Real Magento Community.

Developers Paradise

Developers Paradise introduces a great opportunity to communicate with the Magento community members and have some fun in the sun. The event gathers more than 1,000 participants from 30 countries. For further information and registration, hit this link: Developers Paradise[2].

Magento Unconference

Magento Unconference is a relatively young event, because it was held only once, but it is already a promising affair. Get ready for food, preshow, two aftershows, t-shirts, and of course ecommerce and Magento.

Mage Titans

If you are a Magento developer, then you should pay a closer attention to Mage Titans a conference for Magento developers curated by Magento developers. For further information and tickets, follow this link: Mage Titans[3].

MagentoLive

MagentoLive brings our favorite ecommerce platform to everyone. All events are hosted by the Magento team, so you can get the latest Magento news and ideas as well as share you experience with other participants there. The most intriguing feature of MagentoLive events is the place where they are held: it must be a state-of-the-art venue. And don't forget about killer parties! More information is available here: MagentoLive[4].

---

[2]http://www.developers-paradise.com/
[3]http://www.magetitans.co.uk/
[4]http://magentolive.com/

MageStackDay

Have you asked questions on magento.stackexchange.com? Then you should attend MageStackDay, which is an online hackathon dedicated to answering questions. StackExchange itself introduces a great opportunity to find what you are looking for. This Magento community event increases your chances to get desired information. Check the event here: MageStackDay[5].

Conclusion

If someone says you can become a developer and perform everything without other specialists successfully running your Magento store at the same time, don't believe them. It will take a lot of time to get necessary experience, so I don't recommend that you choose this path. It is almost impossible to simultaneously be a good ecommerce merchant and a top-notch coder, since both require all of your free time and even more. For further information about Magento 1 and Magento 2, visit the Firebear Blog[6].

---

[5]http://magestackday.com/
[6]https://firebearstudio.com/blog/

Index

© Viktor Khliupko 2016
V. Khliupko, *Magento 1 DIY*, DOI 10.1007/978-1-4842-2457-1

Get the eBook for only $4.99!

Why limit yourself?

Now you can take the weightless companion with you wherever you go and access your content on your PC, phone, tablet, or reader.

Since you've purchased this print book, we are happy to offer you the eBook for just $4.99.

Convenient and fully searchable, the PDF version enables you to easily find and copy code—or perform examples by quickly toggling between instructions and applications.

To learn more, go to http://www.apress.com/us/shop/companion or contact support@apress.com.

Printed in the United States
By Bookmasters